The Legend of Veronica in Early Modern Art

In *The Legend of Veronica in Early Modern Art*, Katherine T. Brown explores the lore of the apocryphal character of Veronica and the history of the "true image" relic as factors in the Franciscans' placement of her character into the *Via Crucis* (Way of the Cross) as the Sixth Station, in both Jerusalem and Western Europe, around the turn of the fifteenth century. The author examines how the Franciscans adopted and adapted the legend of Veronica to meet their own evangelical goals by intervening in the fabric of Jerusalem to incorporate her narrative – which is not found in the Gospels – into an urban path constructed for pilgrims, as well as in similar participatory installations in churchyards and naves across Western Europe. This book proposes plausible reasons for the subsequent proliferation of works of art depicting Veronica, both within and independent of the Stations of the Cross, from the early fifteenth through the mid-seventeenth centuries. This book will be of interest to scholars in art history, theology, and medieval and Renaissance studies.

Katherine T. Brown is Director of the Honors Program, Director of Museum Studies, and Associate Professor of Art History at Walsh University in North Canton, Ohio.

Routledge Research in Art and Religion

Routledge Research in Art and Religion is a new series focusing on religion and spirituality as examined by scholars working in the fields of art history and visual studies. Proposals for monographs and edited collections on this topic are welcomed.

Tradition and Transformation in Christian Art
The Transcultural Icon
C.A. Tsakiridou

Tree of Jesse Iconography in Northern Europe in the Fifteenth and Sixteenth Centuries
Susan L. Green

Aesthetic Theology in the Franciscan Tradition
The Senses and the Experience of God in Art
Edited by Xavier Seubert and Oleg Bychkov

The Legend of Veronica in Early Modern Art
Katherine T. Brown

The Legend of Veronica in Early Modern Art

Katherine T. Brown

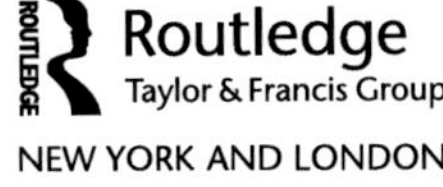

NEW YORK AND LONDON

First published 2020
by Routledge
52 Vanderbilt Avenue, New York, NY 10017

and by Routledge
2 Park Square, Milton Park, Abingdon, Oxon, OX14 4RN

Routledge is an imprint of the Taylor & Francis Group, an informa business

Library of Congress Cataloging-in-Publication Data
Names: Brown, Katherine T., author.
Title: The legend of Veronica in early modern art / Katherine T. Brown.
Description: New York : Routledge, 2020. | Includes bibliographical references and index.
Identifiers: LCCN 2019049306 (print) | LCCN 2019049307 (ebook) | ISBN 9780367197315 (hardback) | ISBN 9780429242922 (ebook)
Subjects: LCSH: Veronica, Saint, active 1st century–Art. | Stations of the Cross. | Franciscan art–Jerusalem. | Franciscan art–Europe, Western.
Classification: LCC N8080 .B76 2020 (print) | LCC N8080 (ebook) | DDC 704.9/4863–dc23
LC record available at https://lccn.loc.gov/2019049306
LC ebook record available at https://lccn.loc.gov/2019049307

ISBN: 978-0-367-19731-5 (hbk)
ISBN: 978-0-429-24292-2 (ebk)

Typeset in Sabon
by Swales & Willis, Exeter, Devon, UK

Front cover: Master of Saint Veronica (Cologne, fl. 1400–1420), *Saint Veronica with the Holy Kerchief*, c. 1420. Bayerische Staatsgemäldesammlungen, Munich, Alte Pinakothek. Image credit: © Bayerische Staatsgemäldesammlungen, Munich, Alte Pinakothek. Photo: Sibylle Forster

Contents

Acknowledgments

My dear friend Dr. Julien Chapuis walked with me through the Staatliche Museen zu Berlin to look for Veronicas, carefully edited multiple drafts, offered wise counsel at critical points, and generously assisted with providing photographs in Berlin. For additional images in Munich, Frankfurt, and Berlin, I am grateful for the instrumental help of Martin Schawe, Stephan Kemperdick, Babette Buller, Marie-Theres Steinke, and Antje Voigt. I extend thanks to Dr. James C. Anderson, jr., Professor Emeritus at the University of Georgia, mentor and friend, for Latin translations and invaluable comments on several early drafts. I also wish to thank Dr. Nancy T. de Grummond, my primary professor as an undergraduate at Florida State University, for her help with a translation and a long-time mentorship. My thanks are also due to Dr. John Skillen, Gordon College in Orvieto, for a scholar-residency during June 2018 and to the American Academy in Rome for an opportunity to research and write as a Visiting Scholar in June 2019. I extend gratitude to Walsh University for a sabbatical during spring 2018 and for a Faculty Scholar award for summer 2018. At Walsh, I have enjoyed working with many supportive colleagues: Dr. Michael Dunphy, Dr. Britt Cooper, Dr. Jennifer D'Agostino, Dr. Brad and Liz Beach, Dr. Mark Rogers, Lisa Madaffer, Diane Belfiglio, and Rachel Hosler. Alyssa Mitchell and Zoe Fete in the Walsh Library helped to secure numerous interlibrary loans, and I have benefited from conversations with all of my current and past students. Jean-Baptiste LeProux spent time talking with me about Veronica in Soulac-sur-Mer in June 2019 and kindly assisted me by locating church inventories. At Routledge/Taylor & Francis, I remain indebted to Isabella Vitti, Editor; Katie Armstrong, Editorial Assistant; Megan Symons at Swales & Willis; and to the four anonymous readers whom they secured for insightful suggestions at an early stage.

I am grateful for two opportunities to speak about this topic at conferences that generated a productive exchange of ideas. My first presentation on Veronica was held at the International Congress on Medieval Studies at Kalamazoo, MI in May 2018 in a session sponsored by Women in the Franciscan Intellectual Tradition and chaired by Sr. Diane V. Tomkinson, O. S. F. My second presentation, based on Chapter 5 about gender, was delivered at the Renaissance Society of America conference in March 2019 in Toronto in a session sponsored by the Hagiography Society and chaired by Barbara Zimbalist. I would also like to thank Jon-Paul Della Pia (B.A. in Art History at Walsh University 2018; M.A. in Art History, University of Toronto, 2019), my former student, who helped me with graphic design on one of the maps. My initial ideas about images of Veronica in art germinated during a seminar that was hosted by the Council of Independent Colleges, sponsored by the Samuel H. Kress Foundation, and held at the High Museum of Art in Atlanta during the summer of 2016. Dr. Libby Bailey has also offered me multiple opportunities to speak and teach at Wesleyan College in Macon, GA.

My friends keep my spirits high, even across long distances, as is most often the case. For their company in real and virtual time, I am grateful to Dr. Liz Carroll, Dr. Michelle Erhardt, Dr. Amanda Gradisek and Greg Leehan, Kate Haw, Steve and Marilyn Kapaun, J. D., Douglas Kline, Nancy and Todd Michel, Danilo Mori, Dr. Amber McAlister, Dr. Amy Morris, Dr. Sheri Shaneyfelt, Dr. Katherine Smith, Dr. Nancy Thompson, Dr. Jeanne Tift, and Enza Valente. I especially thank my parents, Dorothy Ogden Brown and S. Phillip Brown; my daughter, Suzana Brown; my aunt, Sue O. Ballard; and brothers Phillip O. Brown and Stephen W. Brown, J. D., and their families for interest and encouragement.

This book is dedicated to the memory of Dr. Bruce M. Cole (1938–2018), Distinguished Professor of Art History at Indiana University, Bloomington, and Chair, National Endowment for the Humanities (2001–2009). Bruce served as my major professor and chair of my dissertation committee during my graduate school years (1990–1998) at Indiana University. With shared interests in the iconography of Italian painting, the nature and scope of our many conversations are reflected in these pages. I remain in his debt for a host of early opportunities to teach and study the culturally rich and layered meanings of Early Modern art.

This book has been supported by The Renaissance Society of America and The Samuel H. Kress Foundation with a Publication Subvention for Art History, as well as the Faculty Development Fund of Walsh University.

Plates

Color plates are placed between Chapters 3 and 4.

Figures

Introduction

The Legend of Veronica in Early Modern Art explores the origins of the character Veronica – an apocryphal figure in medieval hagiography – as well as *the* veronica, also called the *Vultus Christi* (Latin for Face of Christ) or *Volto Santo* (Italian for Holy Face), which was a swathe of cloth that allegedly bore a miraculous imprint of Christ's features. As Veronica's hallmark attribute, the *sudarium* (Latin for sweat cloth), as it was called since the twelfth century, was one of the most revered relics in Western Christendom and, as such, a prime focal point for millions of pilgrims who sought to glimpse it in Rome during the Early Modern period. The cloth was initially considered a secondary or contact relic because Christ had touched it to his brow during his walk to execution; early accounts make no mention of an image. Circa 1200, the *sudarium* assumed additional significance as a "true image" when its legend expanded to claim that an imprint of Jesus's features made of his sweat and blood had been miraculously transferred (that is, not through the intervention of human hands) onto the cloth. I examine both the legends about the woman and the history of the relic as factors in the Franciscans' choice to insert the character of Veronica into the *Via Crucis* as the Sixth Station by the turn of the fifteenth century. I argue that the Franciscans adopted and then adapted the apocryphal story of this originally anonymous, first-century woman to achieve their own evangelical goals in meeting the spiritual and physical needs of pilgrims to the Holy Land, who were under their aegis in Jerusalem, as well as those whom they sought to evangelize in urban centers across Western Europe.

This monograph acknowledges and builds upon the foundational research on images of Veronica and her relic by Karl Pearson (1887),[1] Jos Palme (1892),[2] and Ernst von Dobschütz (1899),[3] as well as a second generation of publications, including: André Chastel's article "La Véronique" in *Revue de l'art* (1978);[4] Ewa Kuryluk's book *Veronica and Her Cloth: History, Symbolism, and Structure of a "True" Image* (1991);[5] Hans Belting's *Likeness and Presence: A History of the Image in the Age before Art* (1994);[6] Jeffrey Hamburger's *The Visual and the Visionary: Art and Female Spirituality in Late Medieval Germany* (1998);[7] the series of essays in *The Holy Face and the Paradox of Presentation*, edited by Herbert L. Kessler and Gerhard Wolf (1998);[8] Tiziana Maria Di Blasio's *Veronica: il mistero del volto; itinerari iconografici, memoria e rappresentatzione* (2000);[9] the beautifully illustrated catalogue *Il Volto di Cristo*, edited by Giovanni Morello and Gerhard Wolf (2000);[10] and the first chapter of Alexa Sand's broader work, *Vision, Devotion, and Self-Representation in Late Medieval Art* (2014).[11] The present study also complements recent scholarship in *The European Fortune of the Roman Veronica in the Middle Ages, Convivium*

Supplementum (2017), a collection of 21 essays edited by Amanda Murphy, Herbert L. Kessler, Marco Petoletti, Eamon Duffy, and Guido Milanese.[12] This important and impressive collection of essays focuses on the relic and legends as origins of the fame of Veronica, the formation of the early cult to her in Rome, the promotion of reverence to Veronica in liturgy, and the spread of the cult primarily in Italy and France through the fourteenth century. Because the present study begins with requisite synopses of the legends, the history of the relic, as well as theological and sacramental connotations, there is some necessary overlap with the 2017 volume in the initial chapters. However, this book is distinct from and serves as a complement to the former titles in terms of methodology in three essential ways.

Principally, this research examines the Franciscans' role and aims in incorporating Veronica into the Stations of the Cross, which led to an increased production of her image from the early fifteenth through the mid-seventeenth centuries. I consider reasons why the Franciscan friars, as custodians of sacred places in Jerusalem since 1342, may have added a new female character not mentioned by name in the Gospels to serve as an eyewitness to Jesus's life, thereby underscoring his historical authenticity. I evaluate the placement of Veronica as the Sixth Station in the traditional sequence of fourteen stops in the constructed pilgrimage path, both within the irregular topography of Jerusalem and around the grounds and naves of churches in Western Europe. In addition, I draw iconographic parallels among Veronica and other female characters Christ encountered on his Way to Calvary (the Virgin Mary, the Women of Jerusalem, and Mary Magdalene), women who *were* mentioned in the synoptic Gospels. Moreover, I assert that the Franciscans' insertion of Veronica and her image-bearing veil functioned as a foreshadowing of the Resurrection within the narrative frame of the Stations of the Cross, thereby offering pilgrims a glimpse of an eternal, ideal portrait of the divine. Likewise, Veronica's palliative gesture may have played a role in the syncopation of suffering and salve that Christ experienced on his way to crucifixion. By extension, the Franciscan friars may have planned for pilgrims to participate physically and emotionally in a similar alternation of struggle and respite in order to draw them spiritually closer to Christ and their order's founder, Francis of Assisi, with the intention of guiding pilgrims toward personal, purgative repentance.

Second, the present study approaches the character of Veronica through the lens of gender and therefore addresses women's patronage, viewership, and reverence, especially by religious women living in communities. Veronica may have been part of a conscious revival to bring women from the Church's early history forward during the thirteenth and fourteenth centuries, a period when their roles in liturgy and lay activities were being redefined. I also explore possible links to the Second and Third Franciscan Orders, communities that largely comprised women, for whom Veronica may have served as a focal point of devotion and/or role model.

Third, and finally, this monograph expands upon previous studies by focusing on works of art from the Early Modern period. Earlier research has exhaustively studied and reproduced copies of the veronica relic from the fourth to the end of the fourteenth centuries. This study will essentially commence where prior scholarship tapers in terms of chronology. Although I make references to early renditions of Veronica, this book will concentrate on the development of the iconography of Veronica in works of art produced from the early fifteenth through the mid-seventeenth centuries. Selected works from North and South of the Alps in the final chapter are organized into five primary iconographic roles: (1) Veronica as a protagonist who displays the cloth, her identity extending to the *vera icon*; (2) the veronica within the context of related devotional imagery, such as the Man of Sorrows, the *Arma Christi*, or the Mass of Saint Gregory; (3) Veronica as a corollary, subordinate character within a selected scene from the Passion cycle; (4) Veronica actively wiping Christ's brow as the Sixth Station of the Cross; and (5) the relic isolated with the Holy Face as a focal point of devotion. In the image-rich cultural traditions of the Christian West, artistic renditions of Veronica satisfied social and spiritual needs to witness Christ's visage in a direct, forthright manner. Works of art featuring Veronica prominently presenting Christ's countenance on the *sudarium* functioned largely to induce responses of affective piety among pilgrims, reactions that were intensified when placed in tandem with scenes from Christ's Passion. The purpose of this study is to examine the nature of images of Veronica and the ways in which Early Modern artists adopted her character and cloth relic as subject matter toward these ends.

Notes

1 Karl Pearson, *Die Fronica, Ein Beitrag zur Geschichte des Christusbildes in Mittelalter* (Strasbourg: Verlag von Karl J. Trübner, 1887).
2 Jos Palme, *Die Deutschen Veronicalegenden des XII Jahr* (Prague: Verlag des K. K. Deutschen obergymnasiums der Kleinseite, 1892).
3 Ernst von Dobschütz, *Christusbilder; Untersuchungen zur christlichen Legende* (Leipzig: L. C. Hinrichs, 1899).
4 André Chastel, "La Véronique," *Revue de l'art* 40–41 (1978).
5 Ewa Kuryluk, *Veronica and Her Cloth: History, Symbolism, and Structure of a "True" Image* (Cambridge, MA: Basil Blackwell, Inc., 1991).
6 Hans Belting, *Likeness and Presence: A History of the Image in the Age before Art* (Chicago: University of Chicago Press, 1994).
7 Jeffrey Hamburger, *The Visual and the Visionary: Art and Female Spirituality in Late Medieval Germany* (New York: Zone Books, 1998).
8 Herbert L. Kessler and Gerhard Wolf, eds., *The Holy Face and the Paradox of Representation: Papers from a Colloquium held at the Bibliotheca Hertziana, Rome and the Villa Spelman, Florence, 1996* (Bologna: Nuova Alfa, 1998).
9 Tiziana Maria Di Blasio, *Veronica: il mistero del volto; itinerari iconografici, memoria e rappresentatzione* (Rome: Città Nuova Ed., 2000).
10 Giovanni Morello and Gerhard Wolf, eds., *Il Volto di Cristo*, (Milan: Electa, 2000).
11 Alexa Sand, *Vision, Devotion, and Self-Representation in Late Medieval Art* (New York: Cambridge University Press, 2014).
12 Amanda Murphy, Herbert L. Kessler, Marco Petoletti, Eamon Duffy, and Guido Milanese, eds., *The European Fortune of the Roman Veronica in the Middle Ages, Convivium Supplementum* (Turnhout, Belgium: Brepols Publishers, 2017).

1 Veronica in Legend and Literature

Veronica is usually depicted in Early Modern European works of art as a youthful woman who holds a cloth with an image of Christ's visage, as for example in *Saint Veronica with the Sudarium* by the Master of Saint Veronica (Cologne, fl. 1400–1420), datable c. 1420, in The National Gallery, London (Plate 1).[1] The character of Veronica, who symbolizes the "true image" relic that she holds, developed from legends originating in the fourth century, a period in the West marked by a rise in reverence for early Christian saints in general.[2] Although colloquially called a saint, Veronica was neither listed in the *Martyrologium Hieronymianum*,[3] a fifth-century canon of Christian martyrs pseudo-epigraphically attributed to Saint Jerome, nor was she formally canonized. Folklore about Veronica was augmented during the early medieval period by chronicles of pilgrims to the Holy Land from the fourth century forward. By the fourteenth century, both Veronica as a character and the veronica as a relic had secured recognizable places in the literature and popular culture of Western Europe with mentions by Dante, Petrarch, and Chaucer, as well as chroniclers of Church history.

Veronica is largely considered an apocryphal figure who continues to be celebrated as a patroness of photographers and laundry-workers (because her attribute was a verisimilitude on cloth), despite the fact that Charles Borromeo (1538–1584), Archbishop of Milan during the Counter Reformation, dismissed the Office of Veronica in the *Milan Missal*, where once it had been included.[4] Traditionally, Veronica's feast day has been celebrated on July 12, a date with origins in the *Acta Sanctorum* (Acts of the Saints), a hagiography organized by feast day, begun by Heribert Rosweyde (1569–1629) and finished by Jean Bolland (1596–1665), both Flemish Jesuits.[5] Their 68-volume work, edited by the Society of Bollandists, describes the lives of 6,200 saints, with Veronica among them.[6]

Tracing the origins and peripatetic route of the Veronica legend is inherently difficult but possible.[7] Many of the stories about her in the Middle Ages, from the eighth century forward, were embellishments on preceding ones with changes in plot details or new endings. Combinations of disparate stories about her and regional variations developed as the legend spread throughout Italy, France, Germany, and England. Foundational to understanding the eventual character of Veronica was an unnamed woman who was living in Jerusalem during the first century. According to Eusebius of Caesarea (260/265–339/340), in his *Historia Ecclesiastica* (c. 313–324), the woman originated from Caesarea Philippi, a Roman city in the Golan Heights.[8] Alternatively, she may have originated from Tyre, Lebanon.[9] This anonymous woman, also called the *Haemorrhoissa*, was believed to have been healed from a long-term illness by touching the fringes or hem of Christ's cloak as he walked through a crowd, as recounted in Matthew 9:18–26:

> While he was saying these things to them, suddenly a leader of the synagogue came in and knelt before him, saying, "My daughter has just died; but come and lay your hand on her, and she will live." And Jesus got up and followed him, with his disciples. Then suddenly a woman who had been suffering from hemorrhages for twelve years came up behind him and touched the fringe of his cloak, for she said to herself, "If I only touch his cloak, I will be made well." Jesus turned, and seeing her he said, "Take heart, daughter; your faith has made you well." And instantly the woman was made well. When Jesus came to the leader's house and saw the flute players and the crowd making a commotion, he said, "Go away; for the girl is not dead but sleeping." And they laughed at him. But when the crowd had been put outside, he went in and took her by the hand, and the girl got up. And the report of this spread throughout the district.[10]

Synoptic accounts in Mark 5:25–34[11] and Luke 8:43–48[12] vary only slightly. To summarize the story, which occurs within a series of witness accounts of Christ's miracles, the woman had been bleeding for twelve years. Although she had consulted many physicians, depleting her resources, none had been able to cure her. In fact, she had become worse. Because she had heard of Jesus's ability to heal, she reached out for him as he passed in a crowded space. When Jesus felt that someone had touched his clothes, he asked who it was. When she came forward to confess, he announced that her faith had healed her and commanded her to go in peace. The key moment in this narrative is depicted in a fourth-century fresco in the Catacombs of Marcellinus and Peter, located in the outskirts of Rome (Plate 2).[13]

By the fourth century, two parallel legends – one Byzantine and one Western – connected the Gospel accounts of Jesus's miraculous healing of the unnamed, bleeding woman with an individual named Bernice. The Eastern Orthodox version, written in Greek, is likely the earlier of the two legends and was retold in the fourth century by Eusebius of Caesarea, who claimed to have translated two letters exchanged between King Abgar of Edessa and Jesus into Greek from the original Syriac.[14] The protagonist in the apocryphal correspondence is the Arab Christian King Abgar Uchama "the Black" of Edessa (r. 4 BCE–7 CE and 13–50 CE), who had requested Jesus's assistance in curing him of an ailment.[15] Tradition held that Jesus dictated a response to the king, which was delivered by the courier Ananias in the form of a letter, in which Jesus declined a personal visit, implying the need to undergo crucifixion ("I must accomplish everything I was sent here to do"). Instead, Jesus promised that he would send a disciple after his ascension.[16] After Christ's death, the apostle Judas Thomas sent Addai (also called Thaddaeus) to cure Abgar and to convert the people of Edessa,[17] a city in northern Syria. Reference to an image was not originally included in the letters but instead added in later medieval versions of the legend. In these later embellishments to the story, prior to Jesus's death, the king had sent to him an envoy, who was also the king's court painter. Some versions of the legend recount that the painter rendered a portrait of Christ from life and gave it to Abgar. Another version attests that Christ washed his face and dried it, causing his features to be imprinted on the cloth. The main characters and plot in these later versions of the legend are visible in a painted icon, datable to the tenth century, from Mount Sinai in Egypt (Plate 3). In both versions of the story, King Abgar was healed by viewing the image of Christ's face. Mentioned first in the *Doctrine of Addai* (a Syriac text, datable c. 400), the miracle-working image was considered an *acheiropoieton* (an image not created by human hands) and called the *Mandylion*, meaning cloth, napkin, handkerchief, or towel.[18] Both the image and the correspondence were revered relics because of their miraculous abilities, such as allegedly having defended Edessa from a Persian sack in 544. The relics were transferred in 944 from Edessa to Constantinople, where they were housed in the palace chapel.

In the West, an adaptation of the Eastern legend first appears in the Gospel of Nicodemus, also called the *Acts of Pilate*.[19] This apocryphal text was written by the mid-fourth century[20] by several authors in Greek (although the text claims to have been written originally in Hebrew) with translations in Aramaic, Armenian, Coptic, Latin, and Syriac, among other ancient languages. Some – but not all – of the narrative is told from the point of view of Pontius Pilate, the Roman prefect of Judea. The text is organized into two parts: (A) the Trial, Death, and Resurrection of Christ, and (B) a variation on the texts in A but including the Descent of Christ into Hades.[21] Within Part A, in a section about the trial, in which witnesses speak on Jesus's behalf, is the short passage below that forms the entirety of Section VII. Here the given name Bernice (from the Greek *berenikē*, meaning bearer of victory, also transliterated from the Greek as Berenice, or Beronice in Coptic), was used to describe the woman with the hemorrhage:

> And a certain woman named Bernice crying out from afar off said: I had an issue of blood and touched the hem of his garment, and the flowing of my blood was stayed which I had twelve years. The Jews say: We have a law that a woman shall not come to give testimony.[22]

Bernice is speaking in Jesus's defense after he was accused of healing on the Sabbath and thus violating Jewish law.[23] But these few sentences also serve to assert that under Jewish law, a woman could not serve as a witness at trial. Thus, this brief mention of the woman functions as part of a framing narrative for the drama of the trial in which the roles of women are clearly and publicly defined. In terms of unraveling the origin of the legend of Veronica, this initial association of the Greek given name Bernice with the anonymous woman with a hemorrhage from the synoptic Gospels comprises an important confluence and development. There are other unnamed figures in the canonical Gospels who are identified with new first names in apocryphal texts of the fourth century. For example, the soldier who speared Jesus at the Crucifixion is called Longinus for the first time in the *Acts of Pilate*.[24] Additionally, the two thieves crucified on either side of Christ are named Dysmas and Gestas in the same text.[25] Therefore, identification of a previously unnamed character from the Gospels is not a unique occurrence. As the *Acts of Pilate* were probably written in rebuttal to challengers to Christian theology, the new specificity of given names may have augmented the characters' individuality and added credence to the narratives. The names could also have been mnemonic devices in early oral tradition, which were not recorded until the fourth century. Overall, the use of echoing names, such as Veronica – *vera icon*, underscored the authority of the text, which now appeared to reinforce a divine, preordained plan.

As Wolf (2000) has observed, the Eastern and Western versions of the legend share a key similarity in that both revolve around a king who is cured of a physical ailment by looking at an image of Christ imprinted on a cloth.[26] Leprosy, a skin disease, carried negative connotations and could be interpreted as a punishment for sin, idolatry, or paganism. In the imperial context, the health of the emperor could be equated with the prosperity of the public or the state in general.[27] Thus, the "curing" in the legend could have implied the restored well-being (including freedom from sin) of the greater populace and not solely that of the emperor. A simple analogy of skin to cloth can be expanded in this legend to imply the restoration of the spiritual and physical vitality of an emperor and his people by means of the divine grace inherent in an image that was imprinted on fabric.

In an addendum to one of the Latin versions of the *Acts of Pilate* that dates from the eighth century is the story of the *Cura Sanitatis Tiberii* (The Cure of the Health of Tiberius), often hailed as the earliest textual source for the Veronica story.[28] This narrative is the first to call the woman with the hemorrhage Veronica.[29]

> Volosianus said to Caesar Tiberius, "Jesus healed a certain woman of thirty years, from the issue of blood which she was suffering. She possesses an image of the Lord Jesus' love, and this very same image is brought here with her. For this woman has left everything behind her, except this image of God, saying, 'this shroud is my soul's richness, I will not, during my life, depart from it, for this is my hope of salvation, and there is strength and my hope. Where it is, I am with it.'" When Tiberius Augustus heard about the image of Lord Jesus Christ, he ordered that both it, and the woman must be presented to him. When he saw that shroud, which the woman had, that woman said, "you do deserve to touch the hem of Jesus' garment!" Having said this, she looked up, and saw Jesus Christ bowing down towards that image of Jesus Christ. The ground was trembling with Christ's tears falling. To be consolated from his infirmity, the man, who was suffering inside, had already seen a vision which revealed him the power, richness and honour of God, who can make him whole. And immediately he was cured from his weakness and he ordered that the woman, Veronica, must be covered with gold and precious stones, with a public decree.[30]

Thus, by the eighth century, the legend had evolved with elaborations in both character development and plot. In the passage above, readers can notice new information regarding the woman's age of thirty years. If, according to the Gospel accounts, she had been bleeding for twelve years, then she had been suffering from her incurable medical condition since she was eighteen years of age. Also new in this passage, Veronica professes personal devotion and emotional attachment to her image of Christ's face. This additional description is important because later versions of the legend credit Veronica's faith and compassion for the miraculous imprint of Christ's sweat and blood on her cloth. Also, we read that Emperor Tiberius (who becomes the story's protagonist in the West in a parallel to King Abgar of Edessa in the Orthodox version) commands that both she and her image be brought to him in Rome. When the emperor sees her image-bearing relic, he has a vision in which Christ appears before his own image. The emperor is cured of his disease and honors Veronica publicly. In this modified, serpentine version of the legend, a foundation is laid for making the *sudarium* a holy relic.

In Anglo-Saxon literature, Veronica is conspicuously absent from calendars of feast days or prayers. The Venerable Bede (English, 672–735) did refer to the cloth in *De Locis Sanctis* (On the Holy Places),[31] his description of the Holy Land, written c. 703.[32] Bede succinctly describes the sacred places in Jerusalem and environs from the point of view of an ecclesiastical scholar and historian. But because Bede never visited the Levant (he wrote the text in Northumbria), he relied heavily on earlier sources, such as Adomnán of Iona.[33] His mention of the veronica, however, attests to (and helped propel) the relic's renown in England.

The most significant variant and expansion of the *Cura Sanitatis Tiberii* dates from the ninth century and is called the *Vindicta Salvatoris* (The Vengeance of the Savior).[34] Specifically, the text describes Pilate's life after the Crucifixion of Jesus, including the prefect's imprisonment and condemnation. However, the narrative more generally concerns the fate of the Jewish people, who are blamed for and punished because of their perceived role in Christ's death by means of the destruction of Jerusalem in the first century by the Roman emperors Vespasian and Titus.[35] In the *Vindicta Salvatoris*, the story of Tiberius is preceded by another story of a king, Tyrus of Burdigala (a city in Libia), who, after being miraculously healed of a facial cancer, which spread from his nose to his eye, baptized and changed his name to Titus. After his cure, Titus sought Veronica, whom he had heard had an image of Christ.[36] In the text, the name Veronica is specifically used to refer to both the woman with the hemorrhage in an enumeration of Jesus's miracles *and* to the woman who had "the face of the Lord with her."[37] Emperor Tiberius, who suffered from ulcers and leprosy, sent his envoy Volosianus into Judea, in order to bring back witnesses of Christ's miracles to cure his disease. Volosianus met Veronica, who testified that Jesus cured her bleeding. When he demanded that she give him the image of Christ, she resisted. Volosianus then tortured her until she relinquished it.[38] She subsequently prepared to follow him and the portrait to Rome by accompanying them on a ship. When Volosianus asked her directly, "Woman, whom are you seeking?" she replied:

> In truth, I am looking for [the image of] my Lord that the Lord gave to me, not for my merits but out of his mercy, and which you have taken away from me against the law – just as the Jews had taken Christ, whom neither you nor your people have seen, from the world. Even though I have

deserved ill, hand back to me my Lord! And if you do not hand him back to me, I will not release him until I see where they have laid him down. And I will worship him and serve him as long as I live because my redeemer himself lives, and on the last day I shall see God, my savior.[39]

When her sons, daughters, neighbors, and everyone she knew began to cry at her imminent departure for Rome, Veronica's reply in the story is based on a passage in Luke, which connects her legend with the Gospel account of Christ carrying the cross.[40] The line of dialogue that comprises Veronica's response in the *Vindicta* is: "Daughters of Jerusalem, do not weep for me but for yourselves, and weep for your daughters,"[41] which is a variation of Jesus's dialogue in Luke 23:28: "But Jesus turned to them and said, 'Daughters of Jerusalem, do not weep for me, but weep for yourselves and for your children.'"[42] The apocryphal text concludes with Volosianus bringing both the portrait and the woman Veronica, who he claimed had painted the image, to Tiberius. When the emperor saw the relic and worshiped it, he was immediately cured of his leprosy and baptized.[43]

In the mid-eleventh century, the chronicler Marianus Scotus recounted an Anglo-Saxon version of the Veronica legend by summarizing the *Cura Sanitatis Tiberii* and quoting an earlier author he called Methodius.[44] He included in the introduction to the legend of Veronica a Jewish character named Nathan (*Nathanis Judaei Legatio*), whom Tiberius commanded to leave Judea and travel to Rome.[45] Also in this version, the woman with the flow of blood is connected to Veronica within the dialogue of Nathan, indicating a continuation of the merging of these two female identities by the mid-eleventh century:

Nathan answered and said, "Oh! my lord, I can not find out any such thing, nor know I aught thereof; but if thou hadst some time ago been in Judea, thou mightest then have found such a man, yea a chosen prophet, whose name was the Lord Jesus Christ. He himself healed his people of their sins, and also with his word he cleansed lepers, and enlightened the blind, and awoke the dead. And a certain woman was suffering from a flux of blood, even twelve winters; (she was named Veronica), and she approached behind him and touched the hem of his garment, and straightway through that she was healed."[46]

Subsequently, in the twelfth century, a new version of the legend connected it to the *Volto Santo* of Lucca (Figure 1.1), a sculpted Crucifix in the Cathedral of Lucca,[47] which also served as a reliquary for one of the nails used in the Passion.[48] Twelfth-century accounts about the sculpture in Lucca claimed that Nicodemus had formed a wooden statue of Christ in a cruciform pose of his precise height and proportions based on an imprint that his body left on the burial shroud. The cloth was sometimes thought to be the same as the cloth of Veronica.[49] Frugoni (1982) had suggested that there could have been an earlier *acheiropoieton* textile held and revered in the Cathedral of Lucca that predated the sculpture, thereby suggesting a local tradition was the rationale for considering the sculpture a full-length "true image" of Christ.[50] Although the specificity of this proposal remains uncertain, the critical point

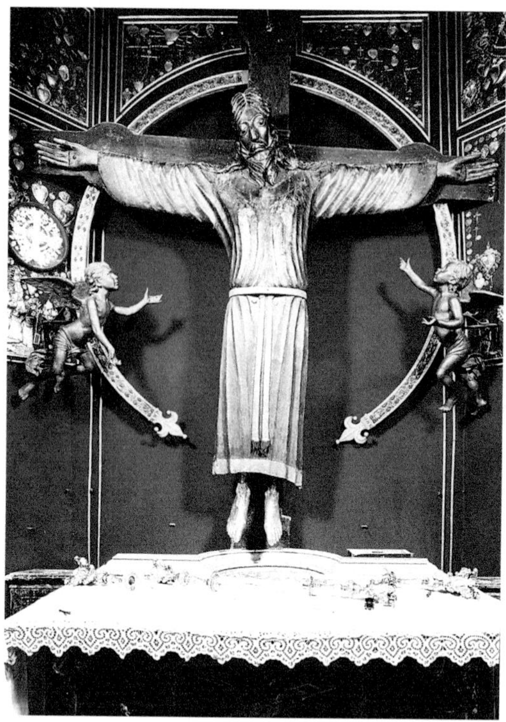

Figure 1.1 Artist unknown, *Volto Santo* of Lucca, early thirteenth century copy of a twelfth century original. Wood. Cathedral of Lucca.
Image credit: Scala/Art Resource, NY

from a broader perspective is that by the twelfth century, the legend of Veronica and her image-bearing cloth had begun to permeate and overlap with other legends about miraculous imprints of Christ's body onto swathes of cloth and related works of art.

It is important to mention here that the Eastern version of the *Mandylion* legend never merged with the Way of the Cross, which provided a reenactment of Christ's Passion cycle, a characteristic solely of the Western version. In the late twelfth century, as noted by Wolf (1998), among the earliest associations of Veronica with the Way to Calvary is Robert de Boron's *Legende de Joseph d'Arimathie*, a French poem well known in France and England during the thirteenth century.[51] Pearson (1887) had noted in his iconographic study that the story of Veronica in the West had two versions: one occurring during the years of Christ's ministry and the second associated with the Passion, with the change of timing in which Veronica appears within the arc of Christ's life datable to the mid-fifteenth century.[52]

Among the later medieval writers to use the Latin version of the woman's name, Veronica, was Giraldus Cambrensis (c. 1146–1223), also called Gerald of Wales, an English Archdeacon. In his *Opera: Speculum ecclesiae* (Works: Mirror of the church), c. 1219, in a section about the relics at Old Saint Peter's basilica, he

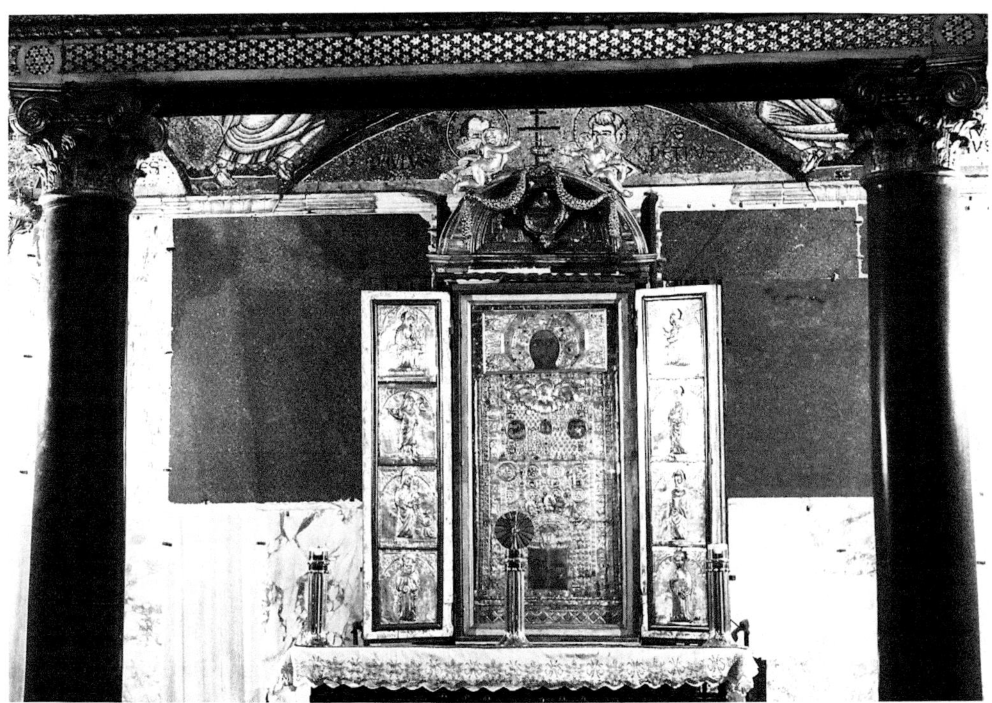

Figure 1.2 *Acheiropoieton* of Christ in a silver frame. Chapel of the Sancta Sanctorum, Palace of San Giovanni in Laterano, Rome. The original probably dates from the fifth or sixth centuries, but the work has been overpainted and heavily restored.

Image credit: VPC Photo/Alamy Stock Photo

distinguishes the *sudarium* relic as the image of Christ's face on a cloth from a painted icon of Christ in a silver frame in the Sancta Sanctorum chapel of the Palace of San Giovanni in Laterano in Rome (Figure 1.2). In his descriptions, he calls both objects *vera icon*, two words which blend to become *Uronica*.

The feminine name *Veronica*, therefore, could stem in part from a late medieval hybridization, fusion, or corruption of the name of the relic. The original given name, however, was Greek, as previously mentioned. Specifically, *Berenikē* (Βερενίκη) was the Macedonian version of the Athenian *Pherenı́kē* (Φερενίκη), meaning "she who brings victory." The Macedonian form became popular during the Hellenistic period under the reign of Alexander the Great, especially for women of the Ptolemy families in Egypt and Seleucids in the Near East.[53] The Latinization to *Veronica* – similar phonetically and syllabically to *Berenikē* – in medieval folklore was re-interpreted (erroneously) to comprise two words: the Latin *vera*, meaning true, and the Greek *eikon*, meaning image.[54] Thus, the Western use of this composite word, and its eventual development into the given name *Veronica*,[55] with its complex cultural etymology, may be an example of the kind of linguistic pun that late medieval ecclesiastical writers often employed to heighten confidence in a divine plan for salvation and to increase the authenticity of some religious narratives. In Giraldus's writings, an excerpt from which is below, the character's given name became interchangeable with the name of her "true image" relic: a cloth (also variously called a towel, napkin, or veil that was an extension of Veronica's clothing) on which was imprinted a preternatural image of the face of the living Christ. Giraldus introduces the passage by comparing the veronica with images of Christ painted by the evangelist Luke. The excerpt begins with a reference to the Lateran image:

> However this image is called *Uronica* as if essential. However another image is held at Rome, which is called *Veronica*, from the lady Veronica who had longed for and had sought to see the Lord by requests; leaving the temple at the same time she had confronted the Lord, saying: "Verona, here [is] that which you were seeking." When that [which she held] had been looked at, he himself receiving her garment, pressed his face into it and left on it his own clearly defined image. This, with similarly great reverence, is seen by nobody, except through the intervention of veils which hang down before it; and this is [located] at St. Peter's. She, however, was that woman, as it is read, who touching the fringed border of the clothing of Jesus had been cured of [a] flow of blood. It is also read [that] because the same woman having been compelled to come to Rome from Jerusalem after the Passion of Christ, and having been forced to bring with her that which she wished to leave behind, [it] was brought at once to Tiberius Caesar with the result that he was cured of an incurable disease from which he had suffered. However some [men] say, playing with the vocabulary, [that] it is to be called *Veronicam* as if a true icon, that is, a true image.[56]

Matthew Paris (English, c. 1200–1259), a Benedictine monk living at St Albans Abbey at Hertfordshire, continued to augment the storyline by recounting in Latin in Volume 3 of his *Chronica Majora* (c. 1240–1259) that Veronica was the woman who gave Christ a cloth on his way to Calvary as an act of mercy and that he pressed his image onto it.[57] The author mentions the veronica in the context of the procession of the relic in Rome in 1208 by Pope Innocent III (papacy 1198–1216) and the subsequent prayers he wrote for it with associated indulgences. Matthew Paris's inclusion of and emphasis on the veronica in his manuscript may have played a role in the early formation of a cult to Veronica in England, which was largely promulgated by Benedictines.[58] Saliently, Matthew Paris was the first chronicler to feature an illumination of the veronica relic (Figure 1.3), which accompanied the following text:

> *On Veronica and the authentication of the same. A.D. 1216*
>
> While in fact the chance of fortune was disturbing the state of the English king with such great turmoils, Lord Pope Innocent, whom the anxiety of an unsteady church was disturbing, reverently carried an image of the face of the Lord, which is called [a] 'Veronica' as is the custom, from the church of Saint Peter all the way to the hospital of the Holy Spirit, with a procession. The image itself, when it had been completed while it was being fitted in its own place, turned itself upon itself so that it was standing in upside down; thus no doubt with the result that the forehead was placed lower, the beard higher. The Lord Pope, fearing too greatly, believed that what had happened was an evil prophecy to himself, and so that he might be more fully reconciled to God, with the counsel of the brothers, composed a certain elegant prayer in honor of the image itself which is called [a]

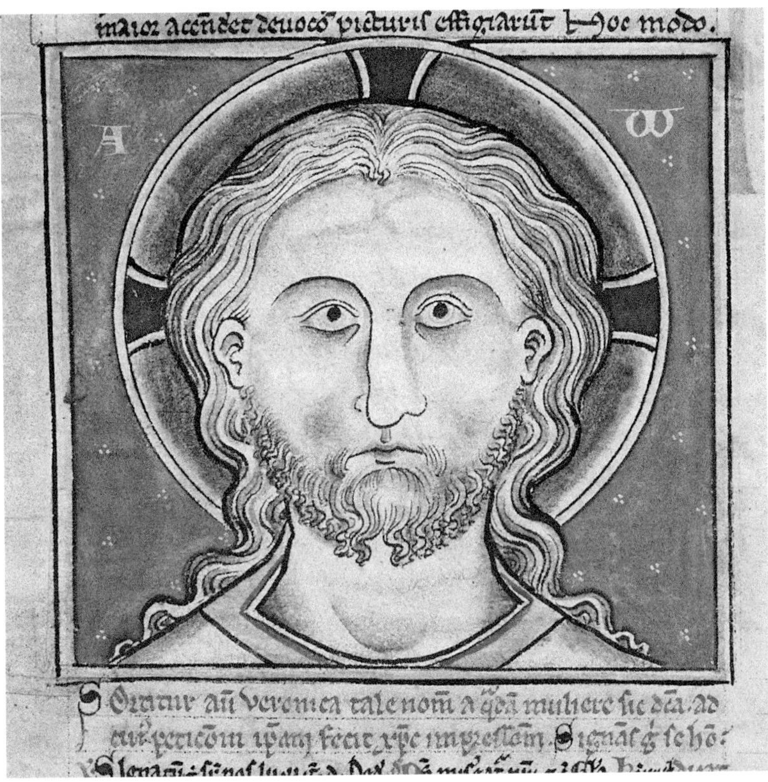

Figure 1.3 Matthew Paris O.S.B. (English, c. 1200–1259), *The Veronica* from the *Chronica Majora*, MS 16II, fol. 53v., c. 1240–1250. Tinted drawing on vellum, pasted to the page; 80 × 85 mm. Corpus Christi College, University of Cambridge.

Image credit: The Parker Library, Corpus Christi College, Cambridge

> 'Veronica,' to which he added a certain Psalm with certain brief verses, and he granted the same indulgence to those saying them for ten days, as is the custom, so that however often it was repeated, as many times as it was said, just so many indulgences would be granted. Therefore many [men] committed the prayer to memory with [its] details, and so that greater devotion might illumine them, they made painted images in this manner.
>
> It happened, however, that the very name 'Veronica' was said [to be] from a certain woman toward whose petition Christ made that very image. Therefore signing himself let [a] human being say [...]
>
> [And then there follows a litany of prayers and requests to be spoken in front of the 'Veronica' image.][59]

On the heels of Matthew Paris, Jacobus de Voragine, O. P. (Italian, c. 1230–1298) drew upon this amalgam of earlier legends and continued to expound upon them. In a chapter titled "The Passion of Our Lord" in the *Legenda Aurea* (Golden Legend), datable c. 1260, Jacobus recounted that Veronica wanted to have a picture painted of Christ so that when she was apart from him, she could look at his image.

The author narrates that she was carrying a linen to a painter when she saw Christ by happenstance. He asked her where she was going, and she told him. He then asked for the cloth, pressed his face to it, and left his image on it. Using dialogue as the primary means for advancing the plot, Jacobus adds that only piety could make the image effective (i.e. heal someone of an affliction).

> During this time Volusian made the acquaintance of a woman named Veronica, who had been in Jesus' company, and asked her where he might find Jesus Christ. She answered: "Alas, he was my Lord and my God, and Pilate, to whom he was handed over through envy, condemned him and commanded that he be crucified." Volusian was grieved at this and said: "I am deeply sorry that I cannot carry out the orders my master gave me." Veronica answered: "When the Teacher was going about preaching and I, to my regret, could not be with him, I wanted to have his picture painted so that when I was deprived of his presence, I could at least have the solace of his image. So one day I was carrying a piece of linen to the painter when I met Jesus, and he asked me where I was going. I told him what my errand was. He asked for the cloth I had in my hand, pressed it to his venerable face, and left his image on it. If your master looks devoutly upon this image, he will at once be rewarded by being cured." "Can this image be bought for gold or silver?" Volusian asked. "No," Veronica replied, "only true piety can make it effective."[60]

As Jacobus de Voragine relied heavily on the *Cura Sanitatis Tiberii*, textual authority drove the augmentation of the Veronica legend. Jacobus's version was important for the legend's codification and dissemination in the West largely due to the book's wide readership with a high number of copies in circulation. Approximately 1,000 copies of the Latin manuscript are extant,[61] with most of the copies having appeared in print by the 1450s. In 1483, the book was printed in English by William Caxton and translated into French and most other Western European languages, including Welsh and Catalan.[62] Featuring not only lives of the saints but also miracle stories about relics, the book was used as the basis of sermons, manuscript illuminations, and paintings during the Early Modern period. The legend's popularity and adaptability facilitated the Franciscans' ability to modify it to their own ends, as will be discussed further in Chapter 3.

In the second half of the thirteenth century, Boniface of Verona (Italian, c. 1270–c. 1317) composed a poem called the *Veronica*, dedicated to Cardinal William de Braye, in which he merges the stories of the veronica in Old Saint Peter's basilica with the *Mandylion*.[63] In the poem, the character of Veronica becomes the wife of King Abgar. In this lyrical text, preserved in a fifteenth-century manuscript in Paris, Boniface exhibits the various ways in which the Eastern and Western traditions of the legend were melding.[64] By the end of the thirteenth century, the legends of Veronica's encounters with Christ and the nature of the imprint of his face onto her cloth were established, albeit in a variety of forms, in both the Orthodox and Western traditions, with the latter eventually eclipsing the former. Folklore about both the woman and her relic sustained familiarity among pilgrims who wrote about the encounter in their journals and travel records during and after visits to Jerusalem and Rome. These stories spread throughout Italy, Germany, France, England, and the Low Countries from the mid-thirteenth through the late fifteenth centuries, forming the foundation for eventual visual iconography.

As an example of the legend's renown in Italy, Dante Alighieri (Florence, c. 1265–1321) alluded to Veronica and her relic (although he does not name her precisely) in his *Vita Nuova* in the context of encountering pilgrims in Rome.[65] Furthermore, the poet mentioned the veronica specifically in Canto XXXI of the *Paradiso* (c. 1320). In this Canto, Dante contemplates the Elect, among whom Beatrice has a place, leaving him with Saint Bernard of Clairvaux (French, 1090–1153).[66] He refers to the veronica in the form of a pilgrim's question:

> As one who comes perhaps from Croatia in order to see our Veronica and, from a long desire, cannot see enough, but says to himself, as long as it is exhibited "My Lord Jesus, my Christ, my true God, and was it like that that you appeared?"[67]

Likewise, Francesco Petrarca (called Petrarch, Tuscany, 1304–1374) alluded to the relic in *Canzoniere* XVI, in which he compares himself to a pilgrim in Rome who seeks the image of Christ's face:

> The old man takes his leave, white-haired and pale,
> of the sweet place where he filled out his age
> and leaves his little family,
> bewildered to see its own dear father disappear;
>
> from there, dragging along his ancient limbs
> throughout the very last days of his life,
> helping himself with good will all he can,
> broken by years, and wearied by the road,
> he comes to Rome, pursuing his desire,
> to look upon the likeness of the One
> that he still hopes to see up there in Heaven.
>
> Just so, alas, sometimes I go,
> my lady, searching, as much as possible,
> in others for your true, your desirable form.[68]

In England, Geoffrey Chaucer (1343–1400) mentioned a veronica (Middle English, *vernycle* or *vernicle*) in the Prologue of *The Canterbury Tales* (1387–1400). The Pardoner had sewn on his cap a veronica,[69] meaning a patch, medal, or badge with an image of the face of Christ, sometimes with the character of Veronica holding the cloth. These were tokens often given to pilgrims in commemoration of their journeys to Rome (Figure 1.4 is an example). This literary reference is significant because it situates the veronica within the context of pilgrimage and other kinds of common relics, such as a swathe of the Virgin's veil.

From the Prologue:

> He'd sewn a veronica on his cap. His knapsack lay before him, on his lap, Chockful of pardons, all come hot from Rome. His voice was like a goat's, plaintive and thin. He had no beard, nor was he like to have; Smooth was his face, as if he had just

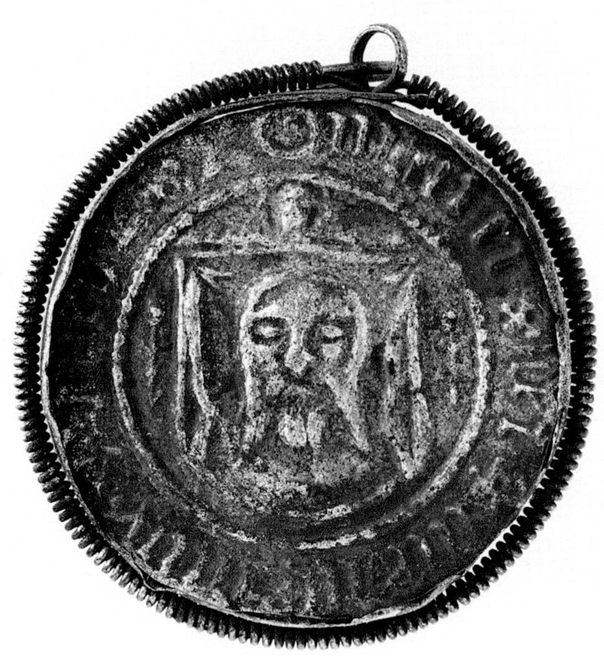

Figure 1.4 Italian (Rome), *Pilgrim Badge with Veronica holding the Vernicle*, fifteenth century. Brass, with design embossed; 33.5 mm diameter. Found Amiens, France. Inscription: o mater:dei:mementon:mey (O Mother of God, remember me). The British Museum, London (1855,0625.16).

Image credit: © The Trustees of the British Museum, London

> shaved. I took him for a gelding or a mare. As for his trade, from Berwick down to Ware You'd not find such another pardon-seller. For in his bag he had a pillowcase Which had been, so he said, Our Lady's veil; He said he had a snippet of the sail St Peter had, that time he walked upon The sea, and Jesus Christ caught hold of him. And he'd a brass cross, set with pebble-stones, And a glass reliquary of pigs' bones. But with these relics, when he came upon Some poor up-country priest or back-woods parson, In just one day he'd pick up far more money Than any parish priest was like to see in two whole months.[70]

As Rhodes (1983) has described, the veronica badge issued at Old Saint Peter's basilica in Rome was one of the most coveted among pilgrims' emblems. Due to its popularity in the Middle Ages, the veronica was easily recognizable in its frontal pose of the face of Christ with a calm expression.[71] Chaucer emphasizes the detail about the veronica by mentioning that the Pardoner wore nothing else on his bare head but the cap. However, the donning of the badge in this context is less an act of piety than an external display of the *appearance* of piety. As a character, the itinerant preacher, who promised cures and pardons in exchange for a fee, had a greater interest in silver and gold than in repentance and spiritual devotion. Chaucer's point may have been that pilgrims fall short of the redemptive nature of Christ's mercy, even as they work, live, and walk with an aim toward salvation. As an emblem commemorative of pilgrimage within a frame story about pilgrims, the veronica badge on the Pardoner's cap may have symbolized to Chaucer that pilgrims (imperfect despite their best intentions) seek a "true image" of Christ, the only one who can ultimately redeem them.[72]

In the early fifteenth century, John Audelay (fl. 1417–1426), an English poet who was chaplain of Knockin, drew inspiration from the legend of Veronica in composing verse.[73] As Fein (2011) has researched and expounded upon at length, one of his devotional poems comprises a set of eight salutations to holy women that are paired with prayers. The culmination of this sequence of salutations is an exchange between the Virgin and Veronica. The two figures are linked, and both were held in esteem because they each carried Christ in their own respective ways: one in her womb and one in effigy.[74] In specific reference to Veronica, Audelay adds a prayer to the image of God, *Salve sancta facies*, that was accompanied by a drawing of the veronica. Devotion to the text and image together granted an indulgence.[75] Audelay's addition of the *Salve sancta facies* is important not only because it links Veronica's attribute to reverence to the divine face but also because of its visionary nature, especially considering that the poet was blind.[76]

> *Salve*, I say, Holé Face of our Saveour,
> In the wyche schynth to us an hevenly fygure,
> An [One] graceus on to se!
> *Salve*, thou settis thi prynt on lynin cloth of witlé [whitish] coloure,
> And betoke hit Veroneca fore love and gret honoure
> Upon here sudoré [sudary].[77]

In a Middle High German adaptation of the Veronica legend called *Veronica II*, the text advises ways to alleviate the effects of loss and the absence of Christ after his crucifixion with the use of the *vera icon* as a substitute, which Weitbrecht (2016) approaches from the perspective of a "converged media enterprise."[78] In summary, the text, composed in Regenbogen's *Briefweise*, counsels that devotion to both the saint and the relic can advance a worshiper along the path to transcendence and salvation.[79] The legend is a conglomerate of stories. It includes aspects of both the Byzantine tradition, which features King Abgar of Edessa, and the Western version, based on the *Acts of Pilate*, which connects Berenice/Veronica to the story of the bleeding woman from the synoptic Gospels.[80] But the German adaptation has some singularities. For example, for the cloth to be effective as a cure, it must be applied directly (come into physical contact with) the wound:[81]

> As Veronica stood at the emperor's bed,
> she applied the cloth to his face and mouth,
> and at once the suffering emperor stood up and was healed.[82]

In French versions of the legend, after the death of the Virgin in the first century, Veronica married Zacchaeus, the tax collector in Jericho whose conversion is told in Luke 19:1–10. She accompanied him from Palestine to Rome. She later married a certain Quercy, who became a hermit renamed Amadour. Driven out of Palestine by persecution, Amadour had wandered, led by an angel, and settled in Rocamadour (in the former Quercy province of Dordogne, France), which was named after him.[83] The couple then joined Martial, a bishop and preacher with whom they collaborated in evangelizing in southwestern Gaul.

Veronica is credited with having brought relics of the Virgin from Palestine via Rome to Soulac-sur-Mer, located at the mouth of the Gironde estuary in southwestern France, during the first century. There, in a Roman temple situated over a natural spring, Veronica established an oratory to the Virgin, the stone retable for which is still visible in the basilica of Nôtre-Dame-de-la-fin-des-Terres, a Romanesque, Benedictine abbey, datable to the eleventh and twelfth centuries (Figures 1.5 and 1.6). A chapel dedicated to Veronica in the northeast transept contains a reliquary that holds a vial of the Virgin's breast milk that Veronica allegedly brought to Soulac (Figure 1.7).[84]

French tradition holds that Veronica was buried in the year 70 in Soulac. However, when the Vikings approached the French coast in the 840s, her remains were moved inland to Bordeaux to protect them from looting. The tomb of Veronica is located in the vaulted crypt of the Church of Saint Seurin

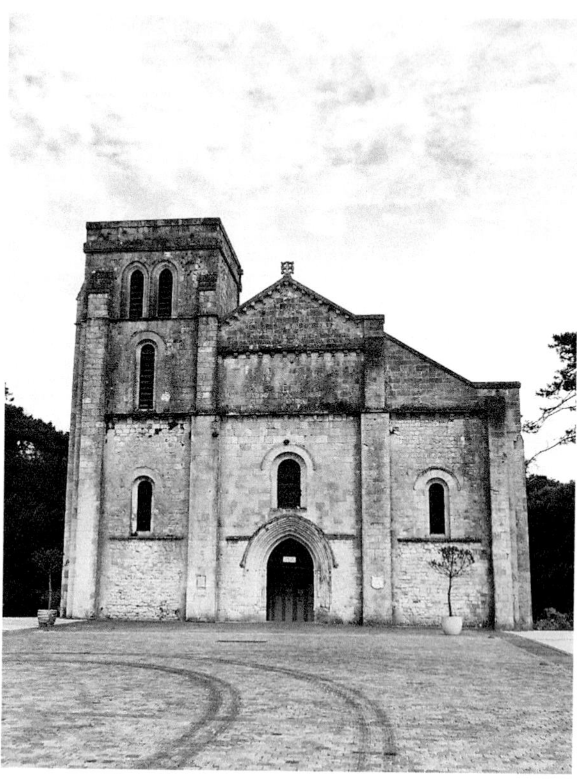

Figure 1.5 Church of Nôtre-Dame-de-la-fin-des-Terres, façade. Soulac-sur-Mer, France.
Image credit: Author

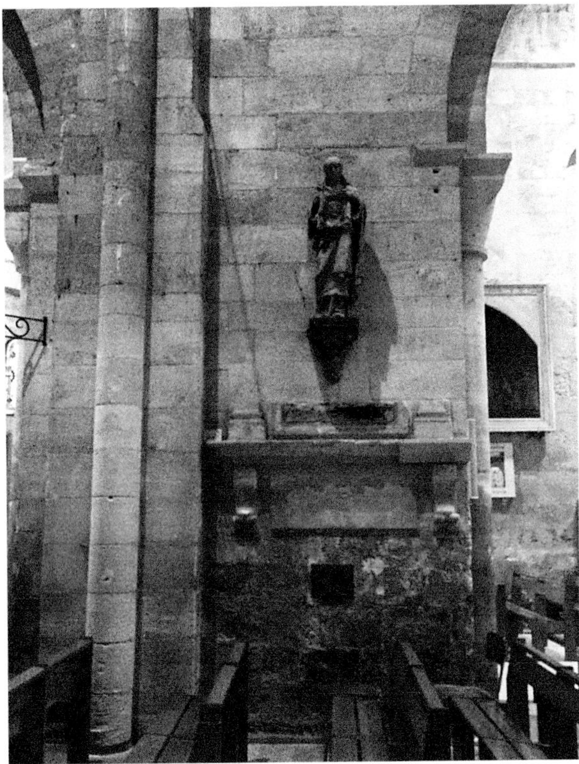

Figure 1.6 Church of Nôtre-Dame-de-la-fin-des-Terres, interior. Soulac-sur-Mer, France. The remains of the retable of the oratory are the rough-hewn stones on the bottom. The sculpture of Veronica above it is a later commemoration.

Image credit: Author

at Bordeaux (Figure 1.8).[85] In part because of her alleged sojourn in France, the legend of Veronica has maintained a special devotion in the country since the late medieval period. At the core of the French cult to Veronica is *La Vengeance de Nostre-Seigneur* (The Vengeance of our Lord), a twelfth-century epic poem, of which there were nine prose versions in Old and Middle French.[86] The text, which describes the Roman destruction of Jerusalem and the conversion of the Roman Empire to Christianity, provided the textual basis of Vengeance plays, which followed dramatizations of the Passion during the Middle Ages, as will be discussed further in the final chapter.

To recapitulate this survey of literary history, parallel legends about Veronica and her image-bearing cloth emerged by the fourth century in both the Eastern Orthodox and Western traditions. Although apocryphal in nature, the stories claimed a tangential connection to the synoptic Gospels through the woman with a hemorrhage, who had assumed the Greek name Bernice by the fourth century. By the eighth century, this unnamed character had become synonymous

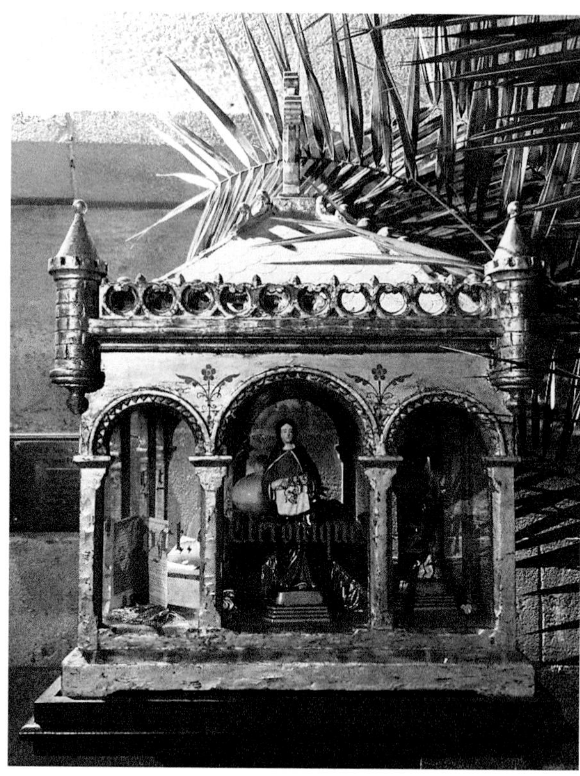

Figure 1.7 Reliquary containing relics of the Virgin brought to France by Veronica. Chapel in the northeast transept, Church of Nôtre-Dame-de-la-fin-des-Terres, Soulac-sur-Mer, France.

Image credit: Author

with the given name Veronica, a medieval hybridization of the Latin and Greek words for her attribute, the *vera icon*. The legend was retold and embellished by Anglo-Saxon writers, as well as by later medieval ecclesiastical historians, notably Giraldus Cambrensis. In the mid-thirteenth century, the English chronicler and manuscript illuminator Matthew Paris recounted a miraculous event during a procession of the cloth in the first quarter of the thirteenth century by Pope Innocent III. Almost contemporaneously, the story was augmented and widely disseminated by Jacobus de Voragine in his *Legenda Aurea*. As the legend spread throughout Europe, variants emerged in English, German, and French traditions. References to both the character Veronica and her *sudarium* can be found in literature and poetry of Italy, Germany, and England. Because of her presence in Soulac-sur-Mer and burial in Bordeaux, a singular French cult to her emerged. These legends and their embellishments served as the textual basis for visual images of Veronica produced during the Early Modern period, as will be explored in the following chapters.

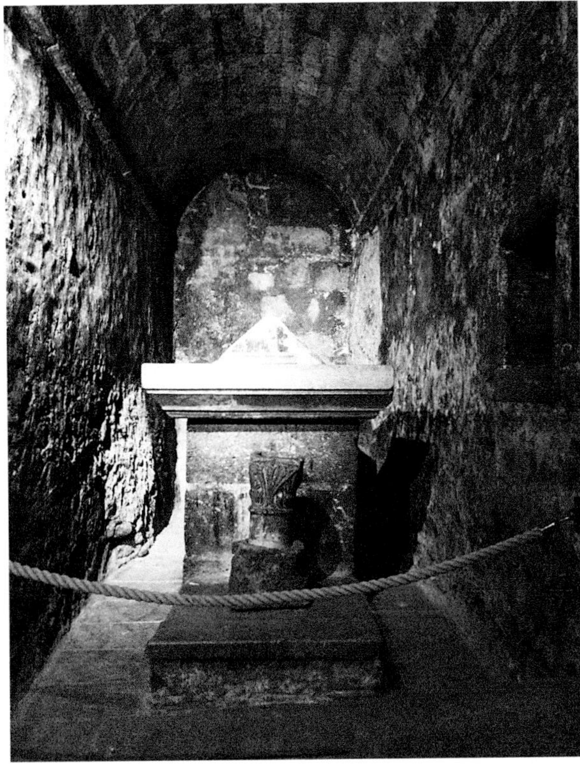

Figure 1.8 Tomb of Veronica, Crypt of the Church of Saint Seurin, Bordeaux, France.
Image credit: Author

Notes

1 The inscription on the saint's halo is in Latin: *Sancta Veronica*. The inscription on Christ's halo is a Greek abbreviation of his name: *ihs.xp.ih.x*. The National Gallery, London, accessed August 31, 2019, www.nationalgallery.org.uk.

2 Peter Brown, *The Cult of the Saints: Its Rise and Function in Latin Christianity* (Chicago: University of Chicago Press, 1982). Brown describes the social and ecclesiastical milieu of the first through fourth centuries, a period during which funerary rites and burial customs expanded to accommodate popular concepts of guardian angels and patron saints. These protective, invisible guides were often identified with early Christian martyrs. Bishops encouraged families to communicate with spiritual avatars that existed in a realm between human and divine experiences and to adorn burial sites with altars and chapels to them.

3 Joh. Bapt. De Rossi, and Ludov. Duchesne, eds., *Martyrologium Hieronymianum: Ad Fidem Codicum, Adiectis Prolegomenis* (Brussels: Typis Polleunis et Ceuterick, 1894).

4 Antoine Degert, "Saint Veronica," in *The Catholic Encyclopedia: An International Work of Reference on the Constitution, Doctrine, Discipline, and History of the Catholic Church*, ed. Charles G. Herbermann, et al. (New York: Robert Appleton Company, 1912), 362–363. For purposes of disambiguation, Degert notes that the Roman Martyrology also records at Milan a Saint Veronica de Binasco of the Order of Saint Augustine on 13 January and a Saint Veronica Giuliani on 9 July.

5 Robert Godding, ed., *De Rosweyde aux Acta Sanctorum: La recherche hagiographique des Bollandistes à travers quatre siècles: actes du Colloque international, Brussels, 5 October 2007* (Brussels: Société des Bollandistes, 2009).

6 Heribert Rosweyde and Jean Bolland, *Acta Sanctorum* (Antwerp and Brussels: Société des Bollandistes, 1643–1940), accessed April 24, 2018, ProQuest, http://acta.chadwyck.co.uk. In the *Commentarius Historicus* section of the *Acta Sanctorum*, under the date July 12, Veronica is listed as: "Hæmorrhoissa nomine, ut volunt, Veronica, Cæsareæ Philippi in Phœnicia (S.)." See also Jan Machielsen, "Heretical Saints and Textual Discernment: The Polemical Origins of the *Acta Sanctorum* (1643–1940)," in *Angels of Light? Sanctity and the Discernment of Spirits in the Early Modern Period*, eds. Clare Copeland and Jan Machielsen (Leiden: Brill, 2013), 103–141.

7 For a synopsis of the evolution of the story, see Andrea Lorenzo Molinari, "Saint Veronica: Evolution of a Sacred Legend," *Priscilla Papers* 28 (2014): 9–15.

8 Eusebius Pamphili, *Ecclesiastical History, Books 1–5*, trans. Roy J. Deferrari, in *The Fathers of the Church: A New Translation*, vol. 19 (Washington, DC: Catholic University of America Press, 2005). The text was originally written in Greek, although there were contemporary translations in Latin, Syriac, and Armenian. Eusebius's book chronicles Church history from the first through the fourth centuries from a distinctly Christian perspective.

9 The idea that the woman originated from Tyre comes from the *Cura Sanitatis Tiberii*, an eighth-century variation of the *Acts of Pilate*, datable to the mid-fourth century. "Then Volosianus said to that young man, 'can you tell me the name of that woman?' He said, 'She is called Veronica, dwelling in Tyre.'" Tuomas Levänen, trans., *Cura Sanitatis Tiberii*, Section 9, www.academia.edu/15436621/Cura_Sanitatis_Tiberii_English_Translation.

10 Michael D. Coogan, Marc Z. Brettler, and Carol Newsom, eds., with contributions by Pheme Perkins, *The New Oxford Annotated Bible with Apocrypha: New Revised Standard Edition*, 4th ed. (Oxford: Oxford University Press, 2010), 1759.

11 "And a large crowd followed him and pressed in on him. Now there was a woman who had been suffering from hemorrhages for twelve years. She had endured much under many physicians, and had spent all that she had; and she was no better, but rather grew worse. She had heard about Jesus, and came up behind him in the crowd and touched his cloak, for she said, 'If I but touch his clothes, I will be made well.' Immediately her hemorrhage stopped; and she felt in her body that she was healed of her disease. Immediately aware that power had gone forth from him, Jesus turned about in the crowd and said, 'Who touched my clothes?' And his disciples said to him, 'You see the crowd pressing in on you; how can you say, "Who touched me?"' He looked all around to see who had done it. But the woman, knowing what had happened to her, came in fear and trembling, fell down before him, and told him the whole truth. He said to her, 'Daughter, your faith has made you well; go in peace, and be healed of your disease.'" Ibid., 1801.

12 "Now there was a woman who had been suffering from hemorrhages for twelve years; and though she had spent all she had on physicians, no one could cure her. She came up behind him and touched the fringe of his clothes, and immediately her hemorrhage stopped. Then Jesus asked, 'Who touched me?' When all denied it, Peter said, 'Master, the crowds surround you and press in on you.' But Jesus said, 'Someone touched me; for I noticed that power had gone out from me.' When the woman saw that she could not remain hidden, she came trembling; and falling down before him, she declared in the presence of all the people why she had touched him, and how she had been immediately healed. He said to her, 'Daughter, your faith has made you well; go in peace.'" Ibid., 1846.

13 For further discussion about the story of the *Haemorrhoissa*, see Barbara Baert (with the collaboration of Emma Sidgwick), "Touching the Hem: The Thread between Garment and Blood in the Story of the Woman with the Haemorrhage (Mark 5:24b–34parr)," *Textile* 9 (2011): 308–352; and Emma Sidgwick, "At once limit and threshold: How the early Christian touch of a hem (Luke 8:44; Matthew 9:20) constituted the medieval Veronica," *Viator* 45 (2014): 1–24.

14 Eusebius Pamphili, *Ecclesiastical History*, 1.13.5–1.13.22. For the Greek text of the two letters with a translation into English and commentary, see Bart D. Ehrman and Zlatko Pleše, *The Apocryphal Gospels: Texts and Translations* (Oxford: Oxford University Press, 2011), 413–417.
15 Ehrman and Pleše, *The Apocryphal Gospels*, 417.
16 Ibid., 413, 417.
17 Ibid., 413.
18 Herbert L. Kessler, "Il *mandylion*," in *Il Volto di Cristo*, eds. G. Morello and G. Wolf (Milan: Electa, 2000), 64–99.
19 For the complete text in Greek with an English translation and commentary, see Ehrman and Pleše, *The Apocryphal Gospels*, 419–489.
20 The date of the middle of the fourth century is accepted by Ehrman and Pleše. However, the authors also consider a proposal of Izydorczyk (1997) that the texts of the mid-fourth century were based on traditions and stories from the previous two centuries. Ehrman and Pleše, *The Apocryphal Gospels*, 420. See also Zbigniew Izydorczyk, *The Medieval Gospel of Nicodemus: Texts, Intertexts, and Contexts in Western Europe* (Tempe, AZ: Medieval and Renaissance Texts and Studies, 1997).
21 Ehrman and Pleše, *The Apocryphal Gospels*, 419.
22 M. R. James, trans., *The Gospel of Nicodemus, or Acts of Pilate* (Oxford: Clarendon Press, 1924), 7. In Greek, she is called Βερνίχη or Βερονίχη. See Charles Wycliff Goodwin, trans. and ed. for the Cambridge Antiquarian Society, *The Anglo-Saxon Legends of St. Andrew and St. Veronica* (Cambridge: Deighton, MacMillan and Co., 1851), vii.
23 Molinari, "Saint Veronica: Evolution of a Sacred Legend," 9.
24 M. R. James, trans., *The Gospel of Nicodemus*, 15.
25 Ibid., 8.
26 Gerhard Wolf, "'Or fu sì fatta la sembianza vostra?' Sguardi alla 'vera icona' e alle sue copie artistiche," in *Il Volto di Cristo*, eds. G. Morello and G. Wolf (Milan: Electa, 2000), 103–211, especially 105–106.
27 Ibid., 105.
28 The full version of the legend in Latin, called *Cura Sanitatis Tiberii Cesaris Augusti et Damnatio Pilati*, comes from a Vatican manuscript of the eighth century, printed by J. D. Manso in the *Supplement to the Miscellanea Stephani Baluzii*, vol. iv, 55. See Goodwin, *The Anglo-Saxon Legends*, vi. For an English translation, see Tuomas Levänen, trans., *Cura Sanitatis Tiberii*, www.academia.edu/15436621/Cura_Sanitatis_Tiberii_English_Translation. The nature of Tiberius's illness is unclear, but the Anglo-Saxon legend recounts that the emperor was so "unsound by reason of various wounds that he became a leper." Goodwin, *The Anglo-Saxon Legends*, 27. Some versions, including the German adaption of the legend, suggest that his illness is moral and related to the destruction of Jerusalem. See Judith Lange, *Die Verslegende «Veronica II»: Hybridedition und Studien zur Überlieferung* (PhD. diss., Aachen University, Germany, 2013); and Julia Weitbrecht, "The Vera Icon (Veronica) in the Verse Legend Veronica II: Medializing Salvation in the Late Middle Ages," *Seminar: A Journal of Germanic Studies* 52 (2016): 173–192. The foundational, critical edition of the *Cura Sanitatis Tiberii* text is Dobschütz, *Christusbilder*, 163–190. The most recent re-examination of and challenge to this scholarship is Zbigniew Izydorczyk, "The *Cura Sanitatis Tiberii* a Century after Ernst von Dobschütz," in *The European Fortune of the Roman Veronica in the Middle Ages, Convivium Supplementum*, eds. A. Murphy, H. L. Kessler, M. Petoletti, E. Duffy, and G. Milanese, 32–49 (Turnhout, Belgium: Brepols Publishers, 2017).
29 "[...] mulierem nomine Vironicam qui Latine vocatur Vasille." The word *vasille*, which may be related to *vexillum* (Latin for military banner), may have been used to refer to the *sudarium* with an image of Christ's face. Goodwin, *The Anglo-Saxon Legends*, viii.
30 Levänen, *Cura Sanitatis Tiberii*, Sections 12 and 13. For the Latin and Middle English versions, with extensive source notes regarding original manuscripts, see E. M. Thompson, "Apocryphal Legends," in *Journal of the British Archaeological Association* XXXVII (London: British Archaeological Association, 1881): 239–253.
31 Bede, *The Complete Works of Venerable Bede, in the original Latin, collated with the Manuscripts and various printed editions, and accompanied by a new English translation*

of the Historical Works, and a Life of the Author, 8 vols., ed. Rev. J. A. Giles (London: Whittaker and Co., 1843).

32 Peter Darby and Daniel Reynolds, "Reassessing the 'Jerusalem Pilgrims': the Case of Bede's *De locis sanctis*," *Bulletin for the Council for British Research in the Levant* 9 (2014): 27–31.

33 Ibid., 29.

34 For the complete text in Latin with an English translation and introduction, see Ehrman and Pleše, *The Apocryphal Gospels*, 537–557. For the Old English text with translation, see J. E. Cross, ed., with contributions by Denis Brearley, Julia Crick, Thomas N. Hall, and Andy Orchard, *Two Old English apocrypha and their manuscript source: "The Gospel of Nichodemus" and "The Avenging of the Savior"* (Cambridge: Cambridge University Press, 1996), 248–293. For a recent critical analysis, see Rémi Gounelle and Céline Urlacher-Becht, "Veronica in the *Vindicta Salvatoris*," in *The European Fortune of the Roman Veronica in the Middle Ages, Convivium Supplementum*, eds. A. Murphy, H. L. Kessler, M. Petoletti, E. Duffy, and G. Milanese, 50–57 (Turnhout, Belgium: Brepols Publishers, 2017). The authors of the latter essay distinguish between and compare two states of the Latin text, one without Volusianus and one that includes this character. Furthermore, the authors assert that the writers who transcribed the text over time did not know about the character of Veronica and instead focused on the image of Christ on the relic.

35 Ehrman and Pleše, *The Apocryphal Gospels*, 537.

36 Mary Swan, "Remembering Veronica in Anglo-Saxon England," in *Writing Gender and Genre in Medieval Literature: Approaches to Old and Middle English Texts*, ed. Elaine Treharne (Cambridge: D. S. Brewer, 2002), 23–27. See also J. E. Cross, ed., et al., *Two Old English apocrypha.*

37 Ehrman and Pleše, *The Apocryphal Gospels*, 543, 549.

38 Ibid., 551–553.

39 Ibid., 553.

40 Molinari, "Saint Veronica: Evolution of a Sacred Legend," 11.

41 Ehrman and Pleše, *The Apocryphal Gospels*, 553.

42 Coogan, et al., eds., *The New Oxford Annotated Bible*, 1874.

43 Ehrman and Pleše, *The Apocryphal Gospels*, 557.

44 Goodwin, *The Anglo-Saxon Legends*, vii.

45 Ibid., ix–xi.

46 Ibid., 29.

47 For a basic introduction to this sculpture's history and iconographic complexities, see Michele Bacci, "The *Volto Santo*'s Legendary and Physical Image," in *Envisioning Christ on the Cross: Ireland and the Early Medieval West*, ed. Juliet Mullins, Jenifer Ní Ghrádaigh, and Richard Hawtree (Dublin, Ireland: Four Courts Press, 2013), 214–233.

48 Anne Derbes, *Picturing the Passion in Late Medieval Italy* (Cambridge: Cambridge University Press, 1996), 121.

49 Raffaele Savigni, "The Roman Veronica and the Holy Face of Lucca: Parallelism and Tangents in the Formation of their Respective Traditions," in *The European Fortune of the Roman Veronica in the Middle Ages, Convivium Supplementum*, eds. A. Murphy, H. L. Kessler, M. Petoletti, E. Duffy, and G. Milanese, 274–285 (Turnhout, Belgium: Brepols Publishers, 2017). Savigni mentions several points of overlap between the sculpture in Lucca and the veronica in Rome, each of which was purported to be a "true image" of Christ.

50 Chiara Frugoni, "Una proposta per il *Volto Santo*," in *Il Volto Santo. Storia e culto*, eds. Clara Baracchini and Maria Teresa Filieri, 15–48 (Lucca: Pacini Fazzi, 1982).

51 Gerhard Wolf, "From Mandylion to Veronica: Picturing the 'Disembodied' Face and Disseminating the True Image of Christ in the Latin West," in *The Holy Face and the Paradox of Presentation*, eds. Herbert L. Kessler and Gerhard Wolf, 153–179, 169 (Bologna: Nuova Alfa, 1998). See Robert de Boron, *Joseph d'Arimathie*, ed. Richard O'Gorman, *Studies and Texts* 120 (Toronto: Pontifical Institute of Mediaeval Studies, 1995),

164–180. The edition by O'Gorman offers both the verse and prose versions with critical notes.

52 Pearson, *Die Fronica*, 76.

53 Behind the Name, "Berenice," accessed June 21, 2019, www.behindthename.com.

54 For more on the etymology of the name Veronica, see Alfred Maury, "Lettres sur l'étymologie du nom de Véronique donné a la femme qui porte la sante face et sur l'origine de son culte," *Revue Archéologique* 2 (Paris: Presses Universitaires de France, 1851): 484–495.

55 Variant spellings include Veronika in German, Hungarian, and Scandinavian languages; Véronique in French; Verónica in Spanish; Weronika in Polish; and Nika in Russian. See Behind the Name, "Berenice," accessed June 21, 2019, www.behindthename.com.

56 Translation by James C. Anderson, jr., electronic correspondence with the author, July 9, 2018. The original Latin can be found in Giraldus Cambrensis, *Opera: Speculum Ecclesiae*, ed. J. S. Brewer, M.A. (London, Her Majesty's Stationery Office, 1873; reprinted by Kraus Reprint, Ltd., 1964): 278–279, as follows:

"Hæc autem imago dicitur *Uronica*, quasi essentialis. Alia autem imago Romæ habetur, quæ dicitur *Veronica*, a Veronica matrona quæ tamdiu desideraverat et orationibus Dominum impetraverat videre; quæ semel exiens a templo Dominum obvium habuit dicentem: 'Verona, ecce quem desiderasti.' Quem cum intuita fuisset, ipse peplum ejus accipiens impressit vultu suo, et reliquit in eo expressam imaginem suam. Hæc in magna similiter reverentia, et a nemine, nisi per velorum quæ ante dependent interpositionem inspicitur; et hæc est apud Sanctum Petrum. Hæc autem illa, ut legitur, mulier fuit, quæ tangens fimbriam vestimenti Jesu a sanguinis profluvio curata fuit. Legitur etiam quod eadem mulier post Christi passionem Romam de Hierosolimis venire coacta, eamque secum portare quam relinquere voluit compulsa, statim ut Tiberio Cæsari allata fuit curatus est a morbo incurabili quo laboraverat. Dicunt autem quidam vocabulo alludentes, Veronicam dici, quasi *veram iconiam*, id est, imaginem veram."

57 Matthew Paris (Matthæi Parisiensis, Monachi Sancti Albani), *Chronica Majora*, vol. 3, ed. Henry Richards Luard, M.A. (London: Her Majesty's Stationery Office, 1872; reprinted Weisbaden: Kraus Reprint Ltd., 1964), 7–8, http://archive.org.

58 Hamburger, *The Visual and the Visionary*, 371. For a refutation of the theory that Matthew Paris instigated the spread of the cult and associated imagery of Veronica in England, see Nigel Morgan, "'Veronica' Images and the Office of the Holy Face in Thirteenth-Century England," in *The European Fortune of the Roman Veronica in the Middle Ages, Convivium Supplementum*, eds. A. Murphy, H. L. Kessler, M. Petoletti, E. Duffy, and G. Milanese, 84–99 (Turnhout, Belgium: Brepols Publishers, 2017). Morgan proposes that Matthew Paris derived his version of the veronica and its associated text of the Office from the Lateran icon by means of a copy held at Westminster Abbey or Palace in London.

59 Translation by James C. Anderson, jr., electronic correspondence with the author, May 28 and June 10, 2018. The original Latin inclusive of the prayers is as follows: "*De Veronica et ejusdem autenticatione*. A.D. 1216 "Dum vero fortunalis alea statum regni Angliæ talibus turbinibus exagitaret, dominus Papa Innocentius, quem vacillantis ecclesiæ cura sollicitabat, effigiem vultus Dominici, quæ Veronica dicitur, ut moris est, de ecclesia Sancti Petri usque ad hospitale Sancti Spiritus reverenter cum processione bajulabat. Qua peracta, ipsa effigies, dum in loco suo aptaretur, se per se girabat, ut verso staret ordine; ita scilicet, ut frons inferius, barba superius locaretur. Quod nimis abhorrens dominus Papa, credidit illud in triste sibi præsagium evenisse, et ut plenius Deo reconciliaretur, consilio fratrum, in honore ipsius effigiei, quæ Veronica dicitur, quondam orationem composuit elegantem; cui adjecit quondam Psalmum, cum quibusdam versiculis, et eadem dicentibus decem dierum concessit indulgentiam, ita scilicet, ut quotienscunque repetatur, totiens dicenti tantumdem indulgentiæ concedatur. Multi igitur eandem orationem cum pertinentiis memoriæ commendarunt, et ut eos major accenderet devotion, picturis effigiarunt hoc modo. "Sortitur autem Veronica tale nomen a quadam muliere sic dicta, ad cujus petitionem ipsam fecit Christus impressionem. Signans igitur se homo dicat,"Signatum est super nos lu[men] v[ultus] t[ui], D[omine]. Ded[isti]. *Ps.* Deus misereatur nostri, etc. Gloria. Kyrieleison, Christeleison, Kyrieleison.

Pater noster. Et ne. *Vers.* Fac mecum signum in bo[num] ut vid[eant]. *Vers.* Tibi dixit cor meum [exquisivit te] fa[cies] m[ea], fac[iem] t[uam] D[omine] r[equiram]. *Vers.* Quærite Dominum et confirmamini, q[uærite] f[aciem] e[jus] s[emper]. *Vers.* Ora pro nobis, beata Veronica. U[t] d[igni]. *Vers.* Domine Deus virtutum converte nos, et ostende. *Oremus.* Deus qui nobis signatis lumine vultus Tui memorial tuum ad instantiam Veronicæ sudario impressam imaginem relinquere volusti, per passionem et crucem Tuam tribue nobis quæsumus, ut ita nune in terries per speculum et in enigmate ipsam adorare et venerari valeamus, ut facie ad faciem venientem judicem Te secure videamus, Qui vivis et regnas cum Deo Patre." Matthew Paris, *Chronica Majora*, vol. 3, 7–8.

60 Jacobus de Voragine, *The Golden Legend: Readings on the Saints*, trans. William Granger Ryan with introduction by Eamon Duffy (Princeton, NJ: Princeton University Press, 2012), 212.

61 William Granger Ryan, Introduction to *The Golden Legend: Readings on the Saints*, vol. 1, by Jacobus de Voragine (Princeton, NJ: Princeton University Press, 1993), xiii.

62 Swan, "Remembering Veronica in Anglo-Saxon England," 24.

63 Marco Petoletti, and Angelo Piacentini, "The *Veronica* of Boniface of Verona," in *The European Fortune of the Roman Veronica in the Middle Ages, Convivium Supplementum*, eds. A. Murphy, H. L. Kessler, M. Petoletti, E. Duffy, and G. Milanese, 250–259 (Turnhout, Belgium: Brepols Publishers, 2017).

64 Ibid.

65 See Dante Alighieri and Mark Musa, *Dante's* Vita Nuova, *New Edition: A Translation and an Essay* (Bloomington, IN: Indiana University Press, 1973), section XL.

66 Dante Alighieri, *The Divine Comedy*, trans. C. H. Sisson (Oxford: Oxford University Press, 1980), 728.

67 Ibid., 489, lines 103–108.

68 "Movesi il vecchierel canuto et bianco
del dolce loco ov' à sua età fornita
et da la famigliuola sbigottita
che vede il caro padre venir manco;

indi traendo poi l'antico fianco
per l'estreme giornate di sua vita,
quanto più po col huon voler s'aita,
rotto dagli anni, et dal camino stanco;

et viene a Roma, seguendo '1 desio,
per mirar la sembianza di colui
ch' ancor lassù nel ciel vedere spera.

Cosi, lasso, talor vo cercand' io,
Donna, quanto e possibile in altrui
la disiata vostra forma vera."

Francesco Petrarca and Mark Musa, *The Canzoniere, or Rerum Vulgarium Fragmenta* (Bloomington, IN: Indiana University Press, 1999), 16–17. Petrarch's poem is in the public domain. The translation by Mark Musa is reproduced here by permission from Indiana University Press.

69 On Chaucer's use of the word *veronica*, see James F. Rhodes, "The Pardoner's 'Vernycle' and His 'Vera Icon,'" *Modern Language Studies* 13 (1983): 34–40.

70 Geoffrey Chaucer, *The Canterbury Tales*, trans. David Wright (Oxford: Oxford University Press, 1998), eBook Collection (EBSCOhost).

71 Rhodes, "The Pardoner's 'Vernycle,'" 34. See also Paul Perdrizet, "De La Véronique et De Seinte Véronique," in *Seminarium Kondakovianum* 5 (Prague: Institute: Kondakov, 1932): 1.

72 Rhodes, "The Pardoner's 'Vernycle,'" 37–38.

73 Susanna Fein, "Mary to Veronica: John Audelay's Sequence of Salutations to God-Bearing Women," *Speculum* 86 (2011): 964–1009.

74 Ibid., 965.

75 Ibid., 1001.
76 Ibid., 966.
77 Ibid., 1001–1002, lines 1–6.
78 Julia Weitbrecht, "The Vera Icon (Veronica) in the Verse Legend Veronica II: Medializing Salvation in the Late Middle Ages," *Seminar: A Journal of Germanic Studies* 52 (2016): 173–192.
79 See Judith Lange, "Die Verslegende 'Veronica II': Hybridedition und Studien zur Überlieferung" (PhD. diss., Aachen University, Zugl, 2013).
80 Weitbrecht, "The Vera Icon," 174.
81 Ibid., 184.
82 "Da Fronica vor des keysers bette stünd,
daz duch leit sie um uber daz antlitz und den mont.
Da stunt der krancke keyser uff und wart gesunt."

Lange, 202, lines 12–14. Translation to English by Julien Chapuis, in electronic correspondence with the author, July 18, 2019.
83 Michel Bourrières, *Saint Amadour and Sainte Véronique* (Paris: Tolra, 1895); and Jean Rocacher, *Rocamadour et son pèlerinage: étude historique et archéologique*, 2 vols. (Toulouse: Association les Amis de Rocamadour, 1979).
84 The gilded wooden reliquary that dates from 1860 contains a small collection of relics of the Virgin Mary brought to Soulac by Veronica, as well as relics from Saints Fort and Francis de Sales. A church inventory of 1628 lists the Marian relic as "Lac beatae Virginis Mariae." In a later inventory of 1676, the same relic is listed as: "Plus une Nostre Dame où il y a du lait de la Vierge pesant un marc et demi et en argent doré." See *Inventaire des Reliques de L'Eglise de Soulac, 9 Juillet 1628, Archives départementales de la Gironde*, H 507, II, and *Inventaire de L'Église de Soulac en L'Année 1676*, in Association des Amis de la Basilique Nôtre Dame de la Fin des Terres de Soulac-sur-Mer, *Nôtre Dame de la Fin des Terres* (Soulac, n.p., 1993), 79–82. I wish to thank Jean-Baptiste Leproux at the Church of Nôtre-Dame-de-la-fin-des-Terres in Soulac-sur-Mer for kindly providing access for me to these inventories in June 2019.
85 On Veronica at Soulac and Bordeaux, see M. Mezuret, *Notre-Dame de Soulac ou de la fin-des-terres: L'Apostolat de Sainte-Véronique en Aquitaine: le tombeau et le culte de Saine-Véronique a Soulac* (Lesparre: J. Rivet Imprimeur-Libraire, 1865); Aurélien des Célestins de l'Ordre de Saint Benoit, *Sainte Véronique, apôtre de l'Aquitaine: son tombeau et son culte à Soulac, ou, Notre-Dame de Fin-des-Terres, Archidiocèse de Bordeaux* (Toulouse: L. Hébraile, 1877); Grégoire Marie Thomas, *Soulac et Notre-Dame de la Fin-des-Terres* (Bordeaux: Imprimerie de l'oeuvre de Saint-Paul, 1882); and Bernard-Marie Maréchaux, *Notre Dame de la Fin des Terres de Soulac* (Bordeaux: Imprimerie Nouvelle A. Bellier, 1893).
86 Alvin E. Ford, ed., *La Vengeance de Nostre-Seigneur: The Old and Middle French Prose Versions: The Cura Sanitatis Tiberii (The Mission of Volusian), the Nathanis Judaei Legatio (Vindicta Salvatoris), and the Versions found in the Bible en français of Roger d'Argenteuil or influenced by the Works of Flavius Josephus, Robert de Boron and Jacobus de Voragine* (Toronto: Pontifical Institute of Mediaeval Studies, 1984).

2 The *Sudarium* Relic as Material Object in the West

Although the history of the veronica relic is integrally intertwined with the evolution of the legend and its many manifestations, this chapter focuses on the object itself and its peregrinations across various locations, each of which affected its viewership, including the periodic *inability* to view it. It is important to clarify at the outset that, just as there were two versions of the legend, there were also originally two "true image" relics. The earlier of the two, the *Mandylion*, was a Byzantine portrait from the sixth century. Brought from Edessa in northern Syria to the Pharos Chapel in the Great Palace of Constantinople during the mid-tenth century, it was revered in the Eastern Orthodox tradition as a divinely produced verisimilitude of Christ's face. The second, Veronica's *sudarium*, became the Eastern cult-relic's rival and eventual successor in the West by the early thirteenth century, both in renown and devotion. Housed in Old Saint Peter's basilica, the veronica was a focal point of veneration in the Roman Church and remains one of its principal relics in the crossing of New Saint Peter's basilica. However, unlike the *Sindone di Torino* (Shroud of Turin), which has been extensively documented, there are neither technical documents nor clear photographs of the veronica, thereby explaining the lack of a reproduction of it in this volume or elsewhere.

It may seem paradoxical to address the materiality of an object that can neither be touched nor examined in proximity. Yet, the history of the veronica relic – including the history of *the idea* of it, aside from any physical properties – is critical for understanding its role in Rome, the hub of spiritual life in the Christian West from the late Middle Ages through the Baroque period. In fact, the veronica embodies one of the central paradoxes of Christianity, which promotes belief through faith alone, yet tolerates and even encourages the display and veneration of relics as tangible proof of the historicity of holy figures or the veracity of events mentioned in the Scriptures. In the story of the Doubting Thomas (John 20:29), after Thomas had placed his fingers in the wound in Christ's side and only then believed that he had risen from the dead: "Jesus said to him, 'Have you believed because you have seen me? Blessed are those who have not seen and yet have come to believe.'"[1] The veronica relic – as either an actual object or the concept of one – encouraged worshipers to follow Jesus's teaching in this verse from John by believing in the divine nature of a material artefact *without* viewing or touching it, as the latter portion of this chapter addresses.

Belting (1994) asserted that the two "true image" cult objects – the earlier Eastern one and its Western counterpart – should be considered together because the veronica inherited the legends of the *Mandylion*, which served as the basis of the relic's reverence in the West.[2] Moreover, during the early thirteenth century, at approximately the same time that the public visibility and veneration of the veronica increased in Rome, the Constantinopolitan relic was lost. The Western relic in essence replaced its Eastern prototype and predecessor. Specifically, the Eastern relic disappeared in the sack of Constantinople in 1204 during the Fourth Crusade,[3] and the precise whereabouts of the Byzantine icon thereafter remain obscure. Two inventories from 1534 and 1740 of the treasury of the Sainte-Chapelle in Paris document a relic belonging to Louis IX that was claimed to be the *Mandylion*, although this object was absconded during the French Revolution.[4] The essential distinction between the Eastern and Western relics, as Belting has pointed out, is that the legend of Veronica in the West was not initially linked to a physical cult-object, whereas the Eastern version from its origins *did* hinge on a relic. As the legend in the West evolved, by the twelfth century, the story mentioned a *sudarium*, which the Romans held and claimed Jesus had used in the first century. But reference to an image on it only appears about 1200.[5] Whereas the Eastern relic was considered a "true image" from the beginning, in the West, the revered object was initially thought of as a contact relic, because Christ had touched it, or as an effluvial relic because the cloth had absorbed his sweat and blood.[6] The holiness of the *sudarium* expanded to comprise a "true image" identity notably at the time of the Eastern icon's disappearance. Both the *Mandylion* and the veronica remain important for the study of the Orthodox and Latin Church's support of the use of icons in liturgy and personal devotion because these two miraculous images of Christ's visage offered testimony of his physical existence and justified the use of images as proof. The imprints of Christ's face, believed to be divinely produced, served as prototypes for subsequent images of him.

By 1204, the Western *sudarium* purportedly bore an imprint of Christ's face. The image was considered an *acheiropoieton*, that is, an image not created by human hands,[7] like its Eastern prototype. As a record of the pre-Crucifixion visage, the veronica can be distinguished from the Shroud of Turin, allegedly a post-Crucifixion imprint.[8] In this aspect, because Christ was alive when the imprint of his features was transferred to Veronica's veil, the cloth was popularly believed to be "more true" than the Shroud of Turin, or at least closer to the living Christ. As Koerner (1996) proposed, and Weddigen (2015) among other scholars since have concurred, by 1500 such divine images were regarded as self-portraits by God.[9] According to Christian theology, Christ was made in God's image, as exemplified by the following three passages from Paul's letters:

> 2 Corinthians 4:4–7: "In their case the god of this world has blinded the minds of the unbelievers, to keep them from seeing the light of the gospel of the glory of Christ, who is the image of God."[10]
>
> Colossians 1:15: "He is the image of the invisible God, the firstborn of all creation."[11]
>
> Hebrews 1:3: "He is the reflection of God's glory and the exact imprint of God's very being, and he sustains all things by his powerful word."[12]

As such, Jesus's visage on the *sudarium* was perceived not simply as a transferral of his physical features to a cloth but moreover a self-portrait of and by God. Status as an *acheiropoieton* helped to refute any claims that the relic was a product of idolatry.[13] On the contrary, it encouraged the worship of God and Christ by means of an image. Furthermore, the belief that the imprint had not been created by human hands facilitated the image's acceptance as one welcomed by God. The veronica relic in essence became the archetype of images of Christ, an effigy that claimed to provide viewers a coveted, one-on-one encounter with the face of their maker and redeemer.[14]

The veronica is historically and thematically associated with an earlier icon in Rome, probably dating from the fifth or sixth century, which also was considered an *acheiropoieton* (Figure 1.2). As mentioned in Chapter 1, this full-length image of an enthroned Christ, holding a scroll in his left hand and his right hand in a gesture of benediction, was believed to have been painted by Saint Luke with the help of angels. The icon remains ensconced in an elaborate silver frame in the Chapel of the Sancta Sanctorum in the Palace of San Giovanni in Laterano in Rome. Although both the Lateran object and the veronica were used in public processions and each were focal points of Roman cults on the image of Christ, the fame and legacy of the latter eventually surpassed the former after the thirteenth century. Thus, although the veronica was neither Rome's first nor only *acheiropoieton,* it eventually became the more renowned of the two within the Church and the city of Rome.

Bynum (1995), in considering the formation and nature of Christian relic cults in the West, has asserted a connection between the reverence for relics and a belief in the resurrection of the body.[15] Theologians of the fourth and fifth centuries, such as Gregory of Nyssa, discussed Christ's Resurrection within the context of relics. Jerome defended relics as a source of virtue, and Augustine respected relics, believed in their ability to work miracles, and considered them part of a plan for a resurrection of the whole body from individual parts.[16] Bynum asserted that the tendency to perceive wholeness despite the fragmentary nature of relics is a uniquely Western phenomenon.[17] Such tenets of early Christian thought were vibrant during the Early Modern period and remain relevant in discerning possible meanings of Veronica's veil as a focal point of veneration.

In outlining a chronology of the veronica's multifarious translocations, we can recall that legends as they had evolved by the mid-thirteenth century held that Veronica took the veil to Rome at the request of Emperor Tiberius (r. 14–37) to heal him of afflictions, probably ulcers and leprosy. In Rome, the curative cloth subsequently remedied illnesses of the Flavian emperors Vespasian (r. 69–79) and Titus (r. 79–81).[18] Versions of the Veronica legend involving the Roman emperors were frequently subjects of works of art, as evident in a Flemish tapestry datable to 1510 in the Metropolitan Museum of Art in New York (Figure 2.1). Either the Flavian emperor Domitian (r. 81–96) gave the cloth to Pope Clement I (whose papacy is dated 88–99, according to Tertullian and Irenaeus), or some traditions claim that Veronica, on her deathbed, bequeathed it to Clement. The object is assumed to have remained in successive papal collections, where it was revered as a relic, since the second century. The cloth was housed at Old Saint Peter's basilica in a chapel dedicated to it probably by the eleventh century.[19] However, as Ann Van Dijk (2013) has described, the relic, like most other sacred objects within the basilica before the thirteenth century, was kept at a distance from worshipers, who could only hope to catch a glimpse of it from the floor level.[20]

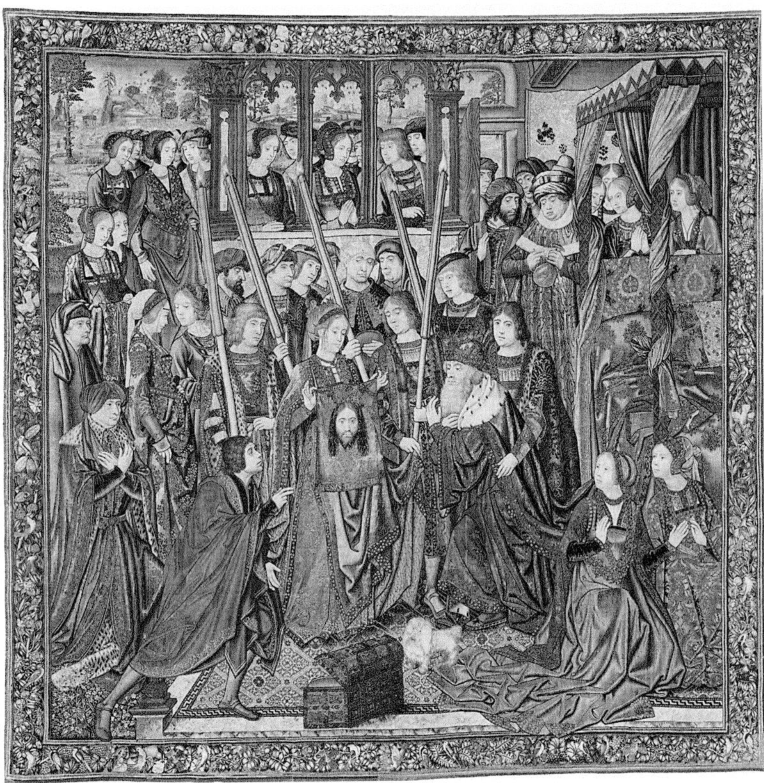

Figure 2.1 Flemish (Brussels), *Emperor Vespasian Cured by Veronica's Veil*, c. 1510. Woven tapestry made of wool, silk, and gilt metal threads. The Metropolitan Museum of Art, New York (1975.1.1914). Robert Lehman Collection, 1975.

Image credit: The Metropolitan Museum of Art, New York

The earliest recorded mention of Veronica's veil as a physical object appears in the late tenth century when a chronicler mentioned that Pope John VII (papacy 705–707) had ordered the construction of an oratory dedicated to Mary "ubi dicitur Veronice"[21] (in the place called Veronica) in Old Saint Peter's basilica, where the Pope had planned to be interred. Ballardini and Pogliani (2013) have proposed a reconstruction of the oratory, which was located in the outer north aisle and was modified when the *Volto Santo* was placed there.[22] Before the oratory's destruction in 1609, Pope Paul V Borghese (papacy 1605–1621) had ordered its descriptions by the Vatican cleric and notary, Giacomo Grimaldi (1568–1623),[23] with drawings by Domenico Tasselli.[24] An account by Nicolaus Muffel in 1452 described that during the papacy of John VII, there were fourteen twisted columns in the oratory, two of which were placed in front of the altar of Veronica.[25] By the year 1018, a scribe named John had been designated as keeper of the cloth: "clerico et mansionario Sanctae Marie in Beronica."[26] Benedictus Canonicus records in 1143 in his *Ordo Romanus* (Roman Order, a document with rubrics for liturgical services) in the *Liber Censuum Romanae Ecclesiae* (Census Book of the Roman Church) a relic "quod vocatur Veronica" (that is called Veronica), although he does not specifically call it an image or describe it.[27] In 1191 the French King Philip II (Philip Augustus), on his way back from the Holy Land, visited Rome, where he was shown the most important relics of Old Saint Peter's basilica. His chronicler described one of them as "a linen cloth that Christ had pressed to his face on which still today that imprint appears most evident as it presents the face of Christ."[28] As Van Dijk describes, by 1193, Pope Celestine III (papacy 1191–1198) had placed the veronica inside a large ciborium (a receptacle for the Eucharistic bread) within the oratory constructed by Pope John VII. The relic was locked securely in an upper register of the ciborium to protect it from religiously fervent crowds. Although periodically on display on a platform, the relic was more difficult to see than other sacred objects at Old Saint Peter's basilica.[29]

The prominence of Veronica's veil increased in Rome during the first quarter of the thirteenth century when its fame was launched as one of the relics most worthy of veneration in Western Christendom. As recounted by Matthew Paris, Pope Innocent III (papacy 1189–1216)[30] paraded the relic between Old Saint Peter's basilica and the *Ospedale di Santo Spirito* (Hospital of the Holy Spirit)[31] in January of 1208 as part of a liturgical celebration during Epiphany.[32] The procession, as illuminated in the manuscript *Liber Regulae Sancti Spiritus in Saxia* (Plate 4), datable 1350, featured a reenactment of the Marriage of Cana, which employed both the veronica and a Marian image from the nearby church, Santa Maria in Sassia.[33] In 1216, Matthew Paris described that when the *sudarium* turned upside down during this procession, Pope Innocent III was initially afraid that the occurrence might have been an omen of God's discontent. However, the Pope took the occasion to declare the object miraculous. He granted a ten-day indulgence to those who recited a prayer that he had written for the veronica,[34] a circumstance that contributed to a rise in the relic's popularity.

Although Pope Innocent III's procession was short in distance, it proved to be important for public exposure and papal endorsement of the veronica relic. From Old Saint Peter's basilica, the hospital is located approximately 700 meters to the southeast, about five minutes' walk along Borgo Santo Spirito, with the building complex situated on the west bank of the Tiber river. The route is roughly the length of two long city blocks, with the basilica of Santa Maria in Sassia at the midpoint (Figure 2.2a–d). The choices of the beginning and terminal sites of the procession represented, respectively, the sacred place where the relic was housed and a health care center for pilgrims. Founded in 727, the *Ospedale di Santo Spirito* is the oldest in Europe.[35] Its original purpose was to care for the Anglo-Saxon pilgrims who had traveled to Rome to visit Saint Peter's tomb. Because the hospital was built on the original site of the *Schola Saxonum*, a charity serving Saxon travelers, the hospital's location was often referenced as *in Sassia* or *in Saxia*. Because Pope Innocent III had refurbished the hospital in 1198, he had a vested interest in showcasing the building and connecting it to the seat of the papacy as an extension of the Church's mission and an emblem of its reach. Thus, the procession functioned in part as an inauguration of the Pope's architectural and charitable achievements.[36] In addition to parading the veronica, Innocent III's celebration connecting Old Saint Peter's to the hospital included a homily, public donations to the city's beggars, and distribution of alms to the approximately 300 patients who were in residence at the hospital at that time.[37]

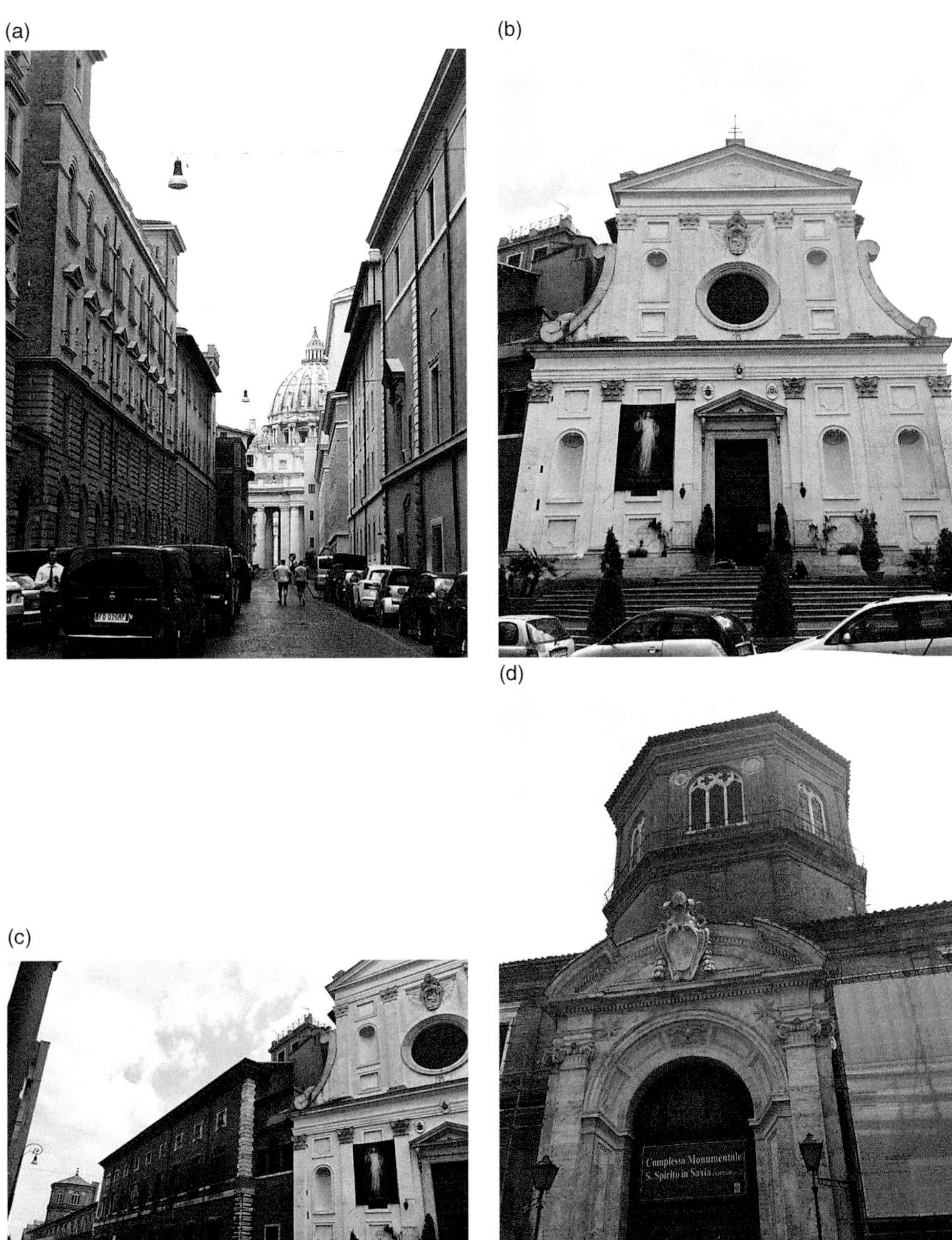

Figure 2.2a–d Pope Innocent III's procession route of the veronica in Rome in the early thirteenth century. (a) The beginning of the route from Saint Peter's basilica down Borgo Santo Spirito. (b) Midpoint at the Church of Santa Maria in Sassia. (c) Santa Maria in Sassia to the *Ospedale di Santo Spirito*. (d) *Ospedale di Santo Spirito* in Sassia.

Image credit: Author

Liturgical instructions for the "Procession with the veil of Veronica" are recorded in Latin in the *Liturgy of the Papal Court and the Franciscan Order in the Thirteenth Century.*[38] In addition to being paraded in annual processions, the object was regularly displayed on Sundays, at Christmas, during Lent, and on Easter. It also held special significance during Jubilee Years, starting in 1300, and on the Feast of Saints Peter and Paul.[39] Bölling (2017) further describes how the veronica was used in papal ceremonies.[40] Collectively, the processions, displays, prayers, hymns, Mass orations,[41] and related indulgences[42] increased the popularity of and widespread devotion to the relic from the first quarter of the thirteenth century forward, enticing pilgrims across Europe to make arduous journeys to see it. Regarding indulgences, Hand (1994) suggested that the Holy Face of Veronica may have been the first indulgenced image and that over time the value of the indulgences associated with the relic increased. Specifically, time spent in purgatory as punishment for a sin was reduced by ten to forty days in the thirteenth century. However, by the late fifteenth century, the punitive time was lowered by ten thousand days or even years.[43]

Also during the first quarter of the thirteenth century, the English writer and statesman, Gervase of Tilbury (Latin *Gervasius Tilberiensis*, c. 1150–1220), in Book III of his *Otia Imperialia* (Recreation for an Emperor), written c. 1210–1215 for Holy Roman Emperor Otto IV, recorded seeing the relic in Rome: "Est ergo Veronica pictura, Domini ueram secundum carnem representans effigiem a pectore superius, in basilica sancti Petri iuxta ualuam a parte introitus dextra recondita" (The Veronica portrait then, presenting a true physical likeness of the Lord from the chest upwards, is preserved in Saint Peter's basilica near the door, on the right-hand side of the entrance).[44] Although a brief mention, the reference crucially documents the relic's location within Old Saint Peter's basilica by the first quarter of the thirteenth century. Contemporaneously, Giraldus Cambrensis (c. 1219) commented on the difficulty in viewing the relic in the basilica. He wrote that the veronica is "seen by no-one except through the curtains which are hung before it."[45]

Pope Innocent IV (papacy 1243–1254) continued the tradition of granting indulgences for praying before the image of Christ's face by adding a second prayer, *Ave facies praeclara*[46] (Hail radiant face), for which one could earn forty days' indulgence.[47] By the end of the thirteenth century, Pope Boniface VIII (papacy 1294–1303) had augmented the relic's visibility by declaring a Jubilee year in 1300 and by naming the relic among the *Mirabilia urbis Romae* (Marvels of the city of Rome). During the Avignon papacy (1309–1376), the relic remained at Old Saint Peter's, where, as described by Di Fruscia (2017), the Canons displayed the veronica in the direction of Avignon.[48] Pope John XXII (papacy 1316–1334), in a letter asking for donations to restore Old Saint Peter's basilica, mentioned a place for divine clemency with an image of the face of the savior.[49] Also during the papacy of John XXII, a second prayer, *Salve sancta facies* (Hail holy face), was composed. Reciting the new prayer before the veronica or a replica of it carried an indulgence of ten thousand days. As the value of indulgences associated with prayers to the veronica continued to inflate, the image's renown increased.[50]

The veil allegedly stayed at Old Saint Peter's basilica through the end of the fifteenth century. William Wey (English, c. 1405/6–1476), a priest from Devon who retired to the Augustinian Priory of Edington in Wiltshire, described in 1458 the cloth and associated indulgences in his pilgrim's journal from Rome, in a section about the relics of Old Saint Peter's basilica:

> The first capital altar is that of Simon and Jude who lie on the same altar. The second altar is that of St. George, in which his body lies. The third is of Pope Leo. The fourth is that of the Blessed Virgin where Mass is sung each day. The fifth is of St. Andrew, the sixth of the Holy Cross and no woman dares enter it. The seventh is to St. Veronica. Each of these altars has, every day, forty years of indulgences and as many Lents and remission of a third part of all sins.[51]

The veil of Veronica is allegedly housed in New Saint Peter's basilica in the southwestern pier that supports the dome at the crossing designed by Donato Bramante in 1506. The shrine to Veronica (Figure 2.3a) is one of the four main reliquaries in the crossing, with the other three dedicated to Helena's fragment of the True Cross, the spear of Longinus, and the head of Andrew. With the reliquaries incorporated into the four massive piers at the core of Bramante's Greek cross design, the relics both radiate out from the tomb of Saint Peter and uphold Michelangelo's sixteen-ribbed dome, a symbol of the vault of heaven. However, as Sanger (2012) has observed, these foremost relics of the Church are not *on display* at the crossing. The piers and accompanying sculptures in niches honor the concept of

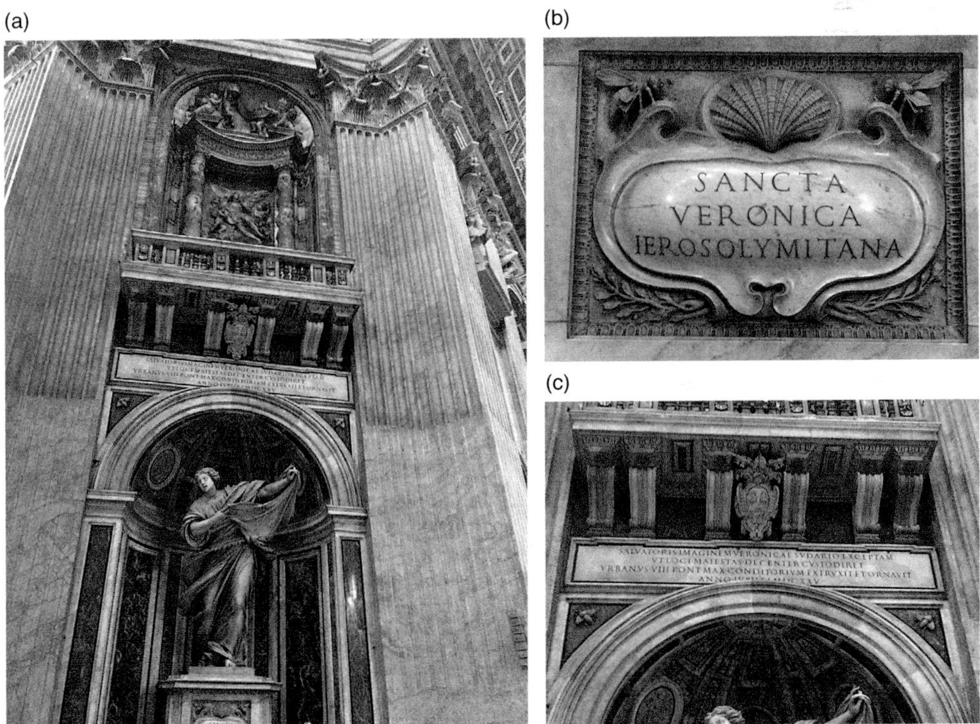

Figure 2.3a–c Shrine to Veronica, first half of the sixteenth century. Marble. Saint Peter's basilica, Rome. (a) Francesco Mochi, *Veronica*, 1629–1640. Marble. (b) Inscription below Francesco Mochi's *Veronica*. Saint Peter's basilica, Rome. (c) Inscription above Francesco Mochi's *Veronica*. Saint Peter's basilica, Rome.

Image credit: Author

sacred objects (and the Church's ownership of them) rather than exhibit them for viewing. Worshipers and visitors are only invited to conjure images of actual relics in their minds.[52] The quadripartite piers that support the weight of the dome can be interpreted as an architectural metaphor for the *idea* of holy objects, each of which has the purpose of assuaging doubt by asserting the Church's possession of tangible proof of the divine. Moreover, as holder of these relics, three of which connected directly to Christ's Passion, the papacy declared Rome as the new Jerusalem.[53]

Reverence for Veronica's veil is commemorated by a Baroque marble statue, datable 1629–1640, by Francesco Mochi (Rome, 1580–1654).[54] The relic is supposedly located above the Mochi sculpture in the chapel under the roundel of Saint Matthew in the spandrel. The shrine-niche features two Latin inscriptions. At the bottom, there is a marble placard that reads: *Sancta Veronica Ierosolymitana* (Holy Veronica from Jerusalem) (Figure 2.3b). At the top in Roman letters is the inscription (Figure 2.3c):

SALVATORIS IMAGINEM VERONICAE SUDARIO EXCEPTAM
UT LOCI MAIESTAS DECENTER CUSTODIRET
URBANVS VIII PONT MAX CONDITORIUM EXTRUXIT ET ORNAVIT
ANNO JUBILORUM MDCXXV

(In order that the majesty of [this] place would fittingly preserve the image of the Savior
caught by the Sudarium of Veronica,
Urban VIII Pontifex Maximus constructed and adorned [this] coffin
In the Year of the Jubilee 1625)[55]

Some Christians have claimed that the Holy Face of Manoppello (Figure 2.4), a cloth with an image of a face that is held in the Basilica del Volto Santo in Manoppello, a small town in Abruzzo, is the original veronica, having been stolen from New Saint Peter's basilica during the construction that began in 1506.[56] In another scenario, the image-bearing cloth was believed to have been looted from New Saint Peter's basilica after the Sack of Rome in 1527 and sold on the streets by Lutheran soldiers but later resurfaced.[57] In 1616, Pope Paul V (papacy 1605–1621) prohibited the production of copies of the relic, and in 1629, Pope Urban VIII (papacy 1623–1644) ordered the destruction of all extant copies.

As a contextual note about copies, the intent of early facsimiles of relics was not to deceive but rather to extend the icon's benevolent powers to a broad viewership and to provide access to Christ by means of duplicate portraiture for those who could not make a journey to Rome to see the original. The copies were not necessarily intended to be exact replicas of a single picture but rather a multiplication of the concept of it. They provided additional opportunities for the faithful to meet the eyes of the divine by means of *vis-à-vis* encounters with Christ. Copies could also function to accompany indulgence prayers or to illustrate chronicles.[58]

In addition to the Manoppello object, at least five other extant images with some degree of resemblance have been claimed to be the original veronica or early copies of it. Among these are likenesses located in the Hofburg Palace, Vienna, Austria; the Treasure of the Cathedral, Prague, Czech Republic; the Monasterio de la Santa Faz, Alicante, Spain; the Cathedral of the Assumption, Jaén, Spain; the Church of San Bartolomeo degli Armeni in Genoa, Italy; and the Matilda Chapel at the

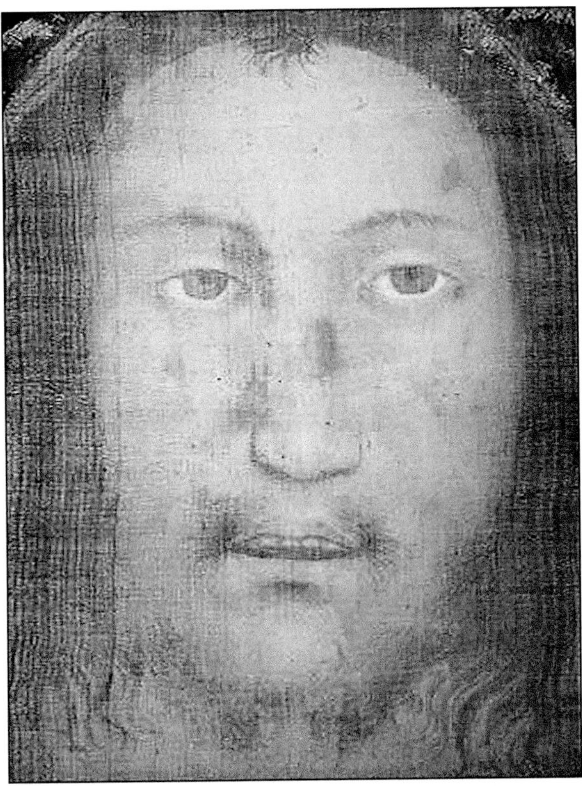

Figure 2.4 Holy Face of Manoppello. Basilica del Volto Santo, Manoppello, Italy.
Image credit: The Picture Art Collection/Alamy Stock Photo

Vatican, but formerly in the convent of San Silvestro in Capite, Rome. The latter image (Figure 2.5) was painted on canvas, affixed to a wooden panel, and encased in a silver frame.[59] Although distinct from each other in visual idiom, each of these copies has in common an inner, cut-out frame that reveals a visage with a three-pronged lower edge to suggest hair and a beard.[60]

In 1545, during the Protestant Reformation, Martin Luther (German, 1483–1546) mocked and criticized the veronica alongside his denouncement of the two head relics of Saints Peter and Paul at the Lateran:

> And yet, on SS. Peter and Paul's day, they display two heads, pretend, and let the common man believe that these are the natural heads of the apostles; so the reverent mob comes running, along with John Doe of Jena. But the pope, cardinals, and their riffraff know quite well that they are two wooden, carved, and painted heads; it is just the same as they do with the cloth of St. Veronica – they pretend it is our Lord's face imprinted on a handkerchief. All it is a small black square board with a shred of cloth hanging on it, and over that hangs another shred of cloth which they pull up when they show St. Veronica; but poor John Doe can see nothing anymore but a shred of cloth

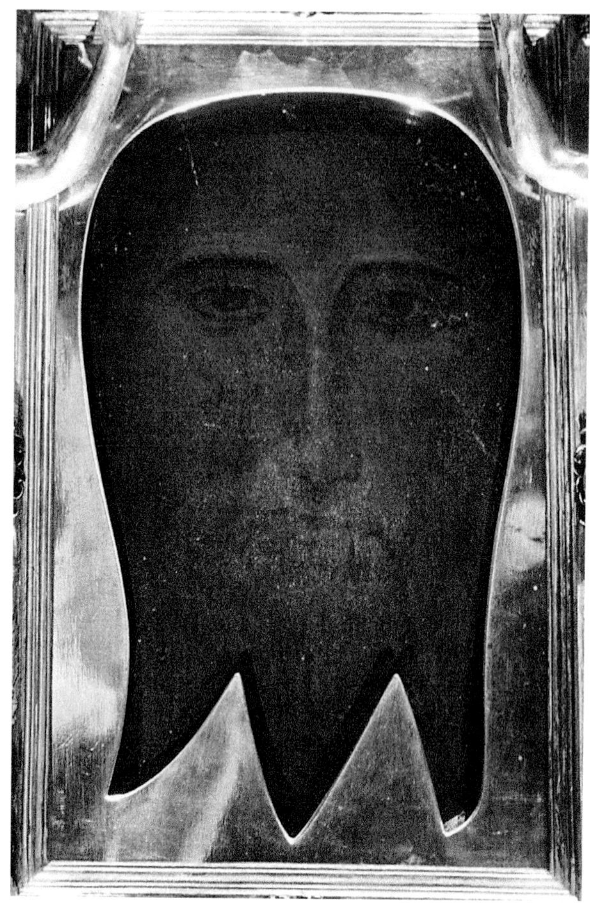

Figure 2.5 *Volto Santo* from the convent of San Silvestro in Capite, Rome. Panel; 40 × 29 cm. Matilda Chapel, Vatican.

Image credit: L'Ufficio delle Celebrazioni Liturgiche del Sommo Pontefice

> in front of a black board – that is called showing and seeing the cloth of Veronica – and there is much pious reverence and many indulgences for such crude lies.[61]

Luther's comments, on par with his disdain for and skepticism about other relics revered by the Catholic church, offer some indication about how the relic was displayed during the sixteenth century, against a black background with a covering and a curtain that could be lifted by a cord for purposes of exposition.

During the Counter-Reformation, Roman Catholics revived an interest in the ostension of and devotion to saints' relics. As Sanger (2012) points out, this reversal of attitude toward relics was in direct response to the Protestants' criticism of them.[62] During the sixteenth century, the Church fostered physical and personal experiences of material objects with spiritual resonance in order to heighten worshipers' sensorial responses to sacred stimuli. Ignatius of Loyola (Spanish, Basque, 1491–1556), founder of the Society of Jesus, opined in his core handbook of religious formation, *Spiritual Exercises* (1522–1524), in a section titled "Rules for Thinking with the Church," that relics should be revered, including in the context of the Stations:

> We should show our esteem for the relics of the saints by venerating them and praying to the saints. We should praise visits to the Station Churches, pilgrimages, indulgences, jubilees, crusade indults, and the lighting of candles in churches.[63]

Furthermore, the 25th Session of the Council of Trent in December 1563 declared regarding the reverence for relics and images of saints:

> Also, that the holy bodies of the holy martyrs and of others living with Christ, which were the living members of Christ and the temple of the Holy Ghost, to be awakened by Him to eternal life and to be glorified, are to be venerated by the faithful, through which many benefits are bestowed by God on men, so that those who maintain that veneration and honor are not due to the relics of the saints, or that these and other memorials are honored by the faithful without profit, and that the places dedicated to the memory of the saints for the purpose of obtaining their aid are visited in vain, are to be utterly condemned, as the Church has already long since condemned and now again condemns them. Moreover, that the images of Christ, of the Virgin Mother of God, and of the other saints are to be placed and retained especially in the churches, and that due honor and veneration is to be given to them; not, however, that any divinity or virtue is believed to be in them by reason of which they are to be venerated, or that something is to be asked of them, or that trust is to be placed in images, as was done of old by the Gentiles who placed their hope in idols, but because the honor which is shown them is referred to the prototypes which they represent[.][64]

Despite this clear Tridentine call to visit and revere relics and images of saints in churches, since the seventeenth century, the veronica at New Saint Peter's basilica has largely waned – if not disappeared – from public view. In 1854, Barbier de Montault, a cardinal and historian, examined the relic while it was on display for veneration. He noted that it was enclosed in a metallic frame that delineated the beard and hair. In describing a face, he noted: "the rest of the features are so vaguely drawn, or rather so completely effaced that I needed the best will in the world to see traces of eyes or nose – one saw only a blackened surface."[65] The cloth in the Vatican was last examined closely in 1907 by the German Jesuit art historian Josef Wilpert, who was allowed to view it with the two panes of glass on either side of its crystal frame (40 × 37 cm) removed. He described the artefact as: "a square piece of light colored material, somewhat faded through age, which bears two faint rust-brown stains, connected one the other."[66] Wilpert further suggested that any actual painted image of a face may have been on a separate cloth of a later addition, probably datable to the end of the twelfth century. Wilpert proposed that this top, image-bearing cloth could have been the one stolen in 1527, leaving the original Roman *sudarium* intact.[67] In my opinion, these two first-hand descriptions tell readers more about what was *not* clear – a defined image of a face – than what was actually extant. Moreover, they tell us more about those who seek the imprint of a face than any actual physical traces of one.

Every year on the fifth Sunday of Lent (Passion Sunday) at New Saint Peter's basilica, a framed reliquary image is briefly displayed on the balcony above Mochi's marble sculpture of Veronica. Accompanying the exposition are a recitation of a modern version of the prayer to the Veil of Veronica (modified from the original written by Pope Innocent III in the early thirteenth century), the singing of antiphons, and the ringing of bells.[68] Given the basilica's scale, it is difficult to discern from the floor any details of the object held by the priests for veneration.

In reflecting on the role of the object in tandem with its legends, debating the authenticity of the relic (whether the physical artefact is *truly* an imprint of Christ's face, or whether the image of the Holy Face was *actually* made without human hands) seems less important from my perspective than recognizing that – culturally, historically, and spiritually – millions of Christians during the Early Modern period believed this to be true. The distinction between the acceptance of the *Mandylion* as an *acheiropoieton* from the outset in contrast to the veronica's later adoption of this status at the turn of the thirteenth century provides some clues regarding the latter's change in rank from a contact relic to a "true image" relic in the West. The early production of copies of the veronica attests to a desire to widen the viewership and spiritual effects of the Holy Face without its power to heal being affixed to a single material object. The descriptions of the cloth at the Vatican by the few clergy or scholars who have seen it are unmistakably vague. Attempts to obscure any traces of a face on the cloth – whether by enclosing the *sudarium* in a ciborium during the papacy of Celestine III, veiling it with curtains as described by Giraldus and criticized by Martin Luther, or holding it up briefly and from a high distance as is the current praxis at New Saint Peter's basilica – kept (and keep) viewers at arm's length and in a perpetual state of yearning to see it, whether motivated by devotion or general curiosity. Although it is instructive to trace the movement and whereabouts of the veronica relic in the West and to outline a chronology of its owners, locations, and viewers, the cultural resonance of the object rests outside of its materiality. The relic is less significant in physical nature than in the hopes of salvation and fears of judgment that its worshipers projected onto it. Embedded in this image-bearing object – although paradoxically largely unviewable – is a collective human desire to meet the divine face to face.

Notes

1 Coogan, et al., eds., *The New Oxford Annotated Bible*, 1915.
2 Belting, *Likeness and Presence*, 208–209.
3 Hamburger, *The Visual and the Visionary*, 317.
4 Steven Runciman, "Some Remarks on the Image of Edessa," *Cambridge Historical Journal* 3 (1931): 238–252.
5 Belting, *Likeness and Presence*, 218–220.
6 On bodily relics in general, and contact and effluvial relics in particular, see Caroline Walker Bynum, *Christian Materiality: An Essay on Religion in Late Medieval Europe* (Cambridge, MA: Zone Books, 2011), Chapter 2, especially 136–139. Other types of contact relics may include earth, dust, water, plants, or any ephemera that touched a saint or a saint's tomb, including *brandea*, which were self-made cloth relics that touched saints' tombs and that could be obtained on pilgrimage, 136. Other kinds of effluvial relics may include vials of blood, tears, or breast milk from a saint or holy

figure. On parallels between the veronica and relics of heads and faces, see Annemarie Weyl Carr, "The Face Relics of John the Baptist in Byzantium and the West," *Gesta* 46 (2007): 159–177.

7 For more on *acheiropoieta*, see Sylvie Barnay, "Il Volto non fatto da mano d'uomo," in *Gesù: Il Corpo, Il Volto dell'Arte*, ed. T. Verdon, 96–103 (Milan: Silvana Editoriale, 2010); and Joseph Koerner, *The Moment of Self-portraiture in German Renaissance Art* (Chicago: University of Chicago Press, 1996), 84–85.

8 The literature on the Shroud of Turin is extensive. See John Beldon Scott, "Seeing the Shroud: Guarini's Reliquary Chapel in Turin and the Ostension of a Dynastic Relic," *The Art Bulletin* 77 (1995): 609–637; Giuseppe Ghiberti, "Il Corpo della Sindone," in *Gesù: Il Corpo, Il Volto dell'Arte*, ed. T. Verdon, 116–123 (Milan: Silvana Editoriale, 2010); and Ferdinando Molteni, "Storia e devozione della Sindone," in *Il Volto di Cristo*, eds. G. Morello and G. Wolf, 276–282 (Milan: Electa, 2000), with accompanying colorplates. As the shroud relates to the veronica, see Andrew R. Casper, "Display and Devotion: Exhibiting Icons and Their Copies in Counter-Reformation Italy," in *Religion and the Senses in Early Modern Europe*, eds. Wietse de Boer and Christine Göttler, 43–62 (Leiden: Brill Publishing, 2013); Michele Bacci, "Alla Ricerca del Volto di Cristo," in *Gesù: Il Corpo, Il Volto dell'Arte*, ed. T. Verdon, 90–95 (Milan: Silvana Editoriale, 2010); and Frank K. Lord, "Image, vision, and faith: Viewers' responses to the Mandylion, Veronica's Veil, and the Shroud of Turin" (PhD. diss., University of North Carolina at Chapel Hill, 2003). The shroud has been studied technically twice (1989 and 2018), with both studies concluding that the cloth is medieval rather than datable to the first century. See P. E. Damon, D. J. Donahue, et al., "Radiocarbon dating of the Shroud of Turin," *Nature* 337 (1989): 611–615; and Matteo Borrini and Luigi Garlaschelli, "A BPA Approach to the Shroud of Turin," *Journal of Forensic Sciences* (July 2018), https://doi.org/10.1111/1556-4029.13867.

9 Koerner, *The Moment of Self-portraiture,* 86; and Tristan Weddigen, "Weaving the face of Christ: on the textile origins of the Christian Image" (University of Zurich: Open Repository Archive, 2015), 84, www.zora.uzh.ch/113276/1/Weddigen.pdf.

10 Coogan, et al., eds., *The New Oxford Annotated Bible*, 2029.

11 Ibid., 2069.

12 Ibid., 2104.

13 Belting, *Likeness and Presence*, 208.

14 Ibid.

15 Caroline Walker Bynum, *The Resurrection of the Body in Western Christianity, 200–1336* (New York: Columbia University Press, 1995), 104–105.

16 Ibid.

17 Ibid., 106. For further discussion of relic fragments as representatives of wholeness, see 308–317.

18 On the Flavian emperors, see Andrew Zissos, ed., *A Companion to the Flavian Age of Imperial Rome* (West Sussex, UK: John Wiley & Sons, Inc., 2016).

19 Belting, *Likeness and Presence*, 537–541.

20 Ann Van Dijk,"The Veronica, the *Vultus Christi* and the veneration of icons in medieval Rome," in *Old Saint Peter's, Rome*, eds. Rosamond McKitterick, John Osborne, Carol M. Richardson, and Joanna Story, 229–256 (Cambridge: Cambridge University Press, 2013), 233–234, 237.

21 Wolf, "'Or fu sì fatta la sembianza vostra?,'" 103.

22 Antonella Ballardini and Paola Pogliani, "A reconstruction of the oratory of John VII (705–7)," in *Old Saint Peter's, Rome*, eds. Rosamond McKitterick, John Osborne, Carol M. Richardson, and Joanna Story, 190–213, 191 (Cambridge: Cambridge University Press, 2013). The article features several three-dimensional, reconstructed models of the oratory.

23 See Federico Gallo, "*De sacrosanto sudario Veronicae* by Giacomo Grimaldi. Preliminary Investigations," in *The European Fortune of the Roman Veronica in the Middle Ages, Convivium Supplementum*, eds. A. Murphy, H. L. Kessler, M. Petoletti, E. Duffy, and G. Milanese, 72–83 (Turnhout, Belgium: Brepols Publishers, 2017).

24 Ballardini and Pogliani, "A reconstruction of the oratory of John VII (705–7)," 191–192. The drawings survive in the Vatican Archives, with several reproduced in Ballardini and Pogliani's article.

25 Ibid., 199. In addition, the oratory was decorated with mosaics, including three scenes of Peter preaching that likely date from the papacy of Innocent III. Ibid., 208, Figure 10.10.

26 L. Schiaparelli, "Le carte antiche dell'Archivio Capitolare di S. Pietro in Vaticano,' *Archivio della Reale Società Romana di Storia Patria* 24 (1901): 393–496, cited in Ann Van Dijk, "The Veronica, the *Vultus Christi* and the veneration of icons in medieval Rome," 243, n. 32.

27 Benedictus Canonicus, *Liber Censuum Romanae Ecclesiae*, vol. II, ed. P. Fabre and L. Duchesne (Paris: Fontemoing, 1910), 141–164, 143.

28 Wolf, "'Or fu sì fatta la sembianza vostra?'", 103.

29 Ann Van Dijk,"The Veronica, the *Vultus Christi* and the veneration of icons in medieval Rome," 237–239. The reliquary, illustrated 238, Figure 12.6, is the subject of a drawing in Grimaldi, *Instrumenta Autentica*, 1620, Vatican BAV, Barb. lat. 2733, fol. 92r.

30 On the role of Pope Innocent III in propagating the cult to Veronica, see Rebecca Rist, "Innocent III and the Roman Veronica: Papal PR or Eucharistic Icon?", in *The European Fortune of the Roman Veronica in the Middle Ages, Convivium Supplementum*, eds. A. Murphy, H. L. Kessler, M. Petoletti, E. Duffy, and G. Milanese, 114–125 (Turnhout, Belgium: Brepols Publishers, 2017). The author examines the Pope's intentions and asks whether his attention to Veronica was motivated by a desire to put the Eucharist at the center of Catholic life or rather if he were trying to augment the pontificate.

31 Van Dijk, S. J. P. and J. Hazelden Walker, *The Origins of the Modern Roman Liturgy: The Liturgy of the Papal Court and the Franciscan Order in the Thirteenth Century* (Westminster, MD: The Newman Press, 1960): 102–103. For more on the link between the hospital and the cult of Veronica, see also Gisela Drossbach, "The Roman Hospital of Santo Spirito in Sassia and the Cult of the Vera Icon," in *The European Fortune of the Roman Veronica in the Middle Ages, Convivium Supplementum*, eds. A. Murphy, H. L. Kessler, M. Petoletti, E. Duffy, and G. Milanese, 158–167 (Turnhout, Belgium: Brepols Publishers, 2017).

32 Wolf, "'Or fu sì fatta la sembianza vostra?'", 104. The procession took place on the Second Sunday after Epiphany. See also Ballardini and Pogliani, "A reconstruction of the oratory of John VII (705–7)," 208.

33 Ann Van Dijk,"The Veronica, the *Vultus Christi* and the veneration of icons in medieval Rome," 239.

34 Matthew Paris, *Chronica Majora*, vol. 3, 7–8. In this text, see Chapter 1, 25–26, n. 59.

35 The *Ospedale di Santo Spirito* is still in operation. The modern building, located at Lungotevere in Sassia, 1, is adjacent to the historic complex that dates to the twelfth century.

36 Carla Keyvanian, *Hospitals and Urbanism in Rome, 1200–1500* (Leiden: Brill, 2015), 83–84.

37 Ibid.

38 S. J. P. Van Dijk and Walker, *The Origins of the Modern Roman Liturgy,* 460–461: "Notandum quod isto die dominus papa Innocentius instituit quod sudarium Christi deferretur ab ecclesia principis apostolorum usque ad hospitale sancti spiritus, quod est ad sanctam Mariam in saxia. Et ibi ostenditur a domino papa omni populo a loco eminenti qui propter hoc aptatus et paratus est. Et ipse dominus papa vadi processionaliter, precedentibus cunctis ordinibus curie et clericis sancti Petri accensis faculis, subsequentibus eumdem papm capellanis suis dicentibus psalmos cum eo. Et dominus papa predicat ibi de evangelio, scilicet *Nuptie facte sunt*, sicut ipse exposuit. Et ibi cantat missam, scola cantante ad introitum *Omnis terra adoret te*. Hiis peractis et finito evangelio, aliquis cardinalis recipit sudarium et reportat unde venit, comitantibus eum canonicis predicte ecclesie sancti Petri. Se quando extrahitur de loco ubi est repositum, tunc cantatur *Te deum laudamus*. In eundo et redeundo dicuntur ps. *Beatus vir qui non abiit* cum sequentibus eum."

39 Jörg Bölling, "Face to Face with Christ in Late Medieval Rome. The Veil of Veronica in Papal Liturgy and Ceremony," in *The European Fortune of the Roman Veronica in the Middle Ages, Convivium Supplementum*, eds. A. Murphy, H. L. Kessler, M. Petoletti, E. Duffy, and G. Milanese, 136–143, 141 (Turnhout, Belgium: Brepols Publishers, 2017).

40 Ibid.

41 A set of Mass orations in the Vatican Archives called *Collecta ad faciem Christi*, datable to the fifteenth century, is analyzed at length by Uwe Michael Lang, "Origins of the Liturgical Veneration of the Roman Veronica," in *The European Fortune of the Roman Veronica in the Middle Ages, Convivium Supplementum*, eds. A. Murphy, H. L. Kessler, M. Petoletti, E. Duffy, and G. Milanese, 144–155 (Turnhout, Belgium: Brepols Publishers, 2017).

42 For an in-depth analysis of indulgences associated with the veronica, as evidenced by letters of indulgence issued forth from prelates across Europe, see Étienne Doublier, "*Sui pretiossisimi vultus Imago*: Veronica e prassi indulgenziale nel XIII e all'inizio del XIV secolo," in *The European Fortune of the Roman Veronica in the Middle Ages, Convivium Supplementum*, eds. A. Murphy, H. L. Kessler, M. Petoletti, E. Duffy, and G. Milanese, 180–193 (Turnhout, Belgium: Brepols Publishers, 2017).

43 John Oliver Hand, *Hans Memling's Saint John the Baptist and Saint Veronica* (Washington, DC: National Gallery of Art, 1994), n.p.

44 Gervase of Tilbury, *Otia Imperialia,* ed. and trans. S. E. Banks and J. W. Binns (Oxford: Oxford University Press, 2002), 604–607. This edition includes the side-by-side Latin text with English translation. Gervase, however, does identify the bleeding woman from the Gospels with Martha, sister of Mary and Lazarus, a variant Western tradition with origins in a sermon by Saint Ambrose or a Pseudo-Ambrose. Ibid., 604, n. 1.

45 Giraldus Cambrensis, *Opera: Speculum Ecclesiae*, 278.

46 Wolf, "'Or fu sì fatta la sembianza vostra?'", 104.

47 Hand, "*Salve sancta facies*," 14.

48 Chiara Di Fruscia, "*Datum Avenioni*. The Avignon Papacy and the Custody of the Veronica," in *The European Fortune of the Roman Veronica in the Middle Ages, Convivium Supplementum*, eds. A. Murphy, H. L. Kessler, M. Petoletti, E. Duffy, and G. Milanese, 218–230 (Turnhout, Belgium: Brepols Publishers, 2017).

49 Wolf, "'Or fu sì fatta la sembianza vostra?'", 104.

50 Hand, "*Salve sancta facies*, 14.

51 William Wey, *The Itineraries of William Wey*, ed. and trans. Francis Davey (Oxford: The Bodleian Library, University of Oxford, 2010), 193.

52 Alice E. Sanger, "Sensuality, Sacred Remains and Devotion in Baroque Rome," in *Sense and the Senses in Early Modern Art and Cultural Practice*, eds. Alice E. Sanger and Siv Tove Kulbrandstad Walker (Burlington, VT: Ashgate Publishing Company, 2012), 203.

53 Blair Moore, *The Architecture of the Christian Holy Land*, 115.

54 On the Mochi sculpture, see Jennifer Montagu, "A Model by Francesco Mochi for the 'Saint Veronica,'" *The Burlington Magazine* 124 (1982): 430–437. Montagu points out that one of the most salient iconographic features of this sculpture is the *sudarium*, which Mochi depicts as the end of Veronica's veil rather than as a separate piece of cloth, 435. On the Baroque style of the sculpture, see Estelle Lingo, "Mochi's Edge," *Oxford Art Journal* 32 (2009): 3–16.

55 Translation by Nancy T. de Grummond, in electronic correspondence with the author, July 17, 2018.

56 On September 1, 2006, Pope Benedict XVI (papacy 2005–2013) visited the object in Manoppello, which for some Catholics lent authority to this interpretation. Benedict's speech on that occasion can be found on the Vatican's website. Benedict XVI, "Pilgrimage to the Shrine of the Holy Face of Manoppello," September 1, 2006, accessed March 25, 2018, http://w2.vatican.va/content/benedict-xvi/en/speeches/2006/september/documents/hf_ben-xvi_spe_20060901_manoppello.html.

57 Belting, *Likeness and Presence,* 220.

58 Wolf, "From Mandylion to Veronica," 172.

59 Belting, *Likeness and Presence*, 210.

60 The exhibition catalogue *Il Volto di Cristo*, eds. G. Morello and G. Wolf (Milan: Electa, 2000), presents many of these copies as colorplates alongside a host of other images of the Holy Face, each with accompanying catalogue entries.
61 Martin Luther, *Luther's Works: Church and Ministry III*, vol. 41, ed. Eric W. Gritsch and Helmut T. Lehmann (Philadelphia: Fortress Press, 1966), 322–323.
62 Sanger, "Sensuality, Sacred Remains and Devotion," 199.
63 Ignatius of Loyola, *The Spiritual exercises of St. Ignatius based on studies in the language of the autograph*, trans. Louis J. Puhl (New York: Vintage Books, 2000), 125.
64 H. J. Schroeder, trans., *Canons and Decrees of the Council of Trent* (Charlotte, N.C.: Tan Books, 1978), 218–219.
65 Barbier de Montault, "Iconographie du chemin de la croix," *Annales Archaéologiques*, xxiii (1867): 232, cited in Flora Lewis, "The Veronica: Image, Legend and Viewer," in *England in the Thirteenth Century: Proceedings of the 1984 Harlaxton Symposium*, ed. W. M. Ormrod, 100–106, 105 (Woodbridge, England: Boyndell Press, 1985).
66 Josef Wilpert, *Die römischen Mosaiken und Malereien der kirchlichen Bauten vom IV. bis XIII. Jahrhundert: unter den Auspizien und mit allerhöchster Förderung Seiner Majestät Kaiser Wilhelms II*, vol. 2 (Freiburg: Herder, 1917), 1117–1125.
67 Ibid., 1123.
68 Gregory Di Pippo, "Passion Sunday: The Veil of St. Veronica and the Stational Liturgy at St. Peter's," *New Liturgical Movement* (March 26, 2012), accessed June 20, 2018, www.newliturgicalmovement.org. The site includes a video of the exposition taken by Lucas Viar in 2008.

3 *Via Crucis*

The Stations of the Cross became commonplace in Western Europe during the Early Modern era and remain so to the present day.[1] In southern Europe by the fifth century, Saint Petronius, bishop of Bologna, had designed a version of the Stations at the basilica of Santo Stefano, a complex known as the *Sette Chiese* (Seven Churches) or *Santa Gerusalemme* (Holy Jerusalem). Santo Stefano is among the earliest examples in the South of a tradition that continued through the late Middle Ages, with important series established by the fifteenth century at Messina and Cordoba. Noteworthy series north of the Alps include the *Kreuzweg* by Adam Kraft in Nuremberg, datable 1487–1490 (Plate 5), and the *Cruysganck* by Peter Sterckx, datable to 1505, in Leuven (Louvain), among many other series in Northern-European urban centers.

F. E. Peters (1985a) claimed a European origin for the Stations. He asserted that liturgy associated with the Way of the Cross developed initially in Europe and only later returned to Jerusalem because public practice there had been discouraged during Muslim rule.[2] As the Franciscans had oversight of the Church of the Holy Sepulcher in Jerusalem, Christian pilgrims were freer to express devotion and to engage in ritual, including processions, in its interior.[3] Worship with prayer and hymns at the five stations inside the church, as reported in 1587 by Jean Zuallart (Ath, Belgium, 1541–1634, called Giovanni Zuallardo in Italian) after a pilgrimage the previous year, was well developed because these stops were located within Franciscan jurisdiction.[4] Conversely, the other nine stations in the city streets were intended to be brief, less formal stops, with only minimal liturgy associated with them. Zuallart had noted that it was not permitted to make any halt or demonstrative gesture at these public spots.[5] Religious expression was thus restrained in the streets of Jerusalem where Muslims would either not have allowed, or strongly discouraged, open displays of religious expression.[6] Descriptions by the Franciscan Elzear Horn (b. Germany, c. 1690–d. Syria, 1744) also indicate that worshipers continued to use modest gestures through the first half of the eighteenth century. He recorded that pilgrims would only say one Our Father and one Hail Mary at each station, without holding a cross, in part to avoid fees or rebuke from Turks.[7] Referring to these accounts, Peters concluded that the development of lengthy, elaborate rituals around the Stations of the Cross had been easier in Europe than in Jerusalem.

Colin Morris (2005) proffered that the Stations as they were established in Europe by the end of the fifteenth century were the product of a confluence of three sources: biblical narrative, the Jerusalem pilgrimage, and Western preferences for devotional practice, with the eventual selection and sequence of events in the European Stations more indebted to Western ecclesiastical writers than to historical evidence in Jerusalem.[8] Likewise, Wharton (2006) argued that Westerners were continuously molding Jerusalem in their minds to meet their own economic needs and aesthetic proclivities. To these ends, Western Europeans, since the Crusades when their economy expanded, encouraged the giving of relics from the Holy Land and the fabrication of souvenirs and replicas, including the Stations of the Cross, as a means of preserving the memory of Jerusalem and revering the city as sacred space even (or especially) when apart from it.[9] In a similar vein, Kirkland-Ives (2009) suggested that, although first occurrences of rituals are difficult to identify, European models likely exerted more influence over the development of the constructed pilgrims' path in Jerusalem than vice versa.[10]

While I concur with Peters, Morris, Wharton, and Kirkland-Ives on most points, I am inclined to qualify the assertion that the West had the greater influence. The concurrent emergence of the Stations of the Cross in Europe and the *Via Crucis* (Way of the Cross) in Jerusalem is indicative of a cross-pollination of form and content via Western travelers who embarked on pilgrimages to the Holy Land. Although the Western influence is most evident in liturgy and practice, the layout of the *Via Crucis* in Jerusalem, as will be explored in this chapter, underwent significant changes in the selection of shrines, including the House of Veronica, as well as the order in which the sites were visited. The gradual codification of the number and sequence of sites in Jerusalem in turn influenced devotional writers and clergy in Europe. Thus, the cross-cultural exchanges largely occurred in both directions. Amidst this discussion of influences, however, my essential questions in this chapter are how and why the Franciscans adopted the legend of Veronica and adapted it to the urban landscapes of Jerusalem and European cities in order to integrate her narrative into the evolving *Via Crucis*. Over the course of the mid-fourteenth through the late sixteenth centuries, the friars developed and promoted the Stations of the Cross as a participatory, devotional practice, which reached a height of popularity in the seventeenth century. This chapter examines their motives and methods, which spawned a rich spiritual and artistic legacy still evident today.

Aside from the authors already mentioned, relatively few sources expound upon the original rationale for the Stations of the Cross, which were essentially designed for Christians to ambulate from one *locus* to the next, either individually or in procession, at any time of the liturgical year but especially during Lent and on Good Friday. There are, however, many studies about specific installations, or the Stations of the Cross in certain regions or periods.[11] The findings of the foundational monograph on the subject by the Jesuit Herbert Thurston (1914)[12] were reinforced by Albert Storme (1984),[13] with each author approaching the subject from both historical and theological perspectives. Da Zedelgem (1949, 2004),[14] a Capuchin who also viewed the subject through a lens of faith, presented the history and function of the Stations in a well-documented book. He asserted that the primary purpose of the Stations was to facilitate spiritual participation in the suffering of Jesus. In his view, the *Via Crucis* testifies to the Church's efforts to provide an abbreviated, intermediary, and practical means for anyone, especially those who could not visit the Holy Land, to meditate on the places and events of Christ's Passion from the Palace of Pilate to the Church of the Holy Sepulcher.[15]

Morris (2005) had further observed that the layout of the Stations of the Cross marked a distinct departure from Palm Sunday processions, which had been a longstanding means to involve laity in liturgy at the beginning of Holy Week. The erection of a series of halting places, which a wide populace could use at any time of the year for personal reflection, can be distinguished from invited (or otherwise restricted) lay participation in a few liturgical processions.[16] A prevailing theory of the purpose of the Stations in Western Europe has been the imitation of pilgrimage to the Holy Land, as indulgences could be earned for walking the Stations either in Jerusalem or in European churches.[17] Lenzi (2016) has recently challenged this view and proposed that the Stations of the Cross may have been an alternative means of religious performance that connected the faithful to the time and place of Christ's life.[18] Lenzi suggests that the function of Stations of the Cross in nave interiors or on church grounds may have been to provide a metaphor for the heavenly Jerusalem rather than a recreation of sites within the historic city of Jerusalem.[19] These multifarious rationales for uses of the Stations are not mutually exclusive. Rather, I see these plausible suggestions as nuanced addenda to a central purpose. The Stations of the Cross developed as an effort to provide Christians with a means to meditate – on-site or by proxy elsewhere – on specific places along Christ's Way to Calvary with the goal of personal repentance.

In terms of form, many early series were simply Roman numerals that could be supplemented by a priest's prayers or a friar's sermons. Each station also typically had a cross incorporated into the design, which Nisbet (1982) suggested may originate from actual wooden crosses used from the first through fourth centuries to designate holy places associated with the Passion in Jerusalem.[20] The addition of works of art in relief sculpture, fresco, mosaic, metalwork, or other mediums as focal points for meditation were later manifestations, with each image corresponding to a number and short title. The series of the Stations promoted artistic and architectural ingenuity as a wide variety of styles, sizes, and mediums were permissible, even encouraged. By the end of the sixteenth century, the Stations had become a standard component of Lenten practice in large part because of the adaptability of works of art to sermons, prayers, and liturgical celebrations.[21]

The Latin noun *statio* originally meant an outpost, especially a military base for night duty. By the thirteenth century, the word *stationes* began to refer to designated stopping points on the *Via Crucis* where a noteworthy encounter or event was believed to have happened to Jesus of Nazareth on his walk to execution. The priest William Wey, writing in 1458, was the first pilgrim to the Holy Land (of whom we know) to use the word *stations* in English to refer to these designated stopping places in Jerusalem. By the end of the fifteenth century, the word *stations* in a broad, vernacular context could mean stops during any procession.[22]

Within the realm of virtual pilgrimage, the placement of holy sites was more subjective and mutable than fixed or actual.[23] The Holy Land could be recreated by the transfer of relics and/or the construction of simulations in faraway cities. As the earth of Jerusalem was considered to be sanctified by Christ's blood, bringing soil samples from the Levant to European cities could be a holy, expiatory endeavor, as exemplified in Pisa and as studied by Ahl (2003).[24] Imaginary maps were another method of generating the effects of virtual pilgrimage, as for example, those created by Matthew Paris in the mid-thirteenth century.[25] Therefore, the erection of Stations of the Cross was one of several means of establishing pilgrimage by proxy. It is important to keep in mind, however, that use of the Stations as a mode for virtual pilgrimage did not imply that the participants could not or did not make the voyage to Jerusalem. Some worshipers *had* gone and had purchased, commissioned, or produced texts and/or works of art as mementos to preserve their recollections and/or to rekindle faith upon return from Jerusalem to Europe.[26] Later versions of the Stations of the Cross produced during the sixteenth and seventeenth centuries in formats such as editions of prints, book illustrations, and sets of enamels or medallions, however, were perhaps more conducive to virtual pilgrimage, especially within the context of convents and monasteries, than intended as mementos from actual, physical walks.[27]

One of the primary motivations for pilgrimage, whether actual or virtual, was the garnering of indulgences, or promises of spiritual rewards in the form of release time from purgatory. The source of the system of indulgences used in both Rome and Jerusalem is typically attributed to Pope Sylvester I (papacy 314–335), whom Constantine and Helena allegedly had requested to codify the practice.[28] By the fourteenth century, the Franciscans held authority over the granting of indulgences to pilgrims in Jerusalem, even though there was no specific connection with a papal decree. As the friars essentially held a monopoly on guided tours of the Holy Land, they issued indulgences and furthered the practice.[29]

The act of processing from one holy site to another in a given sequence likely has origins in the first through fifth centuries, with pilgrims coming to the Holy Land from Europe for this purpose since probably the fourth century. Tradition held that Mary had placed stones near the locations where her son had walked in order to meditate on his death in the immediate aftermath.[30] This idea has apocryphal roots in *Transitus Mariae*,[31] a text datable to the fifth century that aimed to retrace the footsteps of Mary.[32] Many Franciscan guides told pilgrims that the act of walking in Christ's steps and pausing at significant events along his walk to Calvary stemmed from Mary's having done so first. The Dominican theologian, Fratris Felicis Fabri (Fra Felix Fabri, Swiss, c. 1441–1502),[33] wrote in Latin in 1494, after two pilgrimages to the Holy Land in 1480 and 1483, that he had learned that Mary had knelt and prayed at each site where Jesus had fallen while holding his cross.[34] Whether or not Jesus's mother actually followed his path and paused with reverence at various points after his death, the legend of her commemorative route in the first century served as the ideological basis of the Franciscans' guided tours.[35]

Emperor Constantine (r. 306–337)'s granting of religious tolerance in the Edict of Milan in 313, his erection the Church of the Holy Sepulcher (consecrated 335), his own conversion to Christianity, and his mother Helena's discovery and identification of the True Cross were pivotal events that promoted and popularized pilgrimages to the Holy Land beginning in the first half of the fourth century.[36] In fact, the series of stops along Christ's route may have been established during the reign of Constantine by Helena, when she traveled to Palestine in search of the True Cross.

In the last quarter of the fourth century, we can find an indication of a procession through the holy sites in Jerusalem associated with Christ's final walk in an account by Egeria, a female pilgrim, perhaps from Spain, who visited the Levant between 381–384.[37] In one or two letters to her "sisters," who could have been members of a religious society, she describes the sites she saw and the accompanying liturgy she experienced in Jerusalem, including a procession during Holy Week, which traversed the city from Gethsemane to Golgotha,[38] that is, in an east-west direction. The passage below comes from *Peter the Deacon's Book on the Holy Places*, written c. 1137 by Peter the Deacon (c. 1107–c. 1153), a monk and librarian at Monte Cassino. Never having visited the Holy Land, the author relied on three sources: Bede, a Latin guidebook whose authorship is unknown, and Egeria's travel journal.[39] The excerpted passage is from a section about "The Great Week," or the week preceding Easter, and specifically the section on Good Friday:

> From there all of them, including the smallest children, now go down with singing and conduct the bishop to Gethsemane. There are a great many people and they have been crowded together, tired by their vigil, and weakened by their daily fasting – and they have had a very big hill to come down – so they go very slowly on their way to Gethsemane. So that they can all see, they are provided with hundreds of candles. When everyone arrives at Gethsemane, they have an appropriate prayer, a hymn, and then a reading from the Gospel about the Lord's arrest. By the time it has been read everyone is groaning and lamenting and weeping so loud that people even across in the city can probably hear it all.
>
> Next they go with singing to the city, and walking they reach the gate at the time when people can first recognize each other. And from there every single one of them, old and young, rich and poor, goes on through the centre of the city to be present at the next service – for this above all others is the day when no one leaves the vigil till morning comes. Thus the bishop is conducted from Gethsemane to the gate, and from there through the whole city as far as the Cross.[40]

Thus, in his narrative, Peter the Deacon incorporated elements of the fourth-century traveler's account of a candlelit walk from Gethsemane, through a gate and across the city, to "the Cross," presumed to be Golgotha. The passage indicates the beginnings of a procession that commemorated some of the places in Jerusalem associated with Christ's walk on Good Friday. At least one other contemporary account survives. A female saint called Silvia d'Aquileia recorded in her *Peregrinatio Silviae,* written c. 383/384–388, that every afternoon during her stay in Jerusalem she stopped at designated places inside the basilica of the Holy Sepulcher, singing songs and holding a candle.[41] Although the number and order of stops would change over subsequent centuries, the accounts of Egeria and Silvia in the late fourth century demonstrate an early pattern of processing from one holy shrine to another, both in the streets of Jerusalem and within the Church of the Holy Sepulcher, with the purpose of inducing a meditative state of prayer on Christ's suffering. There were likely other early accounts from the fourth century, which are no longer extant.

The original Constantinian Church of the Holy Sepulcher, datable to the fourth century, was damaged and eventually destroyed by fires, invasion, and an earthquake between the seventh and the early eleventh centuries; it was rebuilt in the twelfth century (1114–1149). The church is an enclosed space, comprised of the sites of the Crucifixion and Jesus's rock-cut tomb. The twelfth-century building joins the rotunda over the shrine of the tomb to the remnants of the basilica of Constantine by means of a courtyard. Thus, the building consolidates under one roof the holy sites of Calvary and Golgotha.[42] As a crusader-era structure, its architectural design represented a solution to problems inherent in an uneven site within a dense, urban setting. The goal of the new construction was to provide access to these sacred sites and space for liturgy associated with them.[43] The rebuilding of the church in the twelfth century is germane to the history of the Stations of the Cross because the final five stations (the Tenth through the Fourteenth) are located in the church's interior.

Also during the twelfth century, Saint Bernard of Clairvaux (French, 1090–1153) became a pivotal influence in nurturing Christians' interest in Passion devotion by writing emotionally charged letters and sermons that encouraged readers to imagine vividly the suffering and death of Christ.[44] The practice of inducing spiritual fervor by meditation on the Passion was reinforced by Francis of Assisi (Italian, c. 1181/1182–1226) and his biographer, Saint Bonaventure (Italian, c. 1217–1274),[45] who laid the groundwork in the thirteenth century for a guided itinerary of stops that marked the sites on Christ's final walk. Documentation of a sustained interest in the Stations during the twelfth and thirteenth centuries includes a mention of the *Via Dolorosa* in 1187 by the French pilgrim Ernoul, a squire of the nobleman Balian of Ibelin in Jerusalem.[46] Pringle (2016) also translated and edited a selection of pilgrims' accounts from the Holy Land that date 1187–1291, including an extract of Ernoul's *Chronicle*, c. 1231,[47] and Philip of Savona, O. F. M.'s *Description of the Holy Land* (1285–1289),[48] both of which offer valuable thirteenth-century descriptions. In addition, Folda (1998) described several other journals by Crusader pilgrims to Jerusalem, datable from the span 1099–1291, with the Church of the Holy Sepulcher as a focus.[49]

Franciscan settlements in the Holy Land in the first quarter of the thirteenth century marked a turning point in the history of the Stations of the Cross. Concurrently with the increased visibility of the veronica relic in Rome and the spread of the legend of Veronica from there by means of pilgrims' journals and oral tradition, the Franciscans became caretakers of Christian holy sites in Jerusalem,[50] replacing the Knights Templar in that role.[51] The *Custodia Terræ Sanctæ* (Guard of the Holy Land)[52] was (and remains) a branch of the Order of Friars Minor (*Ordinis Fratrum Minorum*, O. F. M.). Francis of Assisi founded the distinctive custodial priory in 1217 during the Fifth Crusade (1213–1221) for the purpose of protecting both the Christian sites in Jerusalem and the pilgrims who visited them. By 1219, and through the Mamluks' siege of Acre in 1291, the Franciscans established themselves in Palestine, Syria, and Egypt.[53] In Jerusalem in 1229, the friars maintained a house on the *Via Crucis* near the Fifth Station, and in 1272 they occupied the Cenacle (Dining Room, or Upper Room above David's tomb), which was revered as the location of the Last Supper and the descent of the Holy Spirit at Pentecost on Mount Zion. By the mid-1290s, the friars were guardians of both the Church of the Holy Sepulcher and the Tomb of the Virgin in Jerusalem, with permission from the Mamluk Sultan al-Nasir Muhammed (r. 1293–1294 and 1299–1341) in Cairo.[54] In 1309, the Franciscans also settled in Bethlehem. In 1333, Robert of Anjou and Sancia of Majorca, King and Queen of Naples, purchased the Cenacle from the sultans of Egypt and donated it to the Franciscans in order to secure the monks' livelihood there.

Because the Franciscans were largely respected by people of all faiths, including Jews and Muslims, during the Crusades, the friars proved to be effective mediators amidst political and social unrest. In this capacity, they safeguarded and provided access to the sites associated with the life of Christ. The Franciscans' responsibility for the *Custodia* was sanctioned by the papal bull *Gratias Agimus*, issued in 1342 by Pope Clement VI (papacy 1342–1352), who sought to reclaim the holy sites from Muslim control.[55] Thus, from the early thirteenth through the mid-fourteenth centuries in Jerusalem, the Franciscans had the opportunity as guards of the sacred places to begin formalizing, caring for, and promoting the *Via Crucis* (Way of the Cross), alternatively called in Latin the *Via Dolorosa* (Way of Sorrow) or *Via Sacra* (Sacred Way), or in Italian *Il Cammino della Croce* (Walk of the Cross), as a processional route for European pilgrims under their aegis.[56]

Supplemental evidence of an interest in participatory Passion devotion in the mid-fourteenth century can be found in the *Meditationes vitae Christi*, a Franciscan devotional text, datable to c. 1336–1364. In this Tuscan manuscript, there is a reference to pausing with reverence at specific spots where Christ fell within the story of the Three Marys at the Sepulcher:

> Meanwhile, Mary Magdalene and Mary Jacobus and Mary Salome went with precious ointments to anoint the body of Lord Jesus. And as soon as they were outside the gates of the city, they began to bring to mind the pain and the affliction of their Master. And in all the places in which some harm had been done to their Master, they would fall to their knees, and weeping bitterly they said, "Here we encountered him with the cross on his shoulders," and they would kiss the earth, weeping. "And here he turned and said to the women of Jerusalem, 'Do not weep for me, but for yourselves and for your children.' And there, because he was exhausted, he put the cross down and leaned against this stone."[57]

Further indication of the path's development in the mid-fourteenth century, as Blair Moore (2017) has recounted, can be found in the writings of Niccolò da Poggibonsi, a Franciscan friar from Tuscany whose illustrated book, *Libro dei santuarii d'oltramare* (Book of Overseas Sanctuaries),[58] followed a Holy Land visit in 1346–1350. Writing in Italian, the friar described sanctuaries as he had experienced them physically, moving in and around them.[59] In addition, an anonymous contemporary of Niccolò recounted in Italian his visit to the Holy Land. His manuscript, now preserved in Bologna, includes elevations and directions for readers to perambulate within the Church of the Holy Sepulcher in a specified order, as well as instructions on how to continue the walk within and outside the city of Jerusalem, in a manner akin to that of a guidebook. In general, his descriptions are based on materials, sizes, dimensions, distances, and other observations of a tactile nature. Moreover, the writer continues the trend of encouraging affective piety by appealing at various points to readers' emotions, such as grief.[60]

The most popular guidebook to the Holy Land in Renaissance Italy was *Viaggio da Venetia al Sancto Sepolchro et al Monte Sinai* (Voyage from Venice to the Holy Sepulcher and to Mount Sinai), published anonymously in Venice in 1518. Blair Moore (2013), in her search for the origins of this text, concluded that one of the four illustrated versions of the *Libro* by Niccolò da Poggibonsi was likely its prototype.[61] Written in the vernacular, the guidebook includes illustrations to enhance pilgrims' experiences, as well as descriptive prose that parallels the style of contemporary literature in the mid-fourteenth century.[62] Niccolò da Poggibonsi wrote in first person, thereby offering a personalized, eyewitness encounter, and he refrained from replicating previous accounts.[63] This new genre dovetails with the selection of Christ's encounter with Veronica as an independent Station because she too was an eyewitness to Christ's suffering. Veronica's and Niccolò da Poggiboni's perspectives aligned in their first-personal points of view.

In the mid-fifteenth century, the priest and pilgrim William Wey (English, c. 1405/6–1476) traveled to the Holy Land twice in 1458 and 1462 and recorded his itineraries in a manuscript called *Matters of Jerusalem*, datable 1470.[64] Guided by Franciscans,[65] he followed the *Via Crucis*. As the first writer to use and repeat the word *stations* in the context of the *Via Crucis*, he noted that the Sixth Station was dedicated to Veronica. In a section of mnemonic verses (phrases intended to aid memory), he recorded words in Latin, followed by brief descriptions in English:

> Holy Places at the Stations in Jerusalem
> 6 *sudar*: The place where the widow, or Veronica, placed a handkerchief on Christ's face.[66]

Arad (2012), whose research focuses mainly on Wey's map of the Holy Land, reconstructed a chapel that the priest had built in his Edington monastery.[67] As described in Wey's will at the beginning of the manuscript, the chapel was based on the Church of the Holy Sepulcher and was comprised of various liturgical objects and memorabilia from his journeys. The purpose of the chapel was primarily devotional; the room served to increase spiritual reverence for the Holy Land and even to serve as an aid for inspiring virtual pilgrimage.[68] Saliently, the collection of objects within the chapel included a *vernakyl*, a painting of Veronica's cloth on paper.[69]

Of the various iterations of the *Via Crucis* in Jerusalem from the fourth to the end of the sixteenth centuries, the three principal variables have been the selection of events, their numbering or sequence, and the orientation in which a visitor would follow them. Although the number of episodes could range from seven to thirty-three, in its final manifestation the series comprised fourteen periodic places on which to meditate on the events of the Passion. As Kirkland-Ives (2009) has researched, during the late Middle Ages there was a "long version" that encompassed the full Passion and a "short version."[70] Expanded versions included a fluid number of additional scenes, such as the Flagellation, Crowning of Thorns, and Mocking of Christ, among other episodes. The final, condensed sequence comprised fourteen events from the Condemnation by Pilate to the Entombment. As the first and final events, these two scenes eventually came to define the actual sites of the Palace of Pilate on the eastern end and Mount Calvary on the western side of Jerusalem as bookends to the sequential narrative, with other episodes linked to sites located between these two fixed points.

F. E. Peters (1985a) had suggested that pilgrims may have been visiting the stations as part of a circular path on which the Franciscans guided European tourists.[71] In an account by the pilgrim John Rufus called "A Pilgrimage in Jerusalem" within

The Life of Peter the Iberian, written c. 500, the author concluded with a mention of a holy circuit. However, the sites enumerated in his narrative are broader and more comprehensive than those included in the Passion cycle:

> He also went round the holy places on the outskirts: he climbed to the Cenacle of the Disciples, then to the holy Ascension, and from there to the House of Lazarus. After that he took the road which goes from there till he came to holy Bethlehem. After praying there he went to Rachel's Tomb. After praying there, and in the other churches and sanctuaries along the road, he went down to Siloam, and from there up to Holy Sion, where he finished his holy circuit, since he had worshipped in the Savior in all the places.[72]

Likewise, the monk Theodosius the Cenobiarch (Cappadocia, c. 423–529), in his *The Topography of the Holy Land*, written c. 518, organized his descriptions of the Holy Land into two sections, called "The Beginning of the Jerusalem Circuit" and "The Rest of the Jerusalem Circuit," with the word choices in these headings alluding to a circular path.[73] The possibility of a circular route is thought-provoking. But if there were a pilgrim's path in this pattern, it was likely broader in scope and encompassed more shrines in Jerusalem and environs than the series of stops that were traditionally featured in the *Via Crucis*.

At the core of the eventual fourteen stations may have been an abbreviated form of Passion devotion, known as the Seven Falls, which was common in Northern Europe (Table 3.1).[74] Although the number of Falls on Christ's way to Calvary could range widely, there was a predominance of seven in the Low Countries and Germany, as exemplified by Adam Kraft's series in Nuremberg (see Chapter 4). Noteworthy also is that any fall that Christ made during his walk to Golgotha was apocryphal and not recorded by the four evangelists. The only mention of a fall in the narration of the Passion is in Luke 23:27–31, in a metaphorical warning about mountains falling. The passage occurs just after Jesus's meeting with Simon of Cyrene and within the context of conversing with the Women of Jerusalem:

Table 3.1 The Seven Falls compared to the final Fourteen Stations of the Cross

Seven Falls		Fourteen Stations	
		1	Condemnation by Pilate
		2	Carrying of the Cross
1	First Fall	3	First Fall
2	Meeting of his Mother	4	Meeting of his Mother
3	Simon of Cyrene helps him	5	Simon of Cyrene helps him
4	Veronica wipes his brow	6	Veronica wipes his brow
5	Second Fall	7	Second Fall
6	Meeting the Women of Jerusalem	8	Meeting the Women of Jerusalem
7	Third Fall	9	Third Fall
		10	Stripping of Garments
		11	Nailing to the Cross
		12	Crucifixion
		13	Deposition
		14	Entombment

> A great number of the people followed him, and among them were women who were beating their breasts and wailing for him. But Jesus turned to them and said, "Daughters of Jerusalem, do not weep for me, but weep for yourselves and for your children. For the days are surely coming when they will say, 'Blessed are the barren, and the wombs that never bore, and the breasts that never nursed.' Then they will begin to say to the mountains, 'Fall on us'; and to the hills, 'Cover us.'"[75]

Thus, although the word *fall* does appear in Luke's account, it is not in reference to any ambulatory stumble. Instead, the apocryphal emphasis on Christ's Falls may be typologically related to the fall of Adam, whose original sin Christ redeems. Falling down to the ground necessarily yields a pose of prostration, or *proskynesis*, a submissive posture that expresses humility and an acknowledgment of the consequences of sin. An iconographic focus on Christ's Falls was also likely intended to induce empathy and contrition among participants who, in recalling their own misdeeds, segued to a state of repentance. The Seven Falls may underlie the eventual number of stops in the Stations of the Cross, as fourteen is the double of seven. As a prime number, seven was often considered to be a perfect integer in a sacramental context during the Middle Ages.

Da Zedelgem (1949) suggested that the four sympathetic meetings of Christ with his mother Mary, Simon of Cyrene, Veronica, and the Women of Jerusalem may have initially been among the Seven Falls.[76] In the late Middle Ages, the iconographic element of Christ's cross was often absent from these four scenes, with the focus turning to the subordinate characters who had offered assistance. This proposal makes sense because the eventual number of three Falls, along with the four sympathetic meetings that may originally have been Falls, combine to equal the original Seven Falls. In Table 3.1, we can see the core Seven Falls together and in sequence as an overlap with Stations 3–9 in the eventual form of fourteen stations. In the expansion, two stops were added at the beginning, and five supplemented the end.

In the nearly two millennia since the historical Crucifixion, the starting point and sequence for the *Via Crucis* have shifted several times. Prior to 1187 (when Jerusalem fell to Saladin), as Pringle (2016) has articulated, the *Via Dolorosa* began on the eastern end of the city, north of the Temple Mount at the Sheep's Pool (Pool of Bethesda) near the Praetorium (Palace of Pilate), then continued through the area of Haram al-Sharif (Dome of the Rock, the Muslim shrine marking the place of the prophet Muhammed's ascension), toward the Church of the Holy Sepulcher on the western end.[77] However, as the Muslim-controlled Temple Mount area was inaccessible to Christians from the late twelfth to the late thirteenth century, the starting point for the route was altered.[78] By the early fifteenth century, the direction had been reversed; the *Via Crucis* began at Christ's tomb and proceeded eastward. Then, from the late sixteenth century and to the present day, the *Via Crucis* has begun at the Lion's Gate, also called the Gethsemane Gate (within the Eastern Wall of the Old City Walls) at the Antonia Fortress and Praetorium and continued westward in a backwards-Z-shaped path that concluded at the Church of the Holy Sepulcher (see the map and diagram of Jerusalem in Figure 3.1 and Figure 3.2). This eventual return to an east-west orientation corresponds to Egeria's fourth-century description of a directional flow from Gethsemane to Golgotha.

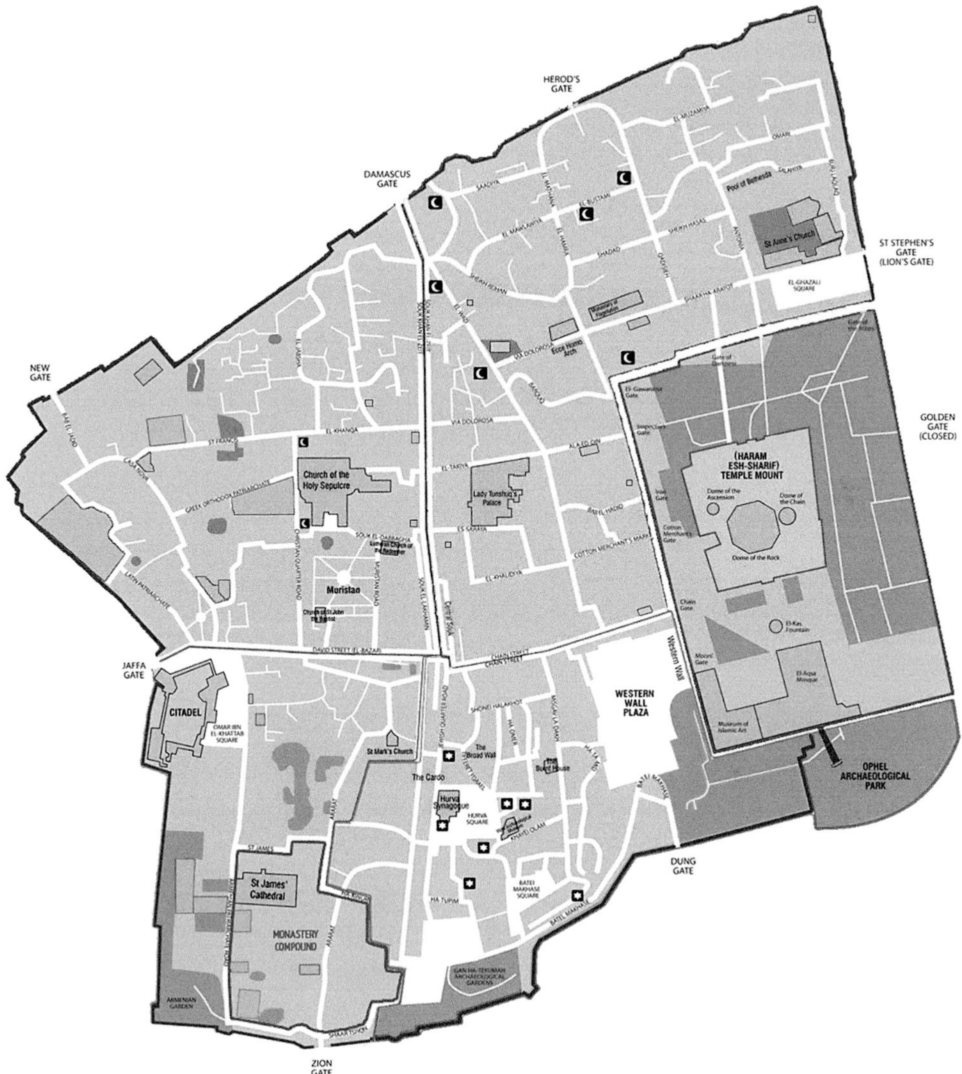

Figure 3.1 Map of Old City Jerusalem.

Image credit: David Bjorgen. Modification (translation of main points of interest into English) by The Curious Game. WikiMedia Commons. Licensed under Creative Commons Attribution-Share Alike 3.0 Unported

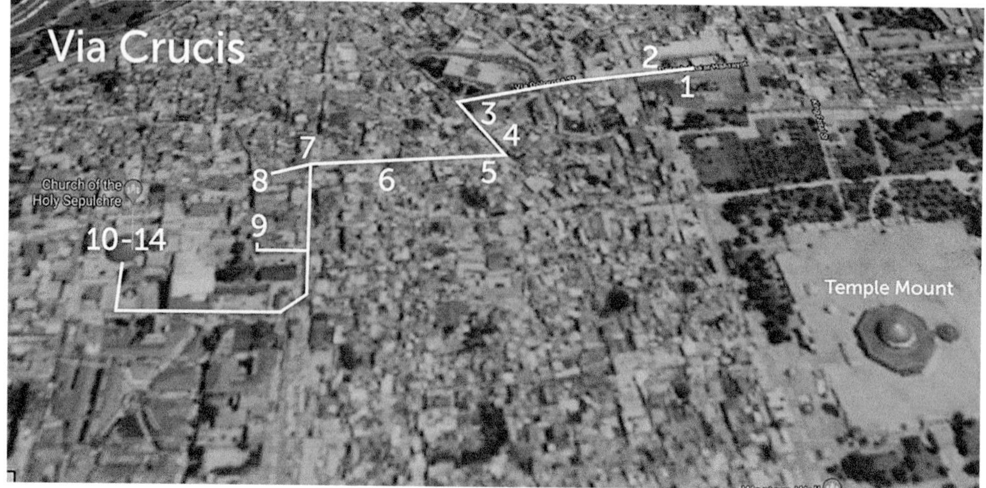

Figure 3.2 Aerial view of Jerusalem with indications of the route of the *Via Crucis*.

Key:

1. Condemnation by Pilate
2. Carrying of the Cross
3. First Fall
4. Meeting of his Mother
5. Simon of Cyrene helps him
6. Veronica wipes his brow
7. Second Fall
8. Meeting the Women of Jerusalem
9. Third Fall
10. Stripping of Garments
11. Nailing to the Cross
12. Crucifixion
13. Deposition
14. Entombment

Image credit: © Google Earth with graphic annotation by Jon-Paul Della Pia

In tracing the change in orientation (and thus beginning point) of the *Via Crucis* in Jerusalem in the early fifteenth century, we can refer to Margery Kempe (c. 1373–after 1438), an English mystic, who described in *The Book of Margery Kempe*[79] her three-week stay in Jerusalem during a Holy Land pilgrimage, on which she embarked c. 1413.[80] A kind of spiritual autobiography, Kempe's account details her journey in the third person; she even calls herself "the creature." The pilgrim tells of her demonstrative spiritual reactions at each holy site, including sobbing and wailing. Interestingly, in the context of orientation, Kempe states being led by "the Gray Friars,"[81] a descriptive phrase for the Franciscans in reference to the color of their habits, and she notes the sequence in which she visited the places associated with Christ's Passion in Jerusalem. She begins by describing the manner in which her guides led pilgrims on an urban itinerary:

> Then the friars lifted up a cross and led the pilgrims about from one place to another where our Lord had suffered his pains and his passion, every man and woman bearing a wax candle in their hand. And the friars always, as they went about, told them what our Lord suffered in every place.[82]

She then describes going to Mount Calvary,[83] the tomb,[84] and the site of the Crucifixion:

> And so overall where that ever the friars led them in that holy place she always wept and sobbed wonderfully, and especially when she came to where our Lord was nailed on the cross.[85]

In the next paragraph, Kempe continues:

> Another day, early in the morning, they went again to the great hills. And their guides told where our Lord bore the cross on his back, and where his Mother met with him, and how she swooned, and how she fell down and he fell down also.[86]

She describes a conclusion of the itinerary at Mount Zion at the place where Christ washed his disciples' feet, the Last Supper occurred, and the Holy Ghost descended.[87]

Although Kempe does not specifically mention the Veronica stop during her progression from one holy site to the next as guided by Franciscan friars, her account is important because it indicates that by the first quarter of the fifteenth century, the Franciscans had singled out a series of stops associated with Christ's final walk, which were visited in a west-east direction. Kempe's account also informs us that the shrines were organized into two clusters, which were visited on sequential days: Calvary first, followed the next morning by the group of sites inside the city walls of Jerusalem. Thus, Kempe visited the holy places in a reverse chronology from the biblical narrative.

In 1458, William Wey had recounted the same west-east orientation of the Stations of the Cross in a section titled "Pilgrimages to the Sites of the Stations" in his journal. Wey recorded that his group started at the Holy Sepulcher and walked toward "a gate facing east through which St. Stephen was led to be stoned."[88] As the Lion's Gate is also known as St. Stephen's Gate, these would have been one and the same. In describing the Stations between the sepulcher and the east gate, he mentioned, "On the right is the place where Jesus pressed his face on to the cloth and handed it to Veronica."[89] In a similar manner, in his journal of 1462, in which he revisited the sites, he recorded:

> These are the ones we visited on 20 July:
> First, the stone with the crosses where Christ fell;
> Second, the street where Christ carried His cross;
> Third, the home of the rich man who was damned;
> Fourth, the crossroads where Christ fell with His cross;
> Fifth, the place where the women wept over Christ;
> Sixth, where Veronica took Christ's face in her handkerchief;
> Seventh, where the Most Blessed Virgin Mary fainted;
> Eighth, the gate through which Christ was led to death;
> Ninth, the pool where the sick were healed when the waters were disturbed;
> Tenth, the two white stones in the wall above the heads of passers-by on which Jesus stood when he was condemned to death by Pilate;
> Eleventh, the school of the Blessed Mary where she learned her letters.
> Along that street, on the other side, is Pilate's house, where Christ was flogged and condemned to death.[90]

We can observe from Wey's enumeration of twelve stations that he processed in a west-east direction. He began at "the stone with the crosses where Christ fell," which can be identified as Calvary, and concluded at the Palace of Pilate. Although Wey's sequence is also in reverse order of the biblical narrative, the meeting with Veronica remains the Sixth Station. Veronica's House, thus, seems to have served as an approximate midpoint for the series of stations as approached from either direction.

A definitive rationale for the change in orientation from east-west in the fourth century to west-east by the mid-fifteenth century will probably never be found. However, one factor to consider is topographical elevation. If pilgrims walked in an east-west direction to follow the sequence of the biblical narrative, they were walking on a gradual incline up to Mount Calvary. In fact, the Franciscan Elzear Horn, writing in the 1720s, had mentioned: "Christ, carrying His Cross, from now on proceeded westward towards Calvary on the Via Dolorosa, which here rises slightly."[91] Conversely, if walking in the opposite direction from west to east, the physical exertion required of ambulatory pilgrims may have been lessened by a descent into the city. Pilgrims' stamina may have played a minor role in the change of direction to the route.

For a brief time at the turn of the sixteenth century, the Veronica stop may have been situated closer to Christ's arrival at Calvary (near the end of the sequence according to biblical narrative), with her placement earlier in the chronology as the Sixth Station a later transposition. Fra Francesco Suriano (Venice, 1450–c. 1529), a Franciscan friar, made two trips to the Holy Land. After an initial sojourn in 1481–1484, he returned to Palestine in 1493–1515 as Guardian, whose duties specified assistance to pilgrims.[92] In his resulting *The Treatise of The Holy Land*, Suriano included a diagram titled "Sanctuaries within Jerusalem," followed by a list of fourteen stops that progressed east-west, beginning at Saint Stephen's Gate and concluding at Mount Calvary. In this version, the House of Veronica immediately precedes Calvary, therefore indicating a temporary placement closer to the site of the Crucifixion and nearer the end of the itinerary. Instead of being numbered, the sites in the diagram and accompanying list are lettered, with some letters of the alphabet skipped, as follows:

A St. Stephen's or Gethsemane Gate
B Entrance to the Haram es-Sharif
C Solomon's Temple or Dome of the Rock
D Pool of Bethesda
E The House of Saint Anne
F The House of Pilate
G The House of Herod
I The Arch on which Christ was sentenced
K Saint Mary of the Spasm
L Where Simon of Cyrene took the Cross
M Where Christ spoke to the women of Jerusalem
N The House of the Epicurean
P The House of Veronica
R Mount Calvary[93]

This placement of the House of Veronica adjacent to the site of the Crucifixion indicates a theological consolidation of the two scenes. However, the new placement of

Veronica's House at the end of Christ's walk at Mount Calvary at the turn of the sixteenth century was short lived. By the end of the sixteenth century, we can notice two key developments: a return to the original east-west orientation and the relocation of Veronica's House from the Calvary end to the midpoint of the path. Both of these modifications are evidenced in *Civitates Orbis Terrarum* (Cities of the World), an atlas edited by Georg Braun (1541–1622) with engravings by Frans Hogenberg (1535–1590) and published in six volumes from 1572–1617 in Cologne.[94] Volume 4, datable to 1588, features a map titled, *Ierusalem, et suburbia eius, sicut tempore Christi floruit, cu locis, in quib "Christ pass"* (Jerusalem, and its outskirts, at the time when Christ flourished, in the place where Christ suffered) (Plate 6). Although imaginary in scope and approach, the map illustrates the *Via Crucis* in a detailed, colored engraving. Exemplary in his rendition of Christ's path, Hogenberg, as artist-cartographer, employs simultaneous narrative as a means for rendering a miniature figure of Christ, who carries his cross in an east-west direction, beginning at the *Palatium Pilati* (Palace of Pilate) and concluding at *Mons Caluaria* (Mount Calvary). We can identify as the sixth encounter the character of Veronica (wearing an ocher tunic), kneeling as she offers her *sudarium* to Christ (donning a brown tunic), while Simon of Cyrene (dressed in blue) still carries the rear end of the cross as a holdover from the previous (Fifth) station. Hogenberg placed Christ's meeting with Veronica at a minor intersection, with the large building at the corner labeled *Dom' Veronice* (House of Veronica). The event takes place inside the city walls and immediately before the large gate, labeled *Porta Vetus Iudiciaria* (Old Judgment Gate), with a subordinate gate called *Porta Genath* just to the north of it. This visionary map of Jerusalem is testament to a codification of the *Via Crucis* as an east-west processional route with Veronica's House at the midpoint by the end of the sixteenth century. The map indicates a revival and solidification of the east-west orientation from the route's Early Christian origins.

The site that is purportedly the House of Veronica (Figures 3.3 and 3.4)[95] is located on a stretch of street with no other stations on it, although the Fifth Station (where Simone of Cyrene helped Christ carry his cross) is at the previous corner. The Sixth Station is situated at roughly the midpoint of the walk, near the Franciscan friars' house, which had been in place since 1229. In terms of logistics and topography, therefore, I suggest that the stop designated to commemorate the apocryphal character of Veronica may have been moved to this point as the Sixth Station with the practical purpose of connecting the first group of Stations (1–5) at the eastern end with the second cluster (7–14) near the Church of the Holy Sepulcher at the western end.

To establish that the stations were clustered into two groups, we can refer to one pilgrim's journal and one published treatise. First, in 1506, the English knight Sir Richard Guylforde recorded in a journal his visit to the holy sites of Jerusalem in two sections, notably using the word *station* for the stops. He calls the first section a "Procession" and mentions that he was led by friars:

> Of the Processyon Done There.
>
> And whan we were thus entred into the sayde Temple of the Holy Sepulcre, y^{e} sayd Tewysday at nyght we were had by and by into y^{e} forsayd chapel of our

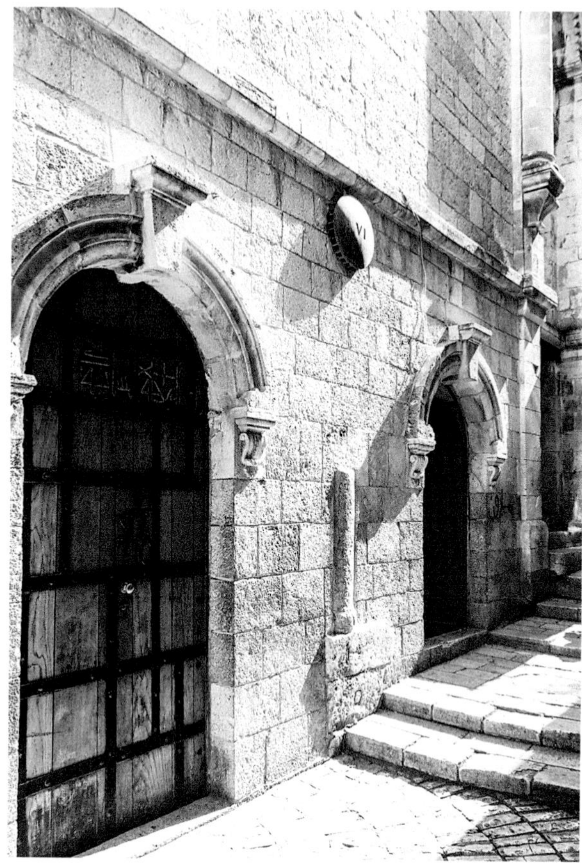

Figure 3.3 Veronica's House, Sixth Station of the Cross, Jerusalem.
Image credit: © Dr. Thomas Liptak, Flickr

> Lady whiche y^e^ freres kepe, and there they made theym redy in ornamente, and began there a very solempne pcessiō; and at euery station was shewed vnto vs by one of ye Frere ye mysteryes and holynes of ye place where they made theyr stacions, and they sange antemes, ympnes, vsicles, and colette appropred vunto ye sayd holy place right solemply and deuoutly.[96]

Guylforde continued by describing the procession going to Mount Calvary where Jesus was crucified and finding post holes where the three crosses had been erected, among other sites.

In a separate, subsequent section, he described visiting a second set of holy places, again led by friars, within the city walls of Jerusalem, beginning with the first stop at the House of Veronica. We can note that he approximated the distance between the Palace of Pilate and Veronica's House by using a pace as a unit of measure:

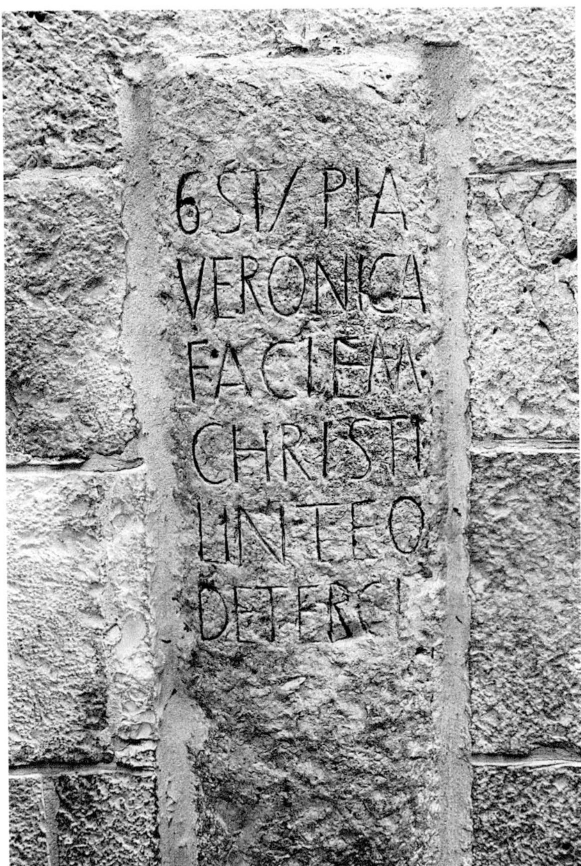

Figure 3.4 Marker outside of Veronica's House, Jerusalem. Inscription: 6ST/PIA VERONICA FACIEM CHRISTI LINTEO DETERCI (6th Station, Pious Veronica wiped the face of Christ with a cloth).

Image credit: Album/Alamy Stock Photo

> Pylgrymages within Iherusalem
>
> And so this day aforesayde we vysyted all ye longe wey by the whiche our Sauyour Criste was led frome the hous of Pylate vunto the place of his crucyfyinge.
>
> And firste, as our way laye, we come to the house of Veronica, whiche is from Pylates house .v. .c. .1. pace, where as our blessyd Sauyour impressyd ye ymage of his face in her wympell whiche is at Rome, and is called there the varnacle.[97]

The most important information to glean from this account is that the Stations were grouped into two distinct clusters, even distinguished and separated by headers in Guylforde's journal.

Secondly, writing in Latin in 1626, the Franciscan scholar P. Franciscus Quaresmi, citing Adrichomius' *Theatrum Terrae Sanctae* (Theater of the Holy Land) of

1590, described the Way of the Cross as comprising two parts with the obstacle of the Judgment Gate as impassable between the two segments:

> Wherefore the *Via Dolorosa* can be divided into two parts: into that part which is within the Holy City, beginning at the palace of Pilate and going continuously to the Gate of Judgments; and that which goes from the Judgment Gate to Mount Calvary. I have divided it thus since the Judgment Gate is closed with a wall [so] it is not possible to go out that way and accompany Christ from it to Mount Calvary.[98]

My proposal then is that the designated location of the House of Veronica had been moved by the end of the sixteenth century from a temporary place at the western end (approaching Calvary) eastward toward the middle of the constructed path with the purpose of bridging a gap and joining the two segments of the *Via Crucis*. On the map from 1588 (Plate 6) we can see the Veronica station just inside the Old Judgment Gate and the manner in which this gate separates the two subsets of stations. The added *locus* also served as an approximate halfway mark within the disorienting urban design of the city and facilitated the movement of pilgrims, many of whom were barefoot and thus probably in pain,[99] and/or who may have been carrying wooden crosses along a zigzag path. Clearly stated, there needed to be a stop at this point on the route to keep the implied, dotted line of stations continuous, thereby ensuring that pilgrims moved efficiently from one station to the next without losing their way. As there were at times likely throngs of pilgrims processing, with many stumbling – either deliberately in imitation of Christ's poses during the Falls or unintentionally from exhaustion or from being pushed from behind – the need for crowd control to prevent trampling was likely a contributing factor as well.

Furthermore, most European visitors to Jerusalem had made long, arduous, and expensive journeys, as Miedema (1998) has reminded us. Upon arrival, however, their stays were often brief and largely guided by Franciscan friars who had strict rules and rarely allowed pilgrims the liberty of meandering individually. The brevity of the stays combined with a paucity of free time to explore on their own could have been disappointing to some travelers, considering the investment and difficulties in having made the pilgrimage. These potential downsides could be offset not only by the promise of indulgences but also by the promotion of the holiness of the sites and the opportunity to view a high number of sacred places in a short amount of time.[100] The impulse, then, for the Franciscans to maximize pilgrims' limited time in the city in light of the high costs of their journeys may have been a contributing factor to the manner in which the friars formalized the *Via Crucis*. The addition of the House of Veronica at a midpoint ensured a cohesive, efficient, and satisfying means for pilgrims to visit as many holy sites as possible during their cursory but intense sojourns.

In 1590, Franciscus Adrichomius had published a treatise called *Theatrum Terrae Sanctae* (Theater of the Holy Land), which described each of the stops on the Way of the Cross with distances noted between them.[101] This late sixteenth-century book represents a codification of the Way of the Cross in Jerusalem as fourteen standard stops sequenced from the Palace of Pilate to Calvary. The treatise proved seminal in the subsequent dissemination of the Stations of the Cross both in the definition of sites and the directional flow for pilgrims, as the text was copied or heavily relied upon by European authors, many of whom had never been to Jerusalem.[102]

The spacing between shrines in European Stations of the Cross frequently demonstrates an attempt to replicate the approximate intervals between sites in Jerusalem, as measured in paces or *braccia* (arms' length), often with an incremental system of indulgences attached. In the sixteenth century, measurements were taken in Jerusalem in order to space stations accordingly in Europe. At first, the Stations were installed outdoors where distances could be replicated. By the end of the seventeenth century, the Stations had moved to the interior of churches where distances were standardized to fit along the aisles, a task facilitated by the even number of fourteen.[103]

Interested in measuring and designing the spaces between stations, Fra Francesco Suriano (Venice, 1450–c. 1529), in his *The Treatise of The Holy Land*, recorded the distances between holy sites, as well as the allotment of indulgences, in a section he called "The Pilgrimage made in the Holy City of Jerusalem."[104] He began:

> In front of the church of the Holy Sepulchre there is a marble slab where Christ stood a while looking up at Mount Calvary where he should be crucified and put to death. Again, going to the left in the city, you come to the House of Veronica, at present demolished; there is an indulgence of 7 quarantines.

After a lengthy list of the indulgences associated with each stop, in a question-response format, he recorded the distances between the shrines:

> Sister. I pray thee tell me how far these places scattered here and there are distant one from another.
>
> Brother. From the Church of the Holy Sepulchre to the house of Veronica is 400 braccia. From there to the house of the rich epicurean is the same.[105]

The locale and direction of the *Via Crucis* in Jerusalem as a late medieval construct is not fully supported by archaeological evidence as the actual path that Christ likely would have taken to Calvary. Archaeological research suggests a more northern path as the probable historical route.[106] The irregular course with several sharp turns can also be explained in part by the fact that the principal streets in Jerusalem, as laid out on a grid in the second century by the Emperor Hadrian (r. 117–138), included two *cardines* (north-south axes) and two *decumani* (east-west axes), necessary because of uneven ground around the Temple Mount. The non-uniform topography of the city may have contributed to the incorporation of the fictional character Veronica into Christ's walk to Calvary in order to claim authenticity for an otherwise crooked path. In summary, the *Via Crucis* should be regarded as a flexible, medieval pilgrimage route constructed primarily to elicit a spiritual response from visitors to the sites rather than a documentary, historical footpath of Christ that can be supported by modern archaeology.

Baldi (1955) outlined a useful synopsis of textual sources, beginning in 1294 and continuing through 1744, which records various manifestations of the *Via Crucis* with labeled diagrams and elevations.[107] Baldi describes the varying numbers and subjects of stops over the developmental arc of the Stations through the mid-eighteenth century. Additional key dates in the late codification of the Stations of the Cross include: In 1686, Pope Innocent XI (papacy 1676–1689) granted the Franciscans permission to erect Stations of the Cross in all of their churches. In 1726 Benedict XIII extended permission to follow the Stations beyond Franciscans to all Christians,[108] and in 1731, Pope Clement XII (papacy 1730–1740) codified the stops with an aim toward correlating the stations to the sites in Jerusalem marked by the Franciscans.[109]

Within the framework of the Stations of the Cross, it is instructive to consider the numeric placement of Veronica as the Sixth Station within the traditional fourteen-station *Via Crucis* (Table 3.2). Specifically, we can notice the relationship of the Veronica stop to Christ's three other sympathetic meetings: with his mother (Fourth), Simon of Cyrene (Fifth), and the Women of Jerusalem (Eighth). These four sympathetic encounters balance Christ's four burdens and stumbles: the Carrying of the Cross (Second) and the three Falls (Third, Seventh, and Ninth). Together the alternation of Falls and salve formed a frame for the ambulatory pilgrim to reenact the syncopation of Christ's suffering and respite. Crisis and catharsis were themes described in the Revelation to John.[110] These opposing yet intertwined emotions are those that the friars may have wanted pilgrims to experience in order for them to connect with the Passion of Christ, whose longsuffering was relieved by four brief respites. It was likely a confluence of factors – the practical need to keep pilgrims oriented and moving, paired with a spiritual motive to encourage vicarious elicitations of Christ's suffering and relief – that resulted in the eventual design of the *Via Dolorosa* in Jerusalem.

The Franciscans also likely added the sympathetic figure of Veronica to heighten pilgrims' empathy for Christ and to help them connect the Passion of Christ to the life of the order's founder, Francis of Assisi, often considered an *alter Christus* because of his reception of the *stigmata* (the wounds of Christ as projected onto

Table 3.2 Stations of the Cross categorized by Crisis or Salve

Station Number	*Crisis*	*Salve*
1	Condemnation by Pilate	
2	Carrying the Cross	
3	First Fall	
4		Meeting of his Mother
5		Simone of Cyrene helps him
6		Veronica wipes his brow
7	Second Fall	
8		Meeting Women of Jerusalem
9	Third Fall	
10	Stripping of Garments	
11	Nailing to the Cross	
12	**Crucifixion**	
13	**Deposition**	
14	**Entombment**	

Francis's hands, side, and feet from a seraphic crucifix at La Verna, as recounted by Bonaventure).[111] In keeping with the Franciscans' mission of evangelization and combating heresy, the friars' goal was chiefly to underscore the humanity of Christ and Francis with an aim toward pilgrims' own repentance and spiritual purging. To these ends, I propose that the Franciscans reconfigured, or augmented, the design for the Stations by adding the stop at Veronica's House at an approximate halfway mark in order to elicit participants' responses that were both physically challenging and personally reflective, all the while moderating foot traffic for practical and logistical reasons.

In comparing Veronica as the main character of the Sixth Station to Simon of Cyrene, her immediate predecessor in the Fifth Station, we can make several observations. Primarily, whereas Veronica is *not* mentioned by name in the Gospels (as discussed in Chapter 1), Christ's encounter with Simon of Cyrene *is* recounted in the synoptic Gospels, albeit in brief mentions in Matthew 27:32, Mark 15:21, and Luke 23:26. In attempting to discern who Simon may have been, we can turn to Mark's account as it offers the most detailed description by calling him a passerby who was coming in from the country and who was the father of Alexander and Rufus. As Cyrene was a Jewish community west of Egypt, Simon may have been returning to Judea from the diaspora with his sons.[112] He was probably a peasant if he was coming in from the country, one who likely would have been considered a foreigner since his place of origin was included in his name. All three synoptic accounts emphasize that the soldiers had *compelled*, or *made*, Simon carry Jesus's cross, thereby indicating that this man had not helped Christ voluntarily. The juxtaposition of Simon of Cyrene with Veronica, whose legendary character was also cast as a passerby, in back-to-back stations, may have served to foil the intents with which each bystander was helping Christ. Whereas Simon of Cyrene had been instructed to help Jesus, the apocryphal character of Veronica did so willingly. As a point of contrast, in John 19:16–17, Christ carries the cross himself. As observed by Derbes (1996), after 1240 Christ carries his own cross in works of art, without the assistance of Simon of Cyrene, which marks a departure from the Byzantine iconographic tradition.[113] The change in referencing John as the primary textual source for works of art depicting the Carrying of the Cross from the mid-thirteenth century forward is decidedly Western in origin.[114]

Ultimately, as interchangeable symbols of compassion, both Veronica as a character and the materiality of her "true image" relic within the Stations of the Cross sequence represented the *Christus vivans* (living Christ) and offered pilgrims a promise of life after death. I assert that the Resurrection, not otherwise pictured or included in the original fourteen stations, was foreshadowed and implied by the presence of Veronica and her veil, which had absorbed and preserved an image of the face of the living Christ. Some modern revisions to the Stations of the Cross omit the station of Veronica.[115] Likewise, the Resurrection is sometimes unofficially added to the *Via Crucis* as a Fifteenth Station, presumably to make the Stations relevant throughout the liturgical year and not solely during Lent. In the Stations' early formation and initial concept, the presence of Veronica, whose name we can recall is etymologically related to the Greek *Berenikē*, meaning bearer of victory, added connotations of her character as holder of, or perhaps testament to, Christ's eventual triumph over death. Veronica's veil thus can be interpreted as a proxy for the flag of the Resurrection. The swathe of cloth served as a reminder that his grave clothes, as the only physical objects found in his empty cave tomb, were interpreted as evidence that he had risen on the third day after his entombment. Alternatively, or in addition, the presence of Veronica holding her image-bearing cloth could allude to, or promise, a second coming.[116]

Pairings of the veronica cloth with other allegories of Christ's triumph over death include its periodic appearance with the lioness and with cubs, as exemplified in the quatrefoil at the apex of *The Man of Sorrows between the Virgin and Saint Catherine of Alexandria*, 1400–1420, by the Master of Saint Veronica (fl. 1395–1415) in the Royal Museum of Fine Arts, Antwerp (Figure 3.5). We can also find images of the character of Veronica paired with the pelican and her young, as for example in the lower border of the illumination *Saint Veronica*, c. 1471, by Lieven van Lathem (Flemish, c. 1430–1493) (Figure 3.6).[117] Furthermore, Veronica can be sometimes be depicted with a phoenix[118] or with a serpent leaving a chalice. A salient example of the latter can be found on the right panel of Memling's Bembo diptych with Veronica

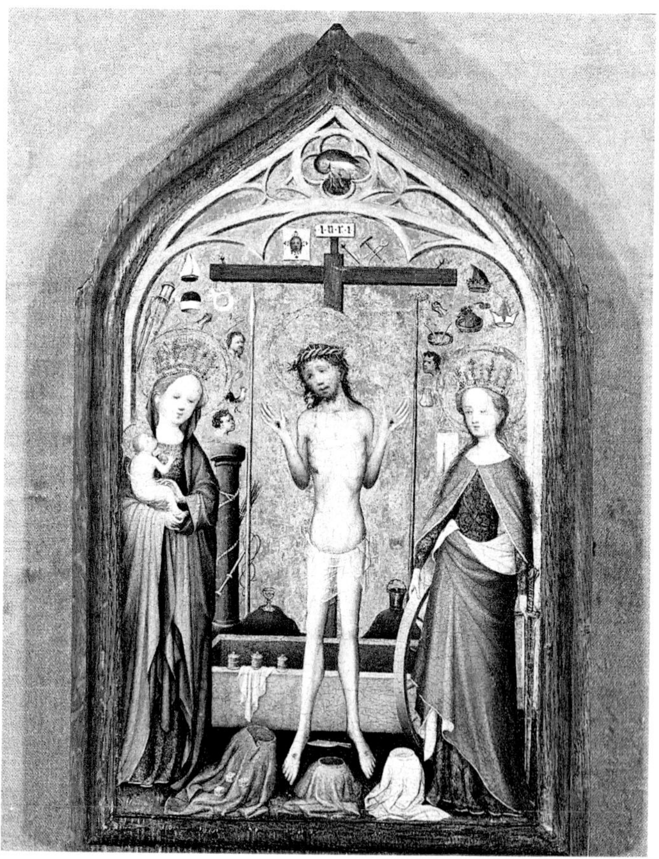

Figure 3.5 Master of Saint Veronica (Cologne, fl. 1400–1420), *The Man of Sorrows between the Virgin and Saint Catherine of Alexandria*, 1400–1420. The Royal Museum of Fine Arts, Antwerp.

Image credit: Scala/Art Resource, NY

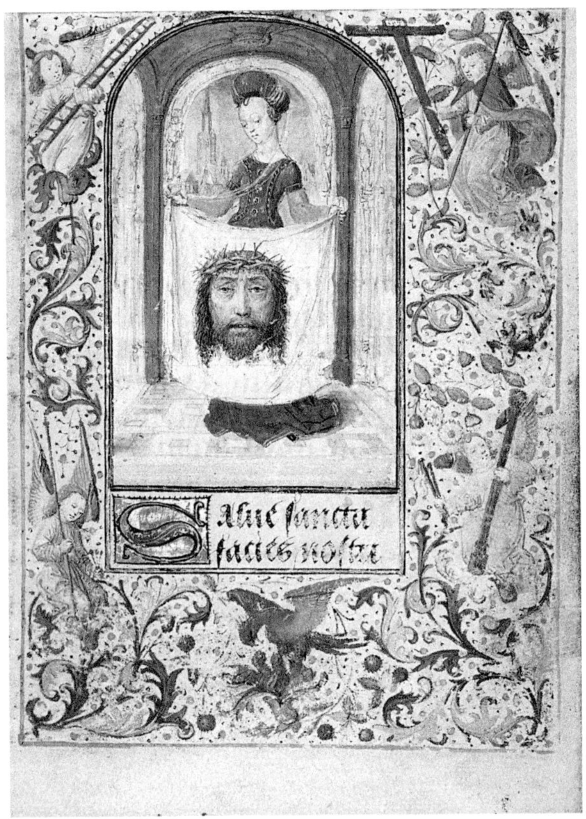

Figure 3.6 Lieven van Lathem (Flemish, c. 1430–1493), *Saint Veronica*, MS 37 (89.ML.35), fol. 2., c. 1471. Tempera colors, gold leaf, gold paint, silver paint, and ink on parchment; 12.4 cm × 9.2 cm. The J. Paul Getty Museum, Los Angeles.

Image credit: The J. Paul Getty Museum, Los Angeles/Open Content Program

on the obverse (Plate 7a) and a chalice with a serpent in it on the reverse (Plate 7b). The chalice refers to a legend about Saint John the Evangelist, who, while preaching at Ephesus, was challenged by a priest at the temple of Diana to drink poison as a test of faith. John made a sign of the cross over the cup and drank the poison without repercussion. In Memling's painting, the writhing serpent symbolizes the poison leaving the cup and thus the power of John's faith to protect him from death. Veronica on the interior of the diptych reinforces this concept of protection against misfortune and triumph over death.[119]

Although largely developed by the Franciscans, the concept of the Stations of the Cross was promoted by other orders, including the Carthusians, Benedictines, and Dominicans. For example, Dominican interest in the Stations can be found in the writings of Heinrich Suso (German, 1295–1366), a mystic who wrote about his cross-carrying reenactments within his monastery.[120] The following century, a Dominican friar called Blessed Alvarez, O. P. (Spanish or Portuguese, b. mid-fourteenth century, initiated 1368, d. 1420), erected an early version of the Stations as a series of oratories

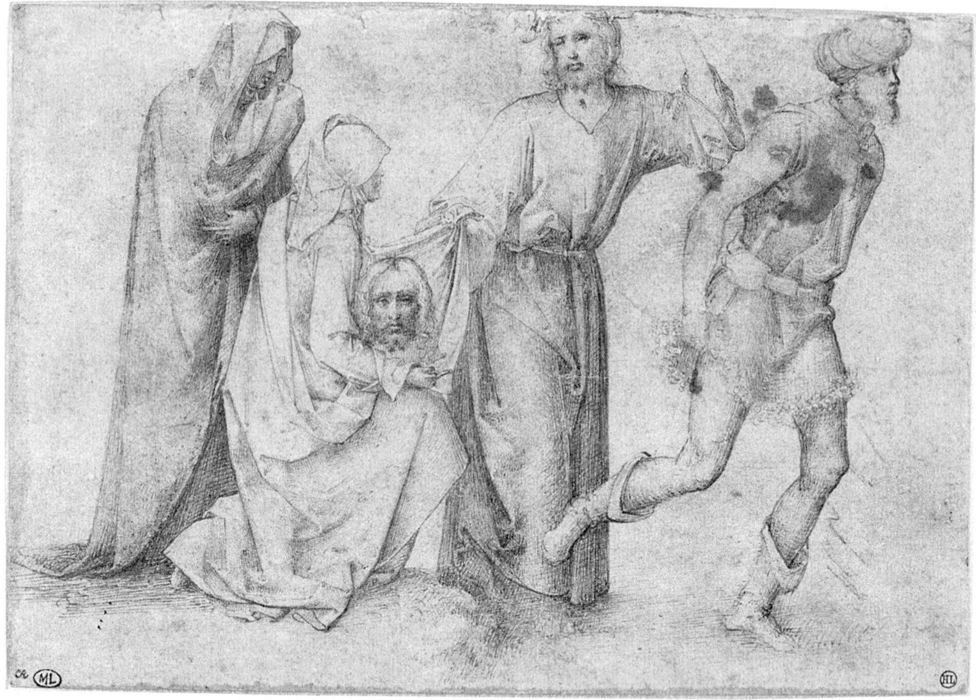

Figure 3.7 Baccio della Porta, called Fra Bartolommeo (Florence, 1472–1517), *Way of the Cross: Veronica showing the Holy Face*, c. 1490–1500. Pen and sepia ink with red chalk and white highlights on beige paper; 14 × 19.6 cm. Musée du Louvre, Paris (RF471r). Collection of Aimé-Charles-Horace His de La Salle; donated 1878.

Image credit: Musée du Louvre, Paris. © RMN-Grand Palais/Art Resource, NY. Photo: Michèle Bellot

in the garden of his monastery, called *Escalaceli* (Ladder to Heaven), at Cordoba after his return from a Holy Land pilgrimage.[121] Later Dominican interest in Veronica is evident by the order's patronage and production of works of art with Veronica as subject. As an example, Fra Bartolommeo, O. P. (Italian, 1472–1517), a Dominican monk from Tuscany originally named Baccio della Porta, produced a pen and chalk drawing of the *Way of the Cross: Veronica showing the Holy Face*, c. 1490–1500, now in the Musée du Louvre (Figure 3.7). The Franciscans' establishment and advancement of the *Via Crucis* in Jerusalem and the Stations of the Cross in Europe were adopted by other orders and eventually by a wide spectrum of Christian denominations, as remains the case today.

Notes

1 Although the visual form and participatory concept of the Stations of the Cross have spread to Africa, the Americas, and Asia, where there are a host of creative examples made especially during the nineteenth and twentieth centuries, for purposes of this study, the focus will be on European series that date during the Early Modern period, considered in relationship to the *Via Crucis* (or *Via Dolorosa*) in Jerusalem.

2 F. E. Peters, "The Procession That Never Was: The Painful Way in Jerusalem," *The Drama Review* 29 (1985): 31–41.
3 Ibid., 34.
4 See Jean Zuallart, *Il Devotissimo Viaggio di Gerusalemme* (Rome: F. Zanetti & Gia Ruffinelli, 1587), www.archive.org.
5 Ibid.
6 Peters, "The Procession That Never Was," 35.
7 "The Friars ... with the blessing of the Superior go forth from St. Saviour's Convent and with very great devotion, barefooted, make the Way of the Cross, which also the faithful of Jerusalem do frequently, especially on Fridays and during Lent; by saying only an Our Father and Hail Mary at each station, they make a great gain of indulgences for themselves and the souls in Purgatory. They exhort pilgrims coming here to do the same, so that, while they go along that Way, outwardly offering due reverence to the Holy Places of the Passion which they meet there, and in body and soul sympathising with the Redeemer suffering in soul and body, they are taught by the same. At the time of Fr. Basil of Caprarola, at one time Guardian of the Convent of Holy Mount Sion, the custom was still in vogue that the Friars with their Superior in procession, but without the cross at the head, on every Friday afternoon after Compline went along the dolorous Way to the House of Pilate and on returning went from the Gate of Judgment to the vestibule of the church of the Holy Sepulchre, and there kneeling said the customary prayers with arms outstretched; but this devotion was abrogated on Jan. 22, 1621, on account of a petulance committed by a young Turk, which so effected the Pasha, the Cadi and the Ministers that the Guardian against justice had to pay 900 pieces of silver [...]." Elzear Horn, *Ichnographiae Monumentorum Terrae Sanctae, 1724–1744*, ed. and trans. Eugene Hoade and Bellarmino Bagatti (Jerusalem: Franciscan Press, 1962), 160.
8 Colin Morris, *The Sepulchre of Christ and the Medieval West: from the beginning to 1600* (Oxford: Oxford University Press, 2005), 360.
9 Annabel J. Wharton, *Selling Jerusalem: Relics, Replicas, Theme Parks* (Chicago: University of Chicago Press, 2006), Chapters 1–2, especially 3 and 50.
10 Mitzi Kirkland-Ives, "Alternate Routes: Variation in Early Modern Stational Devotions," *Viator* 40 (2009): 249–270, 250.
11 Examples include: Fabrizio Tola, "Parole e immagini nella devozione alla Passione di Cristo in Sardegna nel XVII e XVIII secolo: *Via Crucis* e processione dei Misteri," *Theologica & Historica* 25 (2016): 535–561; and Galit Noga-Banai, "*Places of Remembrance*: A Via Dolorosa in Berlin's Bavarian Quarter," in *Between Jerusalem and Europe: Essays in Honour of Bianca Kühnel*, eds. Renana Bartal and Hanna Vorholt, 173–196 (Leiden: Brill Publishers, 2015).
12 Herbert Thurston, S. J., *The Stations of the Cross: An Account of Their History and Devotional Purpose* (London: Burns & Oates, 1914).
13 Albert Storme, *The Way of the Cross: An Historical Sketch (The Holy Places of Palestine)*, 2nd ed. (Jerusalem: Franciscan Printing Press, 1984).
14 Amédée (Teetaert) Da Zedelgem, *Saggio Storico sulla Devozione alla Via Crucis: Evocazione e rappresentazione degli episodi e dei luoghi della Passione di Cristo*, trans. from French by Paolo Pellizzari (Bergamo: Atlas, 2004). Da Zedelgem's original version of this text, *Aperçu historique sur la dévotion au chemin de la croix,* was published posthumously in *Collectanea Franciscana* 19 (1949): 45–142.
15 Da Zedelgem, *Saggio Storico sulla Devozione alla Via Crucis*, 65.
16 Morris, *The Sepulchre of Christ,* 359.
17 Sarah Lenzi, *The Stations of the Cross: The Placelessness of Medieval Christian Piety* (Turnhout: Brepols Publishers, 2016), 3, 198.
18 Ibid., 198.
19 Ibid., 199.
20 Jim Nisbet, *An Illustrated Stations of the Cross: The Devotion and its History* (Mystic, CT: Twenty-Third Publications, 1982).
21 Morris, *The Sepulchre of Christ,* 359–360.
22 Ibid., 318.

23 Robert Ousterhout, "Flexible Geography and Transportable Topography," in *The Real and Ideal Jerusalem in Jewish, Christian, and Islamic Art. Studies in Honor of Bezalel Narkiss on the Occasion of his Seventieth Birthday*, ed. Bianca Kühnel, 393–404 (Jerusalem: *Jewish Art* 23/24, 1997–1998).
24 Diane Cole Ahl, "Camposanto, *Terra Santa*: Picturing the Holy Land in Pisa," *Artibus Et Historiae* 24 (2003): 95–122.
25 See Daniel K. Connolly, "Imagined Pilgrimage in the Itinerary Maps of Matthew Paris," *Art Bulletin* 81 (1999): 598–622; Evelyn Edson, *Mapping Time and Space: How Medieval Mapmakers Viewed their World* (London: British Library, 1999): 118–125; and Melanie Holcomb, "Matthew Paris's Map of the Holy Land" (catalogue entry), in *Jerusalem 1000–1400: Every People Under Heaven*, eds. Barbara Drake Boehm and Melanie Holcomb (New York: The Metropolitan Museum of Art, and New Haven: Yale University Press, 2016).
26 Da Zedelgem, *Saggio Storico sulla Devozione alla Via Crucis*, 71.
27 Kirkland-Ives, "Alternate Routes," 252, with additional bibliography. See also Kathryn M. Rudy, "Virtual Pilgrimages in the Convent: Imagining Jerusalem in the Late Middle Ages," *Disciplina Monastica* 8 (Turnhout, Belgium: Brepols Publishers, 2011): 28–29; and Kathryn M. Rudy, "A Guide to Mental Pilgrimage: Paris, Bibliothèque De L'Arsenal Ms. 212," *Zeitschrift Für Kunstgeschichte* 63 (2000): 494–515. The latter study examines a manuscript in Paris that not only functioned as a personal, devotional aid but also as a guide for earning indulgences through prayer accompanied by images. Rudy concluded that it probably belonged to a Franciscan friar who used it in the context of a convent rather than as an actual guidebook. The manuscript contains a half-page illumination of a standing Veronica, who holds an oversized *sudarium* held up by two angels, under which is the prayer *Salve sancta facies*, 509, Figure 14.
28 Ibid., 494–515, especially 494–496.
29 Ibid., 496.
30 George Cyprian Alston, "Way of the Cross," *The Catholic Encyclopedia*, vol. 15 (New York: Robert Appleton Company, 1912), accessed May 21, 2019, www.newadvent.org.
31 See Agnes Smith Lewis, trans. and ed., *Apocrypha Syriaca: the Protoevengelium Jacobi and Transitus Mariae* (Cambridge: Cambridge University Press, 1902, reprinted 2012).
32 Da Zedelgem, *Saggio Storico sulla Devozione alla Via Crucis*, 69. A Latin adaptation of this text describes Mary stopping to visit each place associated with the life of her son, starting from her house, continuing to Mount Zion, and including places outside of the Passion cycle, such as the sites of Jesus's baptism and ascension.
33 Dorothea R. French, "Felix Fabri," in *Encyclopedia of Medieval Pilgrimage* (Leiden: Brill Publishers, 2012), accessed July 23, 2019, http://dx.doi.org/10.1163.
34 Fratris Felicis Fabri, *Evagatorium in Terræ Sanctæ, Arabiæ et Egypti Peregrinationem*, vol. 1, 1494, ed. Konrad Dietrich Hassler (Stuttgardiæ: Societatis Litterariæ Stuttgardiensis, 1843), www.gutenberg.org, cited in Peters, "The Procession That Never Was," 37.
35 Ibid., 37.
36 Ibid., 33.
37 John Wilkinson, trans. and ed., *Egeria's Travels*, 3rd ed. (Oxford: Aris & Phillips, 1999), 1. Egeria's full name, place of origin, and any title of her writings remain unknown, as only the middle section of her manuscript was found in the late nineteenth century.
38 Ibid., 154.
39 Ibid., 86.
40 Ibid., 154–155.
41 Da Zedelgem, *Saggio Storico sulla Devozione alla Via Crucis*, 70.
42 On the Church of the Holy Sepulcher, see W. Eugene Kleinbauer, "The Anastasis Rotunda and Christian Architectural Invention," in *The Real and Ideal Jerusalem in Jewish, Christian, and Islamic Art. Studies in Honor of Bezalel Narkiss on the Occasion of his Seventieth Birthday*, ed. Bianca Kühnel, 140 – 146 (Jerusalem: *Jewish Art* 23/24, 1997–1998).
43 Denys Pringle, "The Planning of Some Pilgrimage Churches in Crusader Palestine," *World Archaeology* 18 (1987): 341–362, 343, www.jstor.org/stable/124590.

44 Da Zedelgem, *Saggio Storico sulla Devozione alla Via Crucis*, 72. See Saint Bernard, Abbot of Clairvaux, *Life and Works of Saint Bernard*, ed. Dom. John Mabillon; trans. and ed. Samuel J. Eales, 2 vols., 2nd ed. (London: Burns & Oats, Ltd., 1889). As an example of Bernard's description of the "supreme love" that could be inspired the Passion of Christ, see Letter CXC, vol. 2, 590–591.

45 Da Zedelgem, *Saggio Storico sulla Devozione alla Via Crucis*, 73. On Saint Bonavenure, see Bonaventure, *The Life of Saint Francis*, trans. Ewert Cousins, with introduction by Donna Tartt (New York: HarperCollins, 2005); and Jay M. Hammond, J. A. Wayne Hellmann, and Jared Goff, *A Companion to Bonaventure* (Boston: Brill, 2013); and Christopher M. Cullen, *Bonaventure* (Oxford: Oxford University Press, 2006).

46 See Ernoul, *Chronique d'Ernoul et de Bernard le Tresorier*, ed. L. de Mas Latrie (Paris: Société de l'histoire de France, 1871); and Paul Wilhelm von Keppler, *Die XIV stationen des heiligen kreuzwegs eine geschichtliche und kunstgeschichtliche studie zugleich eine erklaerung der kreuzweg-vilder der malerschule von veuron* (Freiburg: Herder, 1904).

47 Denys Pringle, *Pilgrimage to Jerusalem and the Holy Land, 1187–1291* (New York: Routledge, 2016), 135–164.

48 Ibid., 321–360.

49 Jaroslav Folda, "Jerusalem and the Holy Sepulchre through the Eyes of Crusader Pilgrims," in *The Real and Ideal Jerusalem in Jewish, Christian and Islamic Art. Studies in Honor of Bezalel Narkiss on the Occasion of his Seventieth Birthday*, ed. Bianca Kühnel, 158–164 (Jerusalem: *Jewish Art* 23/24, 1997–1998).

50 Xavier John Seubert, "Franciscans in Jerusalem: The Early History," in *Jerusalem 1000–1400: Every People Under Heaven*, eds. Barbara Drake Boehm and Melanie Holcomb, 240–241 (New York: The Metropolitan Museum of Art, and New Haven: Yale University Press, 2016).

51 Wharton, *Selling Jerusalem*, 57–62, 109.

52 For current information on this group's activities, see Custodia Terræ Sanctæ: Franciscan Missionaries Serving the Holy Land, accessed January 15, 2018, http://custodia.org; David D'Arcy, "Custodians of the Holy Land: the Franciscans to Open New Museum in Jerusalem," *The Art Newspaper* (Jan. 6, 2017), https://theartnewspaper.com; and Terra Sancta Museum, accessed April 11, 2018, https://terrasanctamuseum.org.

53 Fra Francesco Suriano, *Treatise on The Holy Land*, trans. Fr. Theophilus Bellorini, and Fr. Eugene Hoade (Jerusalem: Franciscan Press, 1949), 3.

54 Kathryn Blair Moore, *The Architecture of the Christian Holy Land: Reception from Late Antiquity through the Renaissance* (Cambridge: Cambridge University Press, 2017): 122–123.

55 Lenzi, *The Stations of the Cross*, 23; and Blair Moore, *The Architecture of the Christian Holy Land*, 123.

56 The friars maintained their protective role for Christian sanctuaries and pilgrims in Jerusalem through the Mamluk and Ottoman sultanates. Although there have been sporadic interruptions, the friars maintain a custodial role today.

57 Sarah McNamer, *Meditations on the Life of Christ: The Short Italian Text* (Notre Dame, IN: University of Notre Dame Press, 2018), 173–175.

58 Niccolò da Poggibonsi, *Libro d'Oltramare, pubblicato da Alberto Bacchi della Lega* (Bologna: Presso Gaetano Romagnoli, 1881), www.archive.org.

59 Kathryn Blair Moore, "The Disappearance of an Author and the Emergence of a Genre: Niccolò Da Poggibonsi and Pilgrimage Guidebooks between Manuscript and Print," *Renaissance Quarterly* 66 (2013): 357–411.

60 Blair Moore, *The Architecture of the Christian Holy Land*, 134–135.

61 Blair Moore, "The Disappearance of an Author," 357.

62 Ibid., 365.

63 Ibid., 358.

64 The only extant copy of the manuscript, which is considered the original, is in the Bodleian Library (MS Bodl. 565). Wey, *The Itineraries of William Wey*, 17. Wey also travelled to Santiago de Campostela in 1456. In 1458, his journey featured sojourns in Rome, Venice, Jaffa, and Jerusalem. In 1462, he revisited Venice, Jaffa, and Jerusalem.

Ibid., with a map of his itineraries, 20–21. See also Francis Davey, "William Wey: An English Pilgrim's Journey to Jerusalem," in *Pilgrimage: The Sacred Journey*, eds. Ruth Barnes and Crispin Branfoot (Oxford: Ashmolean Museum, 2006): 80–95, with Wey's map of the Holy Land, 88–89.

65 Wey describes the Warden of the Franciscan Brothers granting him permission to visit the Holy Land, 72. Periodically throughout his description of the pilgrimage of 1458 to Jerusalem, Wey mentions the Franciscan Brothers escorting his group of pilgrims, 74.

66 Wey, *The Itineraries of William Wey*, 46–47.

67 Prima Arad, "Pilgrimage, Cartography, and Devotion: William Wey's Map of the Holy Land," *Viator* 43 (2012): 301–322.

68 Ibid., 302.

69 Ibid., 302, 304, with a complete inventory of objects in the chapel, 317.

70 Kirkland-Ives, "Alternate Routes," 250.

71 Peters, "The Procession That Never Was," 36.

72 John Rufus, "'A Pilgrimage in Jerusalem,' in *The Life of Peter the Iberian*, c. 500," in *Jerusalem Pilgrims before the Crusades*, trans. and ed. John Wilkinson (Warminster, England: Aris & Phillips, 2002): 101.

73 The first section, "The Beginning of the Jerusalem Circuit," references places associated with the *Via Crucis*, such as the Tomb of the Lord, Golgotha, and the Praetorium of Pilate. However, the second section, "The Rest of the Jerusalem Circuit," describes sites that fall within a wider geographic radius than stops associated with the Passion cycle. For example, Theodosius names the Pool of Siloam and the Church of Lady Mary. Theodosius the Cenobiarch, "*The Topography of the Holy Land*, c. 518," in *Jerusalem Pilgrims before the Crusades*, trans. and ed. John Wilkinson (Warminster, England: Aris & Phillips, 2002), 107–109.

74 Kirkland-Ives, "Alternate Routes," 256.

75 Luke 23:7–31. Coogan, et al., eds., *The New Oxford Annotated Bible*, 1874.

76 Da Zedelgem, *Saggio Storico sulla Devozione alla Via Crucis*, 85–88. There were also versions of Five Falls.

77 Denys Pringle, *Pilgrimage to Jerusalem and the Holy Land, 1187–1291* (New York: Routledge, 2016), 7–8.

78 Ibid.

79 A copy of the original manuscript, MS 61823, is preserved in the British Library, London, www.bl.uk/manuscripts. Kempe, who claimed to be illiterate, dictated her account to a scribe. See Margery Kempe, *The Book of Margery Kempe: A New Translation, Contexts, Criticism*, trans. and ed. Lynn Staley (New York: W. W. Norton & Company, 2001). In the context of pilgrimage, see also Terence N. Bowers, "Margery Kempe as Traveler," *Studies in Philology* 97 (2000): 1–28.

80 Kempe's journey to the Holy Land included stops in Venice, Ramlah, Jaffe, Assisi, and Rome. She also traveled widely in England and made a pilgrimage to Santiago de Compostela.

81 "And then the Gray Friars who had led her from place to place received her into them and set her with them at meals so that she should not eat alone." Kempe, *The Book of Margery Kempe* 54.

82 Ibid., 50.

83 Ibid., 50–51.

84 Kempe describes the tomb as "the grave where our Lord was buried." Ibid., 52.

85 Ibid.

86 Ibid., 53.

87 Ibid.

88 Wey, *The Itineraries of William Wey*, 75–76.

89 Ibid., 75.

90 Ibid., 128–129.

91 Horn, *Ichnographiae Monumentorum Terrae Sanctae, 1724–1744*, 157.

92 Suriano, *Treatise on The Holy Land*, 3.

93 Ibid., 105. The caption in Figure 7 mentions this diagram and list as being "after the design of Zuallard, reproduced from Sandys Travels."

94 Georg Braun, ed. with engravings by Frans Hogenberg, *Civitates Orbis Terrarum* (Cities of the World), 6 vols (Cologne, 1572–1617). A complete set of zoomable images from all volumes can be viewed online at the Library of Congress, accessed May 31, 2019, ww.loc.gov/resource.

95 The interior of the house, which currently is run by the Little Sisters of Jesus, features the Chapel of the Holy Face, located in a basement with vaulted ceiling.

96 Sir Richard Guylforde, *The Pylgrymage of Sir Richard Guylforde to The Holy Land, A.D. 1506*, ed. Sir Henry Ellis (London: Camden Society, 1851; reprinted New York: AMS Press, 1968), 24–25.

97 Ibid., 28. The original manuscript is preserved in The British Museum, London.

98 This passage from Quaresmi's treatise, *Historical, Theological, and Moral Study of the Holy Land* of 1626, is excerpted from the translation in F. E. Peters, *Jerusalem: The Holy City in the Eyes of Chroniclers, Visitors, Pilgrims, and Prophets from the Days of Abraham to the Beginnings of Modern Times* (Princeton: Princeton University Press, 1985b), 502. The original text in Latin was published by P. Donatus Baldi, *Enchiridion Locorum Sanctorum* (Jerusalem: Franciscan Printing Press, 1955, reprinted 1982), 607, as follows: "Quare via dolorosa in duas partes dividi potest: in eam quae est intra sanctam civitatem, incipiendo a palatio Pilati, et continue prosequendo usque ad portam iudiciariam; et in eam quae est a porta judiciaria usque ad montem Calvariae. Ita illam distinxi quoniam, cum porta judiciaria muro clausa sit, non conceditur per illam exire, et ab ea Christum usque ad Calvarium comitari."

99 Elzear Horn, *Ichnographiae Monumentorum Terrae Sanctae, 1724–1744*, ed. and trans. Eugene Hoade and Bellarmino Bagatti (Jerusalem: Franciscan Press, 1962), 160. In this text, the passage is reproduced on p. 69, n. 7, cited in Peters, "The Procession That Never Was," 503.

100 Nine Miedema, "Following in the Footsteps of Christ: Pilgrimage and Passion Devotion," in *The Broken Body: Passion Devotion in Late-Medieval Culture*, eds. A. A. MacDonald, H. N. B. Ridderbos, and R. M. Schlusemann, 73–92, 79–80 (Groningen: Egbert Forsten, 1998).

101 F. E. Peters, *Jerusalem: The Holy City in the Eyes of Chroniclers, Visitors, Pilgrims, and Prophets from the Days of Abraham to the Beginnings of Modern Times* (Princeton: Princeton University Press, 1985b), 501–502.

102 Peters, "The Procession That Never Was," 38.

103 Ibid., 39.

104 Suriano, *Treatise on The Holy Land*, Chapter 39, 102–103.

105 Ibid., 103.

106 Many archaeological fragments from the *Via Crucis* datable from the reigns of Herod to Hadrian, along with a three-dimensional topographical map of Jerusalem, are in the collection of (and on display at) the Terra Sancta Museum, housed in the Monastery of the Flagellation in Jerusalem, accessed April 11, 2018, https://terrasanctamuseum.org. About the discovery of the location of Jesus's Trial in 2014, see Ruth Eglash, "Archaeologists find possible site of Jesus's trial in Jerusalem," *The Washington Post* (Washington, DC), January 4, 2015, accessed July 11, 2018, www.washingtonpost.com.

107 Baldi, *Enchiridion Locorum Sanctorum*, 593–616. A woodcut on page 614 from Elzear Horn's journal of 1725 perhaps best illustrates how Veronica's House as the Sixth Station physically joined the two segments. See Horn, *Ichnographiae Monumentorum Terrae Sanctae, 1724–1744*.

108 Peters, "The Procession That Never Was," 39.

109 Kirkland-Ives, "Alternate Routes," 250.

110 See Adela Yarbro Collins, *Crisis and Catharsis: The Power of the Apocalypse* (Philadelphia: The Westminster Press, 1984), Chapters 3 and 5.

111 Bonaventure, *The Life of Saint Francis*, 138–150. For an analysis of Francis's reception of the *stigmata* and his role as an *alter Christus* as subjects for Franciscan artistic programs in Florence in the fourteenth century, see Nancy M. Thompson, "The Franciscans and the True Cross: The Decoration of the Cappella Maggiore of Santa Croce in Florence," *Gesta* 43 (2004): 61–79.

112 Coogan, et al., eds., *The New Oxford Annotated Bible,* 1822, n. 21.
113 Derbes, *Picturing the Passion,* 114, 128.
114 Ibid., 121.
115 For example, Pope John Paul II (papacy 1978–2005)'s celebration on Good Friday in 1991 and Pope Benedict XVI (papacy 2005–2013)'s procession in 2008 in the Roman Colosseum omitted the apocryphal Veronica stop and added new "Scripture-based" stations, such as the Crowning of Thorns. These twentieth- and twenty-first-century modifications demonstrate a sustained fluidity of the Stations of the Cross.
116 Wolf, "'Or fu sì fatta la sembianza vostra?'", 108.
117 For a second example, see the Master of the Madonna Strauss, *Man of Sorrows with Mary Magdalene*, c. 1400, reproduced in color in *Il Volto di Cristo*, eds. G. Morello and G. Wolf (Milan: Electa, 2000), 134–135.
118 Nino Zchomelidse, "Liminal Phenomena: Framing Medieval Cult Images with Relics and Words," *Viator* 47 (2016): 260–261.
119 Hand, *Hans Memling's Saint John the Baptist and Saint Veronica.*
120 Kirkland-Ives, "Alternate Routes," 252.
121 The Rt. Rev. Michael Beckett, O. P., "Blessed Alvarez of Cordova," *The Order of Preachers Independent* (February 19, 2015), accessed May 30, 2019, www.theorderofpreachersindependent.org.

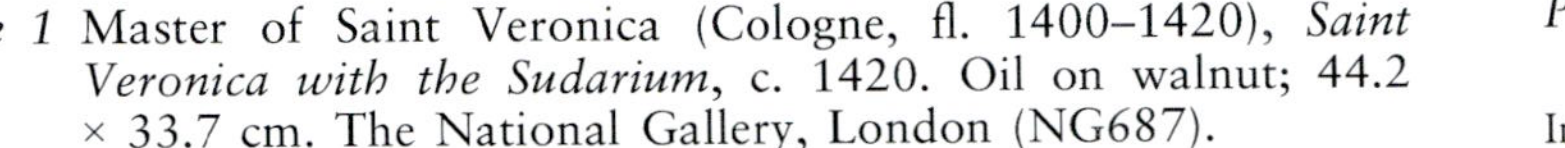

Plate 1 Master of Saint Veronica (Cologne, fl. 1400–1420), *Saint Veronica with the Sudarium*, c. 1420. Oil on walnut; 44.2 × 33.7 cm. The National Gallery, London (NG687).

Image credit: © The National Gallery, London/Art Resource, NY

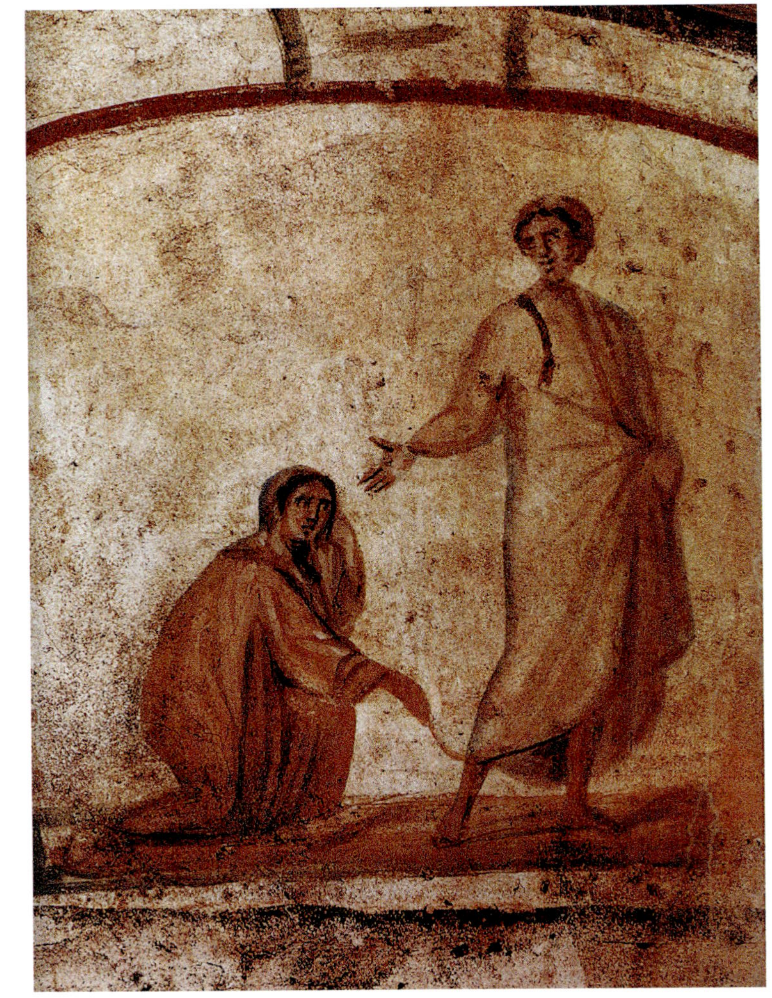

Plate 2 Early Christian, *The Healing of a Bleeding Woman*, 4th century. Fresco. Catacombs of Marcellinus and Peter, Rome.

Image credit: The Picture Art Collection/Alamy Stock Photo

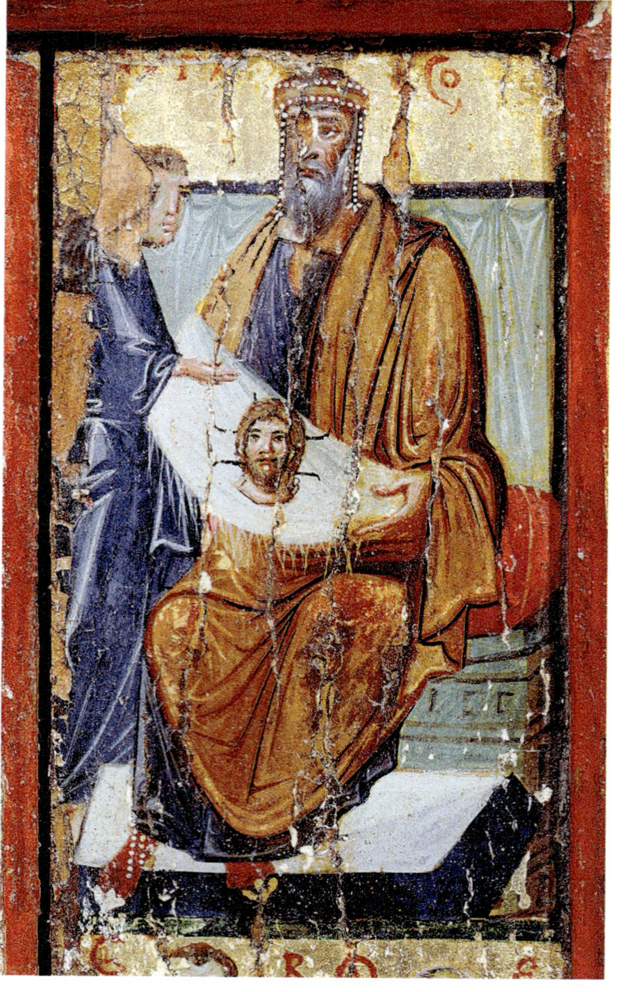

Plate 3 Artist unknown, Icon depicting the *Legend of King Abgar receiving the Image of Edessa from Thaddeus*, after 944. Encaustic on panel. Saint Catherine's Monastery, Mount Sinai, Egypt.

Image credit: © DeA Picture Library/Art Resource, NY

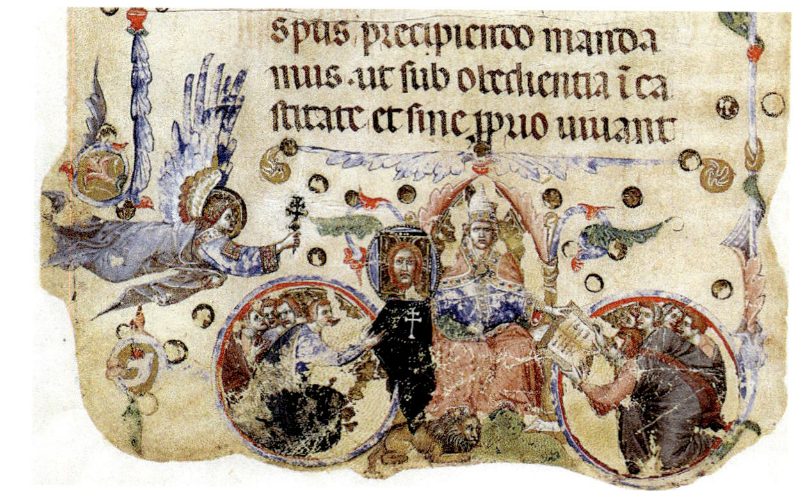

Plate 4 The Procession of Pope Innocent III carrying the veronica in 1208, from *Liber Regulae Sancti Spiritus in Saxia*, MS 9193., c. 1350. Archivio di Stato di Roma.

Image credit: Archivio di Stato di Roma

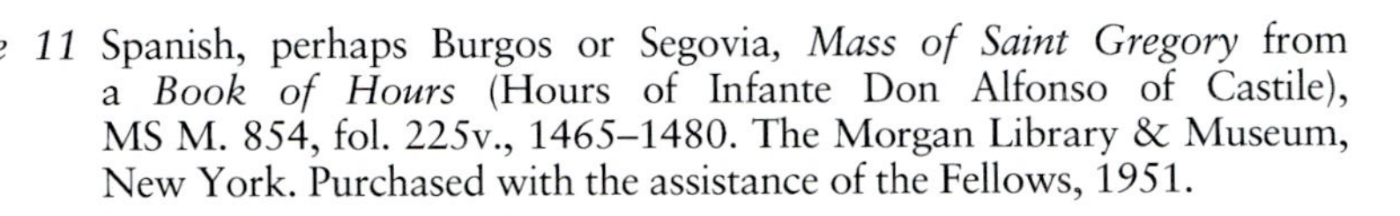

Plate 11 Spanish, perhaps Burgos or Segovia, *Mass of Saint Gregory* from a *Book of Hours* (Hours of Infante Don Alfonso of Castile), MS M. 854, fol. 225v., 1465–1480. The Morgan Library & Museum, New York. Purchased with the assistance of the Fellows, 1951.

Image credit: The Morgan Library & Museum

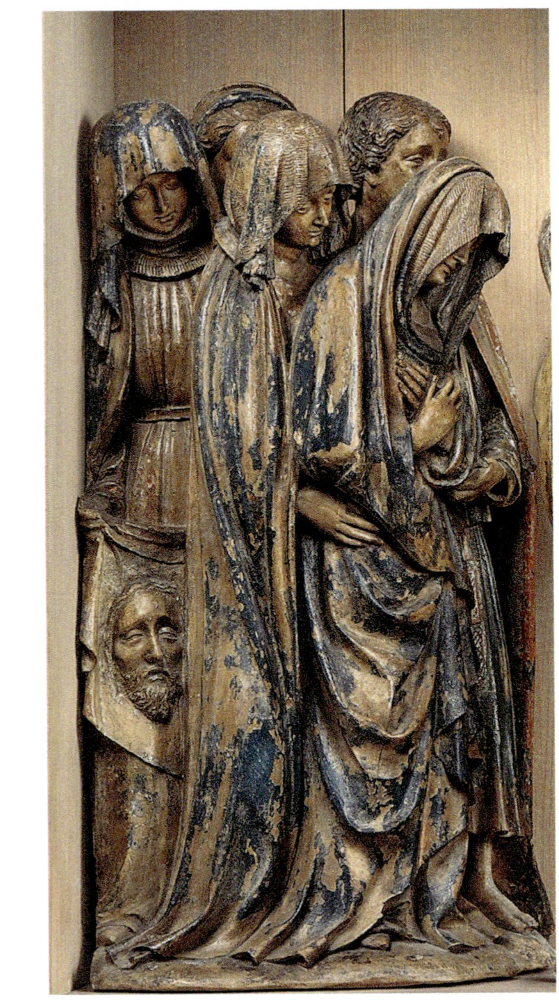

Plate 12 Lorch in the Rhine Valley, *Veronica*, detail of *Christ bearing the Cross*, c. 1425. Terra-cotta with remnants of polychromy. Staatliche Museen zu Berlin, Skulpturensammlung und Museum für Byzantinische Kunst (Inv. 8499). For the complete work, see Fig. 6.19.

Image credit: Staatliche Museen zu Berlin – Preußischer Kulturbesitz. Skulpturensammlung und Museum für Byzantinische Kunst. Photos: A. Voigt, Berlin

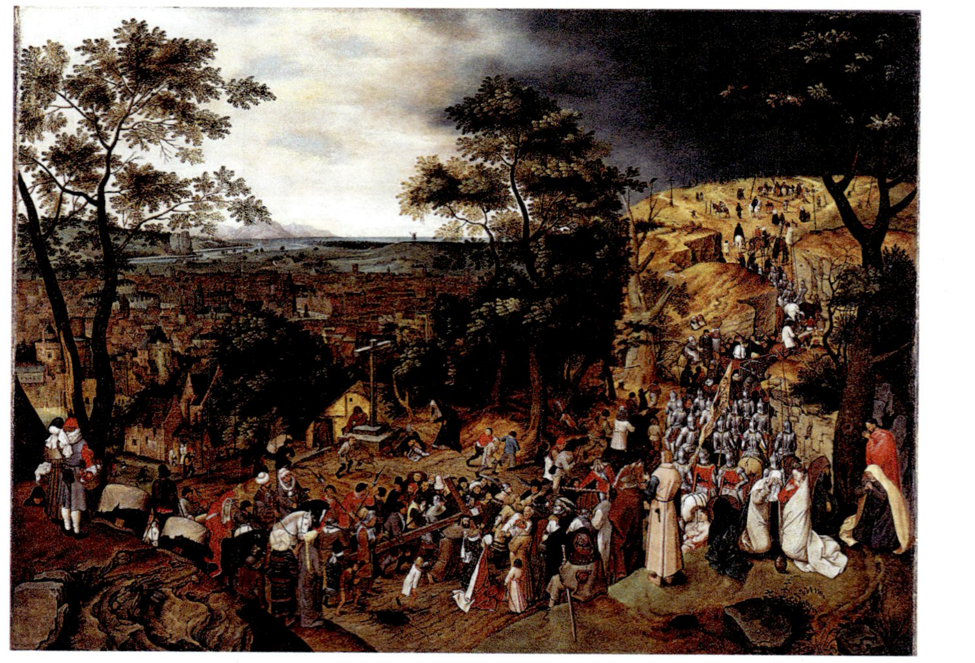

Plate 13 Pieter Brueghel the Younger (Flemish, 1564–1838), *Carrying of the Cross*, 1606. Gemäldegalerie der Staatlichen Museen zu Berlin, (Inv. Nr. 721).

Image credit: © Foto Gemäldegalerie der Staatlichen Museen zu Berlin – Preußischer Kulturbesitz. Photo: Jörg P. Anders

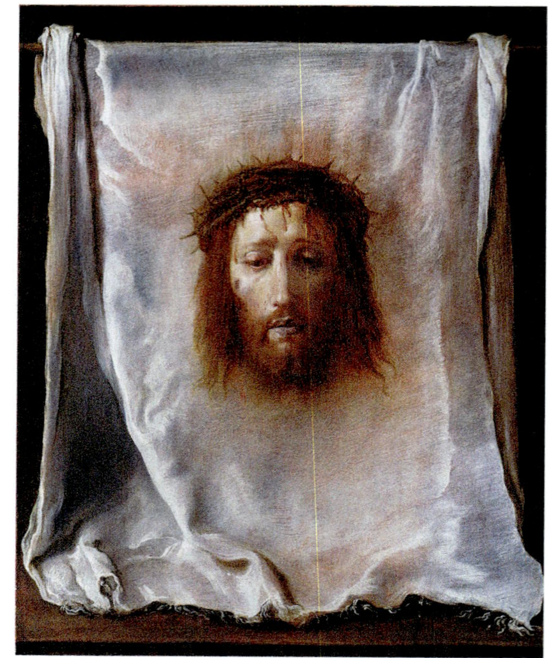

Plate 14 Domenico Fetti (Rome, c. 1589–1623), *The Veil of Veronica*, c. 1618–22. Oil on panel; 80.6 × 66.3 cm. National Gallery of Art, Washington. Samuel H. Kress Collection (1952.5.7).

Image credit: National Gallery of Art, Washington

4 Jerusalem Abroad and Theological Rationales

Jerusalem and Rome were (and are still) major pilgrimage destinations that are connected theologically and historically. Of course, not all pilgrims during the Early Modern period visited both cities, although many did or planned to do so. Pilgrims could receive indulgences in both places, and many guidebooks included maps and descriptions of both Christian destinations. Advertisements in prose or poetry that aimed to entice visitors to each city could be found in *libri indulgentiarum* (indulgence books), a type of guidebook popular in the late fourteenth and fifteenth centuries.[1] For example, the English poem, "Stacyons of Rome," c. 1400, enumerated the relics and associated indulgences in the main churches there.[2] Some indulgence books listed the number of years released from purgatory that could be garnered by visiting specific shrines. Often Rome was considered the safer option, but Jerusalem, as the locale of Christ's Passion and tomb, was regarded as the holier place. As observed by Miedema (1998), unlike visitors to Jerusalem, who were guided by Franciscans, pilgrims in Rome were at greater liberty for self-pacing.[3] Many relics were moved from Jerusalem to Rome,[4] where they went on display in the Seven Pilgrim Churches, with the *sudarium* of Veronica in Saint Peter's basilica among the most sought after and revered (as discussed in Chapter 2). Both sacred cities thus provided the ability to view relics. The major distinction between Jerusalem and Rome in regard to reenacting the Passion was sequence. Whereas the *Via Crucis* in Jerusalem offered a logical progression for visiting the sites (although the number of shrines was variable and the direction changed), in Rome visitors wishing to see Passion relics in the order of the biblical narrative would have to crisscross the city several times to view them in separate basilicas. However, personal preferences could be better accommodated in Rome, as pilgrims could direct themselves with maps and manuals, make their own selections, and afford more time at each place.[5]

In comparing pilgrims' experiences with Passion devotion in Rome and Jerusalem, it is worth noting a numerological correlation between the Seven Pilgrim Churches in Rome[6] and the 14 Stations of the Cross in Jerusalem, each a multiple of the prime number seven. Because visiting each of the major churches in Rome was comparable to stopping before each of the stations in Jerusalem, also with indulgences attached yet without a defined sequence, there may have been an attempt to connect spiritually rich experiences in both destinations with a familiar and related number of stops. In addition to a probable basis in the Seven Falls, as discussed in Chapter 3, seven held connotations as the number of the days of creation and days of the week, as measures of both divine and secular time. There were also seven gifts of the Holy Spirit, seven demons that Jesus cast out of Mary Magdalene, seven sacraments, seven hours of Divine Office, and seven principal chapels in Saint Peter's basilica. Furthermore, the number of virtues (three theological plus four cardinal virtues) and the number of deadly sins were both seven.

Kirkland-Ives (2009) describes several other somatic and kinetic devotional practices that paralleled the development of the Stations of the Cross, such as prayer sequences for the Seven Sorrows of the Virgin.[7] We can note that the last four Sorrows indicate significant overlap in theme with the Stations of the Cross:

1. The Prophecy of Simeon
2. The Flight into Egypt
3. Jesus Lost in the Temple
4. The Meeting of Mary and Jesus on the Way to Calvary
5. The Crucifixion
6. The Lancing of Jesus's side and the Descent from the Cross
7. The Burial by Joseph of Arimathea.

Likewise, there were other numbered devotions, such as the Five Wounds of Christ, which probably developed as mnemonic devices or ways to outline sermons for a largely illiterate populace. Such list-making was a tactic favored by the Franciscans. For example, their corded belt was (and still is) punctuated by three knots, which symbolize their three monastic vows (poverty, chastity, and obedience), with each knot comprising five coils that could help the friars recall the Five Wounds of Christ. In his *Treatise on the Holy Land*, Suriano used lists as a means of organizing his text, including his enumeration of areas in the interior of the Church of the Holy Sepulcher and numbered petitions at holy sites within the city. The Rosary, a prayer with Dominican origins, guides meditation on events in the lives of Christ and Mary with sets of beads. Essentially tactile counting devices, rosary beads function to guide supplicants in keeping track of the repetition of their prayers in three sets (Joyful, Sorrowful, and Glorious) of five Mysteries each. In summary, the Stations of the Cross were not an isolated development but rather one in a broad spectrum of numbered, sequenced meditative practices that the mendicant orders employed as methods of guiding prayer or outlining sermons with the aim of simplifying complex theological tenets inherent in biblical narratives.[8]

Installations of the Stations of the Cross in Europe were designed as participatory, active spaces. In Nuremberg, as one example among many in European cities, Adam Kraft (German, c. 1455/1460–1509) sculpted an abbreviated Stations of the Cross known as the *Seven Falls of Christ*, at the turn of the sixteenth century for a local patron, the knight Martin Ketzel, after his return from Jerusalem (Plate 5).[9] Nuremberg's identification with Jerusalem stemmed from a set of relics that was in the German city's possession, among which was the Holy Lance, alternatively identified as the spear with which Longinus had pierced Christ's side,[10] or as Saint Maurice's spear. Kraft's *Seven Falls of Christ* began near Nuremberg Castle and followed the road out of the city toward Saint John's cemetery. Series of relief sculptures, such this set in Nuremberg, although stationary, became infused with the movement of participants in procession. Therefore, fixed installations of the Stations of the Cross could transform an ordinary European street into a theater set evocative of Jerusalem, a setting fit for a city that safeguarded the Imperial Regalia (*Reichskleinodien*), which included relics from the Holy Land. The placement of Kraft's stops along a road that led out of the city toward a cemetery reinforced the purpose of the Stations as a self-guided, spiritual journey of repentance, often but not always at the end of life, a path that paralleled Christ's walk to the site of his death and the transferral of his body to its place of burial.

Wittkower (1978), Wharton (2006), and Terry-Fritsch (2014–2015) have explored the somaesthetic (relating to bodily perception) qualities of Italian *Sacri Monti* (Holy Mounts) as site-specific series of multi-media works of art that invite meditative practices, similar to those of the Stations of the Cross.[11] A salient example is the installation of Sacro Monte di Varallo in Lombardy, a participatory site designed in the 1480s by the Milanese Franciscan friar Bernardino Caimi, who had returned to Italy in 1478 after serving as custodian of the Church of the Holy Sepulcher in Jerusalem. At Varallo, life-sized figures constructed of polychrome wood or terra-cotta were dressed in real clothes, shoes, and hair to heighten a realistic effect. Franciscan friars led pilgrims along a set path, often at night with dramatic lighting, such that the sensorial experience was personalized.[12] Wittkower had proffered that Caimi's primary motive was to bring the Holy Land experience to Europe for safety reasons, as Turkish power in the area by the end of the fifteenth century had made pilgrimage dangerous.[13] The desire to visit sites in Jerusalem vicariously from the safety of city centers and rural areas in Europe was also likely a contributing factor to the development of the Stations of the Cross, especially during and after the Crusades.

About 1499–1500 at San Vivaldo near Florence, Franciscan friars erected a series of chapels to simulate a sequence of sacred sites in Jerusalem.[14] The purpose of these installations was not necessarily to replicate Jerusalem and Bethlehem precisely. Rather, the intent was to stage locales, even in hilly or mountainous terrain that was very different from Palestine's topography, where supplicants could vividly imagine themselves in the settings associated with events in Christ's life and experience spiritual ecstasy through physically challenging walks.

Subsequent reproductions of holy sites associated with the life of Christ and the Virgin were erected at *Sacri Monti* in Orta, Varese, Oropa, Crea, and Graglia.[15] Notably at Sacro Monte di Orta in the Piedmont, amidst the series of 20 chapels organized as stations that date c. 1580s–1770, sculpted figure groups depict scenes from the life of Saint Francis in juxtaposition to frescoes about the life of Christ.[16] As conceived by the Abbot Amico Canobio and constructed by the friar Cleto da Castelletto Ticino, the scenes begin with the birth of Saint Francis and the speaking crucifix at San Damiano, continue through Saint Francis before the Sultan, and conclude with his canonization.[17] This installation in particular underscores the Franciscan impulse to evangelize by leading pilgrims and passersby toward a physical and emotional closeness with both Christ and Francis through sequenced itineraries that employ works of art and architecture to promote pauses for spiritual reflection. The juxtaposition of these narrative scenes with natural surroundings, or the superimposition of religious scenes onto landscapes and cityscapes, are intentions also evident in the development of the Stations of the Cross. Ultimately, the *Sacri Monti* and the Stations of the Cross, despite different forms, share artistic and spiritual explorations of the mysteries of Christ's suffering and death. Moreover, these two modes of participatory devotion evidence a collective human desire to seek everlasting life by emulating the Passion, inherent in which was the promise of Resurrection.

Apart from the Passion, the apocryphal character of Veronica appears in tandem with key episodes in the life of Christ, especially the Incarnation and related scenes of the Visitation and Nativity; the Adoration of the Magi; the Last Supper; and the Resurrection; as well as the corresponding liturgical celebrations for each of these events. The legend of Veronica has served as a complement to these narratives by underscoring Christ's presence in them. In traditional Catholic liturgy, the veronica relic has been commemorated on the Second Sunday after Epiphany, a celebration that often included a reenactment of the Wedding at Cana. As Hamburger (1998) observed, the feast day of the relic of the Holy Face was originally connected with epiphanies.[18] As a symbol of the Incarnation, the veronica reminded worshipers of Christ's sustained spiritual presence even during his physical absence, a paradox at the core of Christian theology and liturgy.[19] As an example of the iconographic pairing of Veronica with the Incarnation in Early Modern works of art, we can see Veronica as a corollary figure to a Visitation in a French manuscript from the mid-fourteenth century (Figure 4.1). A second example, a Swiss fresco of the same era, depicts the Nativity of Christ adjacent to Veronica, who holds out her veil with the imprint of Christ's face behind the infant in the manger. Although fragmentary and in poor condition, this fresco at the Church of Saint-Étienne (constructed

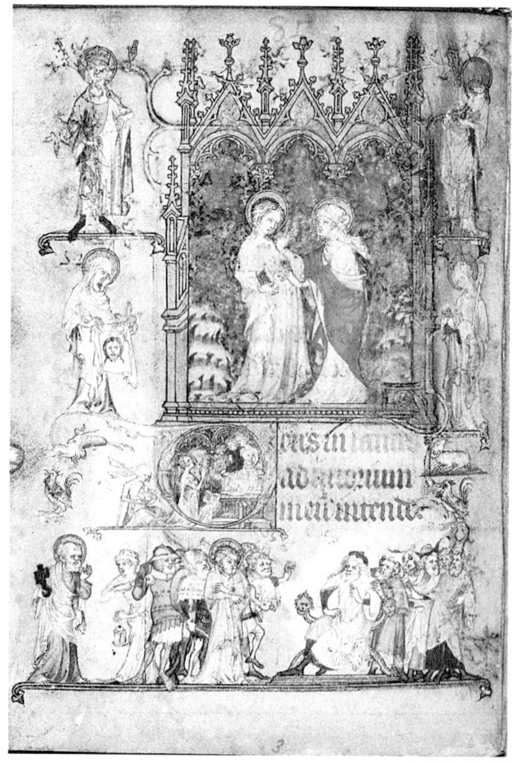

Figure 4.1 Flemish, *The Visitation; St. Veronica, St. Louis, St. Denis and another male saint* in the margins; *Christ before Pilate with the Betrayal of St. Peter*, in the lower margin (*Lauds*) from *The Hours of Yolande of Flanders*, MS 27, fol. 44v., 1353–1363. Bodleian Library, Oxford.

Image credit: Album/Alamy Stock Photo

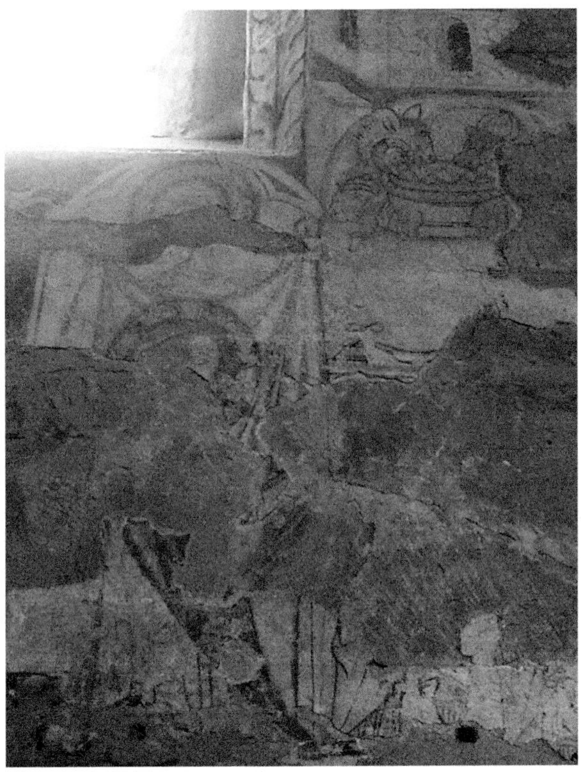

Figure 4.2 *Veronica* with a *Nativity*, fourteenth century. Fresco. Church Saint-Étienne, Moudon, Switzerland.

Image credit: Public Domain. Photo: Julien Chapuis

1281–1425) in Moudon, Switzerland testifies to a sacramental correlation between Veronica and the Incarnation, or Christ's physical inauguration into the world (Figure 4.2). As a third example of Veronica with her cloth pictured in conjunction with Epiphany, she is paired with an Adoration of the Magi in a Netherlandish manuscript, *Da Costa Hours*, datable c. 1515, in the Morgan Library in New York (Plate 8). Similarly, as a fourth example, a Holy Face is painted on the *predella* (the base of an altarpiece) directly under an Adoration of the Magi in the center panel of a German triptych, c. 1519, in the Staatliche Museen zu Berlin (Figure 4.3a–b).

In terms of the Last Supper and its ceremonial reenactment on Maundy Thursday and during the Eucharist, Christ's disembodied face on the veil of Veronica equated his body with the host.[20] As Hamburger (1998) has discussed at length and with insight, the veronica became an integral focal point of popular piety in part because the relic symbolized the Eucharistic bread. The coin-like shape of the Holy Face is reminiscent of the disc-shaped wafer.[21] In addition, because the floating head of Christ on Veronica's cloth could represent his entire body by synecdoche (an analogy in which a part represents the whole), the *Volto Santo* served as a metaphor for the full corporality of Christ.[22] Blair Moore (2017) has further suggested that the white cloth bearing the imprint of Christ's face in works of art about the

(a)

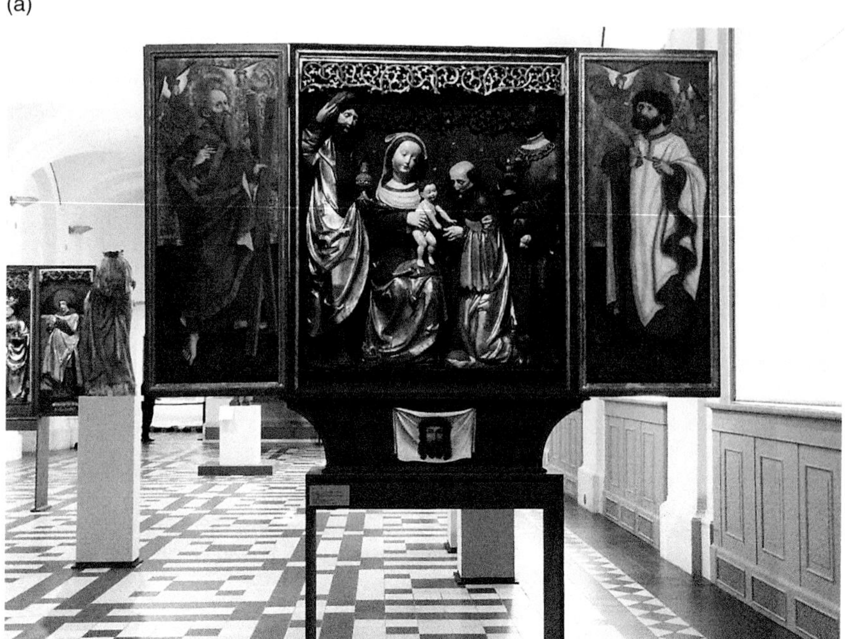

(b)

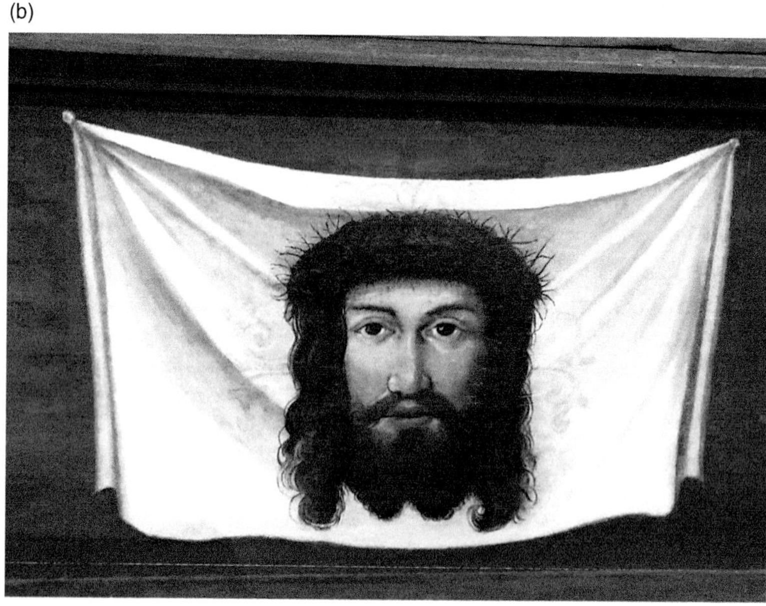

Figure 4.3a–b German (Munich?), *Winged altarpiece with Adoration of the Magi* (with detail of the veronica painted on the *predella*), c. 1519. Staatliche Museen zu Berlin, Skulpturensammlung und Museum für Byzantinische Kunst.

Image credit: Author

veronica is evocative of the color of the Eucharistic bread, as well as the hue of the sandy ground of Golgotha on which Christ's blood was shed, thereby sanctifying that soil.[23] As examples of the pairing of the veronica with the Eucharist in German art of the fifteenth and sixteenth centuries, the Holy Face on the veil of Veronica was often painted on the *predella*, as mentioned above (Figure 4.3a–b), or on the reverse of retables (Figure 4.4a–b).[24] The low placement on large altarpieces encouraged worshipers to lean over the painted veronica in order to read an inscription under the image.[25] Furthermore, the placement of the *sudarium* directly above or near pyxides or other liturgical containers for wafers on the altar aligned the Holy Face with the consecrated host. Another connection between Veronica and the celebration of the Eucharist can be noticed in the position of the figure's arms as she holds out her cloth with Christ's visage imprinted on it, as evident in Hans Memling's *Veronica* of 1470 in the National Gallery, Washington (Plate 7a). This gesture is reminiscent of the pose of a priest who elevates the host at the peak moment in the celebration of the Mass;[26] however, Veronica's arms are not lifted as high as a priest's arms would be raised. Although the theology of the Eucharist is fundamentally based on the corpse of Christ, the rite also hinges on the body's transcendence over death to everlasting life, a dichotomy about physicality and immortality that is also implied in Veronica imagery.

Transubstantiation, the Catholic doctrine according to which the bread and wine used during the celebration of the Eucharist change into the body and blood of Christ, was affirmed by Pope Innocent III in Canon 1 of the Fourth Council of the Lateran, which was called by a Papal Bull in 1213 and held in large assembly in 1215.[27] A related liturgical celebration is the Feast of Corpus Christi (Latin for Body of Christ), which was established in 1267 as the Thursday after Trinity Sunday (the Sunday after Pentecost). The purpose of the Feast of Corpus Christi was to reinforce the Eucharistic wafer and wine as the embodiment of the True Presence of Christ's body and blood, according to the tenets of Transubstantiation. This liturgical celebration was formalized roughly contemporaneously with revived interest in the veronica relic in Rome and may have played a role in fueling pilgrims' motivation to see it. Early Modern celebrations of the Feast of Corpus Christi included processions and religious pageantry, elements of which can also be found in celebratory practices associated with the veronica in Rome.

By metaphorical extension, if the Holy Face of Christ on the veronica relic is a symbol of the host, then Veronica who displays the image-bearing cloth can be likened to a monstrance (a liturgical object with an open or transparent receptacle for the exposition of the consecrated host for veneration). The character of Veronica presents the face of Christ to worshipers in the same way that the monstrance exhibits the wafer for adoration. On a symbolic level, the purposes of the monstrance in liturgy and Veronica imagery in art are the same: to hold and show the body of Christ for those who seek spiritual closeness with him. Notably, the monstrance was one of the principal attributes of the Franciscan saint, Clare of Assisi,[28] especially as depicted in late Renaissance and Baroque art.[29]

Chiefly, the character of Veronica and the attribute of her veil allude to Christ's Resurrection and his victory over death. In paintings such as those by the Master of Saint Veronica (Plate 1) and Memling (Plate 7a), the youthful but resilient Veronica demonstratively holds the image-bearing cloth outward like a banner (usually depicted parallel, or almost parallel, to the picture plane to maximize viewing); she

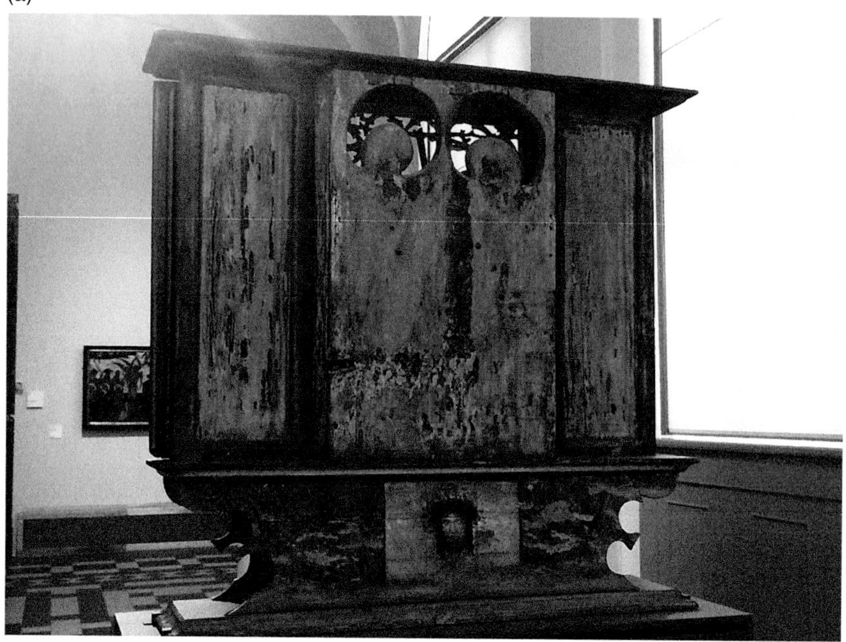

(b)

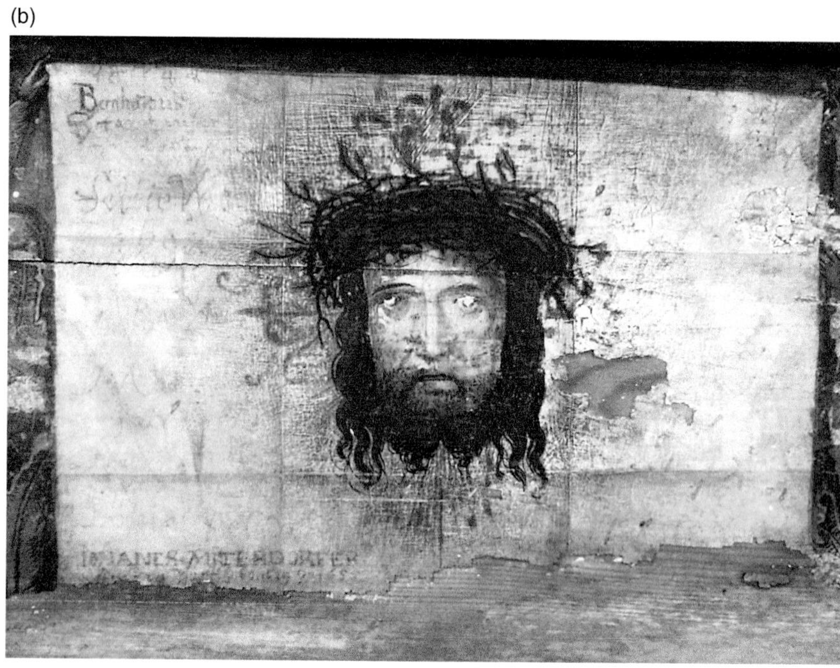

Figure 4.4 a–b German, Reverse of a retable (with detail of the veronica on the *predella*), fifteenth century. Staatliche Museen zu Berlin, Skulpturensammlung und Museum für Byzantinische Kunst.

Image credit: Author

symbolizes the *vera icon*. Veronica and her cloth transcend time and place by offering a glimpse of eternity. As Weddigen (2015) among other scholars have observed, the thinness of the cloth suggested that what is apparent now and what remains forthcoming are separated only by a thin membrane.[30] This metaphor is perhaps best exemplified by two paintings in which Veronica holds a translucent veil folded into 20 squares. The first example is by an anonymous Netherlandish artist of the fifteenth century (Figure 4.5). The second painting of Veronica is one of three works in the Städel Museum in Frankfurt known as the Flémalle Panels, created around 1430 in the Tournai workshop of Robert Campin, in which the young Rogier van der Weyden was employed (Figure 4.6).[31] Here the Veronica is rendered in middle-age, with a wrinkled face that is sorrowful or worried, an expression that serves as a foil to the youthful, solemn visage of Christ on the cloth. The discrepancy in their ages may allude to the inevitable passage of time for human existence and Christ's ability to transcend it, even after his death. Likewise, the implication is that earthly cares will be absolved by Christ's divinity and grace.

We can also consider Veronica's *sudarium* in light of sacramental connotations with fabric. Cloth, often worn as an added layer of protection for skin, alluded to

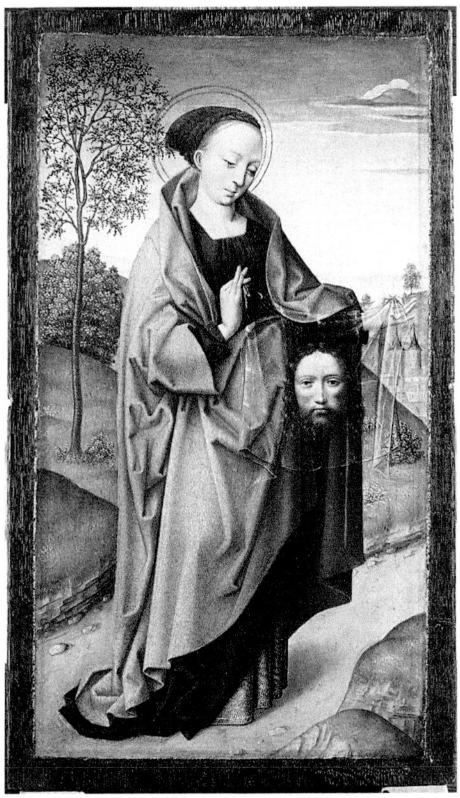

Figure 4.5 Flemish, *Saint Veronica with the Veil of Christ*, fifteenth century. Oil on wood; 30.5 x 17.5 cm. Musée de Brou, Bourg-en-Bresse, France.

Image credit: © RMN-Grand Palais/Art Resource, NY. Photo: Christian Jean

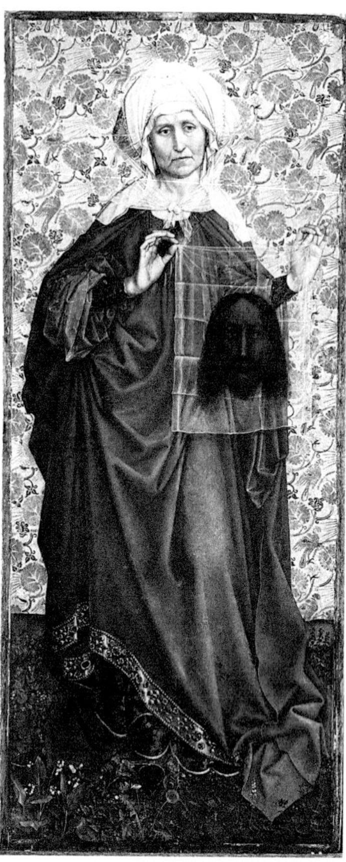

Figure 4.6 Master of Flémalle (Workshop of Robert Campin, Netherlandish, c. 1375–1444), *Veronica displaying the Sudarium*, 1430. Mixed technique on oak; 151.8 x 61 cm. Städel Museum, Frankfurt.

Image credit: © Weilheim, Artothek. Photo: Ursula Edelmann

the Incarnation, the theological concept of a deity in the flesh. Moreover, we can consider parallels of Veronica's cloth with fabric and garments associated with the lives of Mary and Christ. Weaving, historically an activity considered women's work, was associated with feminine devotion, prayer, and meditation.[32] The craft of weaving was tied to Mary in particular because as a child – according to the *Protoevangelium* (or Proto-Gospel) *of James*, a pseudoepigraphical text datable to the mid-second century – she was selected as a virgin from the House of David to spin the purple and scarlet threads to make a cloth, or curtain, for the temple.[33] A reference to the temple curtain can be found in Matthew 27:51 in his account of the Crucifixion, just after Jesus's last breath: "At that moment the curtain of the temple was torn in two, from top to bottom."[34] Thus, the story about Mary having woven this curtain in the *Protoevangelium* may have been a way to provide historical and sacramental context for this dramatic occurrence at the moment of Christ's death. Veronica's cloth is also reminiscent of fragments of the Virgin's tunic and maphorion (a garment covering the head and shoulders), contact relics held at Blachernae in Constantinople, which were believed to be curative and protective. A signature attribute for the *Madonna della Misericordia* (Mary of Mercy) – also a medieval visual pastiche adopted and disseminated by the Franciscans beginning in the early thirteenth century – is her ample mantle, which was a readily recognizable symbol for the concept of mercy.[35] In sum, Veronica's veil complemented and aligned her character with the role of Mary, who wove the temple curtain as a child and who later protected devotees with a mantle, her hallmark article of clothing. In some works of art, Veronica's clothes imitate Mary's garments in style and color. For example, returning to the Memling (Plate 7a), Veronica wears in a layered ensemble a blue cloak, a red tunic, and a white veil, a pattern and color scheme reminiscent of traditional depictions of Mary's clothing.[36]

Regarding parallels between Veronica's cloth and various other swathes of fabric associated with Christ (apart from the hem of his garment, which was touched by the woman with the hemorrhage, as discussed in Chapter 1), we can recall his swaddling clothes at the Nativity and his burial shroud at the Entombment. At both the advent and terminus of his earthly existence, Christ's body was wrapped in fabric, with each type of cloth symbolizing a turning point in his lifespan and a significant change in his nature. The apocryphal cloth of Veronica that miraculously bore Christ's features lent a sense of permanence beyond his incarnate life and implied that his divine presence surpassed the limits of a human lifespan. These three different cloth garments served as metaphors for periods of time: his swaddling clothes (the beginning, birth, Nativity, Incarnation); the burial shroud (the end, death, Entombment); and the *sudarium* (everlasting life, divine presence, Resurrection). Types of cloth, therefore, not only served as storytelling props within the narratives of Christ's life but moreover symbolized different states of being and concepts of time.

In German sculpture and painting, we can find parallels in both composition and intent between the ways in which angels hold up the Christ child in a cloth in a devotional still that appears extracted from a Nativity but without a narrative context (Figure 4.7) and angels who display the veronica cloth with the Holy Face (Plate 9 and Figure 4.8). The compositions are roughly symmetrical with Christ as focal point (as an infant or Holy Face), flanked by angels who present him to viewers. In the first example with the infant, the angels even tilt the child in the cloth outward, almost parallel to the picture plane, with the purpose of facilitating prayer toward him and showing his body fully to viewers. Although the connections between images of the infant Christ and the veronica held by angels are largely formal, the shared intent to display the physical and spiritual manifestation of Christ in the world is the more significant point of comparison.

The Holy Face as depicted on Veronica's cloth in Early Modern works of art can also be interpreted according to Christian numerology. The bisection of the frontal face, often emphasized by a central part in the hair and a straight nose, reflected the dual nature of Christ as human and divine. Likewise, the symmetry of the face could encapsulate the two states of human existence (alive and dead) and thus suspend time as Christ was simultaneously both. The tripartite beard and hair evoked the Trinity. The cruciform nimbus, as evident in a painting by the Master of The Legend of Saint Ursula, c. 1480–1500 (Figure 4.9), implied a division of the

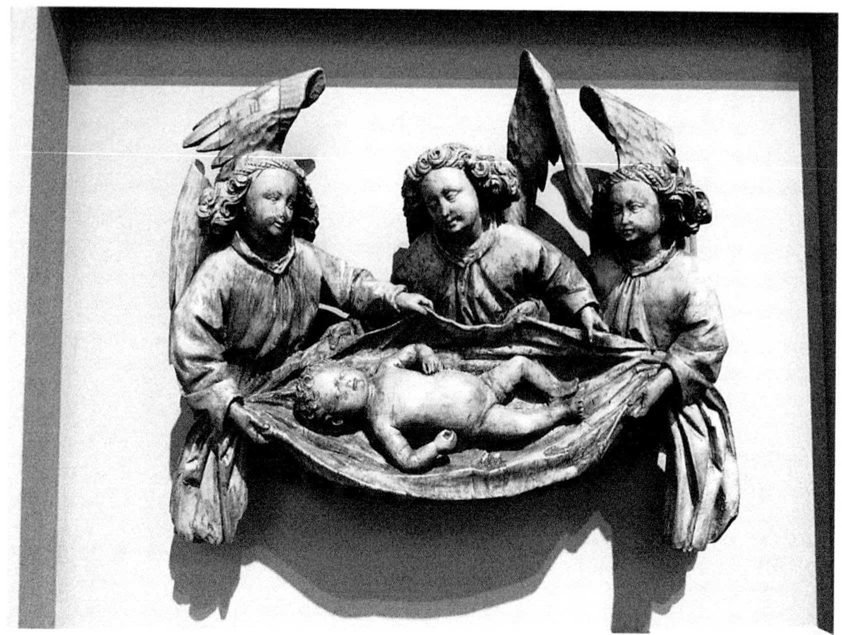

Figure 4.7 Circle of Hans Multscher (Ulm 1427–1466/67), *Three Angels with the Christ Child*, c. 1430–1440. Limewood. Staatliche Museen zu Berlin, Skulpturensammlung und Museum für Byzantinische Kunst.
Image credit: Author

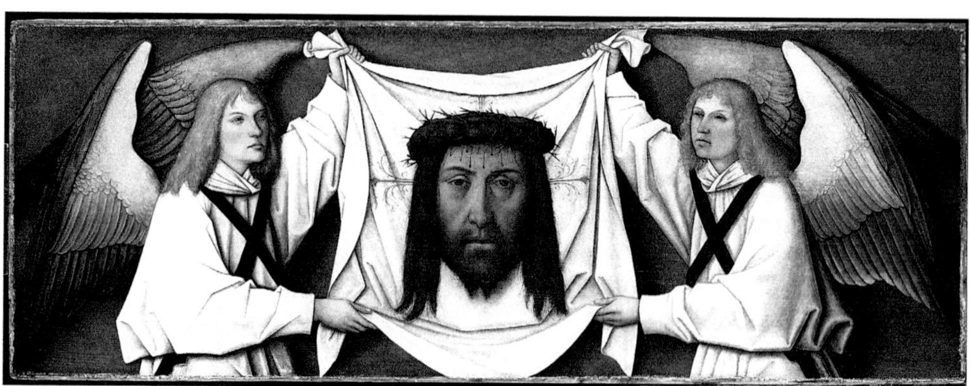

Figure 4.8 Bartholomäus Zeitblom (German 1455/60–1518/22), *Veronica's Veil Held by Two Angels*, 1496. Gemäldegalerie der Staatliche Museen zu Berlin (Inv. Nr. 606A).
Image credit: © Gemäldegalerie der Staatlichen Museen zu Berlin – Preußischer Kulturbesitz

circular head into quadrants, with four recalling the number of evangelists, the fourth day of creation (on which God completed the physical universe with the sun, moon, and stars), as well as the four seasons and four cardinal directions as references to earthly time and place. The general design of a circle divided into quadrants by a cross is also reminiscent of Early Modern spatial concepts of Jerusalem, which was envisioned as a city comprised of concentric circles intersected by a *cardo* and *decumanus*, the principal north-south and east-west thoroughfares. Christ's head with the cruciform nimbus superimposed on a square or rectangular cloth resembled in general form the design of Jerusalem on crusader maps produced during the Latin kingdom of Jerusalem.[37]

The numbers three and four, as factors of 12, were also thereby connected to the number of Tribes of Israel in the Hebrew Bible, the number of apostles in the New Testament, and the number of gates guarded by angels in Jerusalem as described in Revelation. The placement of an A and Ω (the *Alpha* and *Omega*, the capitalized first and last letters of the Greek alphabet) on either side of Christ's head, as evident in the illumination by Matthew Paris (Figure 1.3), reinforced a symmetrical composition not only formally but also conceptually into the beginning and end of time. Of course, time in this context did not solely

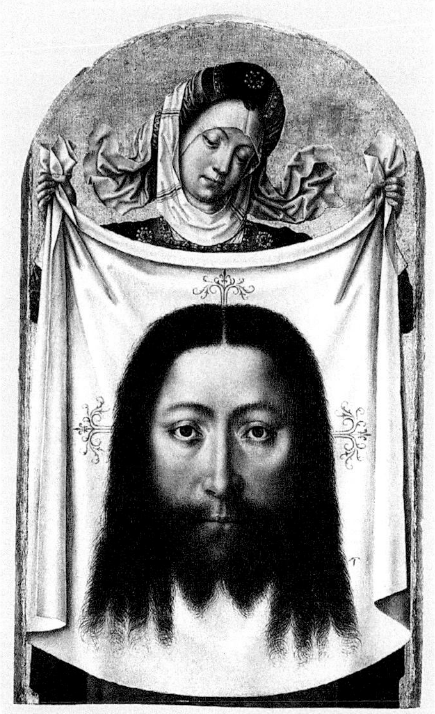

Figure 4.9 Master of The Legend of Saint Ursula (Flemish, 1436–c. 1504/05), *Saint Veronica with the Sudarium*, c. 1480–1500. Oil on oak panel; 31 x 25 cm. Private Collection.

Image credit: Public Domain. Photo: Web Gallery of Art

imply the boundaries of Christ's temporal lifespan but, moreover, his existence throughout time eternal.[38] The apocalyptic nature of veronica imagery in Early Modern art is thus not surprising considering that many Christians probably assumed that they would only see the face of Christ at the end of their own time, that is, at the moment of their judgment.

An important common thread among these various theological or sacramental considerations is that the Holy Face on the *sudarium* provided visual access to Christ as the most important intercessor between God and mankind. Veronica as holder of the image of Christ's face paralleled the role of most other saints from the twelfth century forward; that is, saints were widely regarded as interceding on behalf of the faithful during the vulnerable period between death and judgment.[39] A prevailing belief in the Early Modern period was that saints could sway God's verdict of Heaven, Purgatory, or Hell if they had been venerated during the supplicant's lifetime. Thus, Veronica as a character was widely revered as a saint who could offer intercession. Moreover, the Holy Face imprinted on the veil that she held up for viewers provided a point of mediation with Christ, the most accessible member of the Trinity.[40] The desire for absolution from sin, or at least a reduction of time in Purgatory, especially at the end of one's life, was a major impetus for the commissioning of works of art featuring Veronica holding the Holy Face. This iconography provided a focal point for contrition and, as one approached death, facilitated the reckoning with God by means of an encounter with Christ's visage. Likewise, the image could serve as a recipient of prayers as acts of penance.

The rich theological and sacramental overtones in works of art about Veronica are indicative of Early Modern viewers' reliance on images to supplement faith. Works of art played a crucial role in the Church's securing and maintaining authority over spiritual matters, as well as the implementation of evangelical ministries. As such, images were important visual companions to prayers, sermons, and devotional writings, which featured linguistic wordplay, including words with double meanings and acrostics (phrases or compositions in which the first letter of each line forms a word) used by ecclesiastical writers to underscore a divine plan and to increase the credibility of religious narratives. The Holy Face on Veronica's *sudarium* as a subject in art complemented scenes of events in Christ's life from the Incarnation to the Resurrection and reinforced the significance of accompanying liturgical celebrations.

Notes

1 J. R. Hulbert, "Some Medieval Advertisements of Rome," *Modern Philology* 20 (1923): 403–424, especially 404–405, http://jstor.org/stable/433697.

2 Nita Scudder Baugh, ed., *A Worcestershire Miscellany Compiled by John Northwood, c. 1400, edited from British Museum MS Add. 37.787* (Philadelphia, n. p.: 1956), 40–42. The "Stacyons of Rome" is Section VII.

3 Miedema, "Following in the Footsteps of Christ," 84–85.

4 Ibid. See also on saints' relics in Rome, Alan Thacker, "Rome of the Martyrs: Saints, Cults and Relics, Fourth to Seventh Centuries," in *Roma Felix – Formation and Reflection of Medieval Rome*, edited by Éamonn Ó Carragain and Carol L. Neuman de Vegvar (Burlington, VT: Ashgate Publishing Company, 2007), 13–50.

5 Miedema, "Following in the Footsteps of Christ," 84–85.

6 The original (since 1300 and before 2000) Seven Pilgrim Churches in Rome were the basilicas of Saint Peter (*San Pietro*), Saint Paul outside the Walls (*San Paolo fuori le*

Mura), Saint John Lateran (*San Giovanni in Laterano*), Saint Mary Major (*Santa Maria Maggiore*), Saint Lawrence outside the Walls (*San Lorenzo fuori le Mura*), Holy Cross in Jerusalem (*Santa Croce in Gerusalemme*), and Saint Sebastian outside the Walls (*San Sebastiano fuori le Mura*).

7 Kirkland-Ives, "Alternate Routes," 259.

8 Ibid., 264–265.

9 Stephen Brockmann, *Nuremberg: The Imaginary Capital* (Rochester, NY: Camden House, 2006), 25.

10 Ibid., 14, 296.

11 Rudolf Wittkower, "'Sacri Monti' in the Italian Alps," in *Idea and Image: Studies in the Italian Renaissance*, 175–183 (London: Thames and Hudson, 1978); Wharton, *Selling Jerusalem*, 97–101; Allie Terry-Fritsch, "Performing the Renaissance Body and Mind: Somaesthetic Style and Devotional Practice at the Sacro Monte di Varallo," *Open Arts Journal* 4 (Winter 2014–2015): 111–132.

12 Terry-Fritsch, "Performing the Renaissance Body and Mind."

13 Wittkower, "'Sacri Monti' in the Italian Alps."

14 Morris, *The Sepulchre of Christ*, 362; and Tsafra Siew, "Translations of the Jerusalem Pilgrimage Route at the Holy Mountains of Varallo and San Vivaldo," in *Between Jerusalem and Europe: Essays in Honour of Bianca Kühnel*, eds. Renana Bartal and Hanna Vorholt, 113–132 (Leiden: Brill Publishers, 2015).

15 Wittkower, "'Sacri Monti' in the Italian Alps," 180.

16 Ibid., 180–181.

17 For a complete set of photos and description, see Il Sacro Monte di Orta, accessed April 21, 2019, www.orta.net/sacromonte/index.html.

18 Hamburger, *The Visual and the Visionary*, 322–323.

19 Ibid., 323.

20 Zchomelidse, "Liminal Phenomena," 260; Wolf, "From Mandylion to Veronica," 168; and Hamburger, *The Visual and the Visionary*, 322–323.

21 Hamburger, *The Visual and the Visionary*, 322–323.

22 Ibid., 333–337.

23 Blair Moore, *The Architecture of the Christian Holy Land*, 114.

24 The gouged eyes are the result of later vandalism.

25 Louis Réau, *Iconographie de L'Art Chrétien*, vol. 3 (Paris: Presses Universitaires de France, 1959; Millwood, NY: Kraus Reprint, 1983), 1316.

26 Hamburger, *The Visual and the Visionary*, 336.

27 See Rev. John Evans, M. A., *The Statutes of the Fourth General Council of Lateran, recognized and established by subsequent councils and synods down to the Council of Trent* (London: L. and G. Seeley, 1843).

28 Holly Flora and Arianna Pecorini Cignoni, "Requirements of Devout Contemplation: Text and Image for the Poor Clares in Trecento Pisa," *Gesta* 45 (2006): 61–76, 72.

29 Nirit Debby Ben-Aryeh, *The Cult of St Clare of Assisi in Early Modern Italy* (Burlington, VT: Ashgate Publishing Company, 2014), 106–107.

30 Weddigen, "Weaving the face of Christ," 96.

31 The precise attribution of the works is a matter of scholarly debate. See the Städel Museum, Frankfurt, Digital Collection, accessed August 20, 2019, https://sammlung.staedelmuseum.de/en/work/the-flemalle-panels-st-veronica-with-the-veil.

32 Barbara Baert, "Weaving," in *Weaving, Veiling, and Dressing: Textiles and their metaphors in the Late Middle Ages*, eds. Kathryn M. Rudy and Barbara Baert, 39–40 (Turnhout, Belgium: Brepols Publishers, 2007).

33 Bart D. Ehrman, *Lost Scriptures: Books that Did Not Make It into the New Testament* (Oxford: Oxford University Press, 2003), 67.

34 Matthew 27:51. Coogan, et al., eds., *The New Oxford Annotated Bible*, 1788.

35 See Katherine T. Brown, *Mary of Mercy in Medieval and Renaissance Italian Art: Devotional Image and Civic Emblem* (New York: Routledge, 2017).

36 Hand, *Hans Memling's Saint John the Baptist and Saint Veronica*, n. p.

37 Blair Moore, *The Architecture of the Christian Holy Land*, 95.

38 The placement of the first and last letters of the Greek alphabet on either side of Christ's face may also have suggested that Matthew Paris, who would have had no knowledge of what the relic looked like, may have modelled his image of the veronica on apocalyptic imagery of Christ. Suzanne Lewis, *The Art of Matthew Paris in the Chronica Majora* (Berkeley and Los Angeles: University of California Press, 1987), 129.

39 Miedema, "Following in the Footsteps of Christ," 73.

40 Ibid., 74.

5 Viewing Veronica through the Lens of Gender

A traditional definition of gender represents an expansion of the word's original meaning, which referred to grammatical forms of nouns and pronouns associated (often arbitrarily) with concepts of male, female, or neuter. Contemporary usage of the word *gender* encompasses a spectrum of social identities in fluid range from masculine to feminine, which can be constructed by individuals in relationship to societal expectations, based on biological sex or an individual's sense of self. As Lindquist (2017) has presented, because the makers of many Early Modern works of art remain anonymous, and production was often collaborative, the purpose of employing gender as a methodological tool is not to uncover or redefine the identity of any particular artist or group. Rather, examining artistic production through the lens of gender can add layers of meaning and aid our understanding of how art reflects societal roles determined by sex (biological or perceived) during specific historical periods. The dominant cultural thrust of Christianity, under whose auspices much medieval and Renaissance art was commissioned and viewed, outlined specific roles for men and women, which determined their levels of permissible involvement in (or exclusion from) liturgical and lay activities. Reviewing the iconography, patronage, and viewership of Early Modern works of art through the lens of gender can be an insightful means of reaching a fuller understanding of their cultural, historical, and spiritual resonance.[1]

Veronica, as a female character synonymous with the relic of the Holy Face, is a complex hagiographical subject, which can be nuanced by consideration from a gendered perspective. As a point of distinction, this approach is not necessarily feminist, an adjective describing movements that have advocated for women's rights to be equal to those of men. Although some Early Modern works of art have been used to further feminist aims, especially during the nineteenth and twentieth centuries, it would be difficult to pinpoint medieval works of art that were made with a demonstrative feminist intent.[2] The goal of this chapter, thus, is to employ a gendered methodology in looking at historical images of Veronica in order to broaden our perception of them rather than to use them anachronistically to further any specific agenda.

We can begin by recalling that one of the chief points of distinction between the Byzantine version of the Holy Face legend and its Western counterpart was a female as linchpin character.[3] Whereas in the Eastern version, the connection between King Abgar and the healing image of Christ was a male emissary painter, in the West, the critical link was an empathetic woman with a cloth. The apocryphal character of Veronica, with her holy cloth as an extension of her identity, symbolized the grace necessary to bridge disease to a cure, or as an expansion of that metaphor, from sin to salvation. That the Western version of the legend of the "true image" relic hinged on a female character was probably a contributing factor in the story's eventual merging with the Gospel account of the unnamed woman with a hemorrhage.

None of the synoptic Gospel writers specified the cause or nature of the woman's blood flow. But if her blood were menstrual, then she would have been considered ritually unclean and therefore would have made Jesus impure by touching him.[4] The association of a woman's menses with contamination stems from the Hebrew Bible, specifically a passage in Leviticus 15:19–24:

> When a woman has a discharge of blood that is her regular discharge from her body, she shall be in her impurity for seven days, and whoever touches her shall be unclean until the evening. Everything upon which she lies during her impurity shall be unclean; everything also upon which she sits shall be unclean. Whoever touches her bed shall wash his clothes, and bathe in water, and be unclean until the evening. Whoever touches anything upon which she sits shall wash his clothes, and bathe in water, and be unclean until the evening; whether it is the bed or anything upon which she sits, when he touches it he shall be unclean until the evening. If any man lies with her, and her impurity falls on him, he shall be unclean seven days; and every bed on which he lies shall be unclean.[5]

Furthermore, if the blood flow were longer than the regular monthly period (as was the case for the woman with the hemorrhage, who bled for twelve years), Leviticus 15:25 continues:

> If a woman has a discharge of blood for many days, not at the time of her impurity, or if she has a discharge beyond the time of her impurity, all the days of the discharge she shall continue in uncleanness; as in the days of her impurity, she shall be unclean.[6]

Thus, in the accounts of the synoptic Gospels, the woman's touching of the hem of Jesus's clothes (a physical encounter with the divine) removed not only the woman's longsuffering but also likely the cultural taint associated with her having a gynecological problem.[7] The Gospel accounts of the *Haemorrhoissa* and the apocryphal legend of Veronica were then thematically connected not only by a female protagonist but also by the leitmotif of blood, because the miraculous visage on Veronica's *sudarium* was imprinted by Christ's blood and sweat.

Regarding the Franciscans' role in adapting and promulgating the Veronica story, we must ask why the friars chose to insert a woman into the Stations of the Cross series, especially giving her conciliatory gesture toward Christ a distinct *locus* as the Sixth Station. If the fluxing woman mentioned by Matthew, Mark, and Luke were Veronica, or if she were widely believed to be the same character, then her role as an addendum to the Stations could be a clever inversion of and analogy to the storyline in the Gospels. In the same way that Christ's garment healed the woman's suffering (as symbolized by her excessive blood), so too Veronica's *sudarium* became the holy cloth that absorbed Christ's pain (as symbolized by his blood and sweat). Therefore, in the Gospel accounts and subsequent apocryphal texts, a holy cloth had the potency to cure those who touched it, and blood served as a readily recognizable symbol for human suffering, especially as it related to women. The Franciscans may have aimed to capitalize on the immediacy of these resonant idioms by selecting a female character whose condition and actions were comparable to Christ's hardship in a novel, singular station.

In the Stations of the Cross, we can notice two opposing uses of cloth: its application for salve and its removal for shame. Specifically, Veronica's use of a cloth for purposes of aid in the Sixth Station contrasts with the violence of the Romans who stripped Christ of his garments and cast lots for his clothes in the Tenth Station. Whereas the soldiers ripped cloth to humiliate and harm him, Veronica had offered Christ the *sudarium* as a humble token of comfort. With the use of a cloth as conspicuous and consistent prop, the choice of Veronica as an independent station with a female protagonist may have served in part as a foil to the torturous actions of the Roman mob.

Moreover, Veronica's charitable act underscored the roles of the other females present during the Passion. Veronica can be aligned with the crowd of women of Jerusalem, the Virgin Mary, and Mary Magdalene.[8] The latter two characters often appear together in stational scenes of the Crucifixion (Twelfth), Deposition (Thirteenth), and Entombment (Fourteenth). Figure 5.1 provides a complete set of Limoges enamels in which to view the role of women comparatively, with Veronica as the Sixth Station at far left of the middle register. All of these women grieve and offer comfort to Christ during his final walk, albeit in different ways: his mother greets him while he is carrying the cross; the women of Jerusalem weep for him; and Mary Magdalene washes his feet with her tears as she mourns. The Gospel writers' accounts of women present at the Crucifixion provide a broad context for the presence of women in the Stations of the Cross, as described, for example, in Matthew 27:55–56:

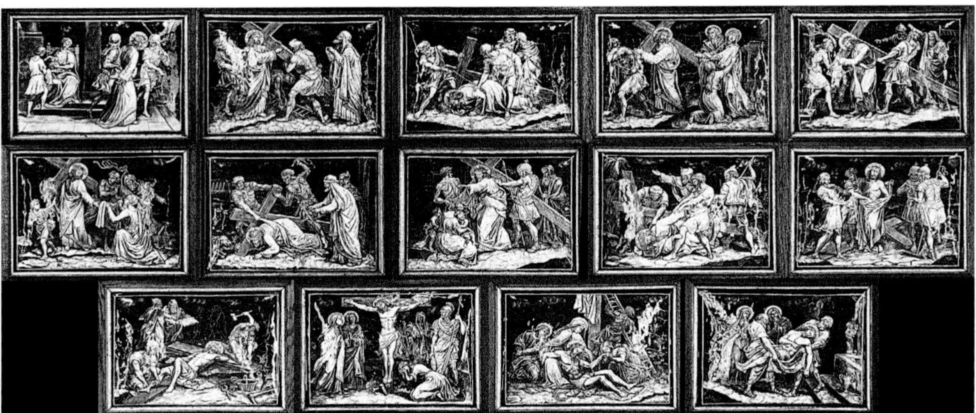

Figure 5.1 French, *Fourteen Stations of the Cross*, sixteenth century. Limoges enamel. From the Church of Nôtre-Dame-des-Champs d'Avranches, Manche, Normandy, France.

Image credit: Public Domain. WikiMedia Commons. Photo: Tango 7174. Licensed under Creative Commons Attribution-Share Alike 4.0 International, 3.0 Unported, 2.5 Generic, 2.0 Generic, and 1.0 Generic

> Many women were also there, looking on from a distance; they had followed Jesus from Galilee and had provided for him. Among them were Mary Magdalene, and Mary the mother of James and Joseph, and the mother of the sons of Zebedee.[9]

Thus, the presence of an apocryphal Veronica during the events leading up to the Crucifixion could be more credible if she were considered to be one among a large assembly of women. Moreover, the compassion underlying her gesture, however minor and anecdotal, functioned in part to reiterate the roles of other women who are described as both named characters and generally as part of a crowd in the Gospel accounts of the Passion.

In addition, we can consider the Franciscan selection of Veronica *vis-à-vis* their developing views of women's roles in the Church and auxiliary lay activities. The Franciscans in part may have been looking back to the early Church and consciously seeking to emulate and revive it. Their choice to highlight a first-century woman reflects a deliberate act of propelling early Christian characters into the forefront of fourteenth-century liturgy, Church governance, and spirituality. Important for this discussion is the thesis of Schüssler Fiorenza (1983), who re-examined the history of Christianity, in terms of both New Testament writings and ecclesiastical structure, from a critical feminist perspective. In her polemic against androcentric texts and church patriarchy since the first century, Schüssler Fiorenza reconstructs and recognizes the roles of women in establishing an apostolic past. Although she does not address the Franciscans directly, her approach to hermeneutics (the study of interpreting literary texts such as the Bible) and especially her redress of the roles of several unidentified women in the Gospels (such as the woman who anoints Christ) are important when considering the Franciscans' recognition of women's largely anonymous contributions in Christ's lifetime, as well as to their own spiritual lives during the gradual redefinition of monastic and lay roles in the fourteenth century.[10]

A second key female character who may have been another viable choice as the subject of an independent station was Helena of Constantinople. In fact, the place where Helena allegedly had discovered and identified the True Cross had been one of the principal sites located outdoors near the Church of the Holy Sepulcher, where pilgrims could obtain an indulgence.[11] The location must have been frequently featured on the Franciscans' tours, because many pilgrims describe the stop in their journals. For example, in 1288, the Dominican Ricoldo of Monte Croce mentioned the site associated with Helena in his enumeration of outdoor places:

> Going up by the way along which Christ went up carrying his cross, we found the place where he said: "Daughters of Jerusalem, do not weep for me." There they show the place of the swoon of our Lady, when she was following her son as he carried the cross. And there, next to the street they show a commemorative house. There they show the place where Christ stood with his cross and wearily rested for a spell. Then there is a cross-street which comes into the city and where they met Simon of Cyrene coming from his country house, that he might bear the cross of Christ. Next to it is a place which once belonged to the Friars Minor. Going indirectly up by the street where Christ went up, we found the place where, they say, Helena identified and singled out the cross of Christ from those of the thieves by its raising someone from the dead. Then going forward we entered the church or the place of the tomb.[12]

The pilgrim's repeated use of the phrase "they show" probably refers to the Franciscan guides. Although the author does not mention Veronica by name, he describes a "commemorative house" where Christ stood with his cross and rested for a while that was located near an intersection (cross street) and in proximity to the house of the Friars Minor. This description may have indicated an outdoor pause at the alleged House of Veronica, although the author does not clearly identify the stop as such. However, the *locus* associated with Helena, whom the author does name specifically, was placed just before the entrance to the church of the Holy Sepulcher. Perhaps there had been a quandary over the arc of development of the *Via Crucis* regarding which of these two female characters – Veronica or Helena – would be highlighted in the final group of stations. Helena's high social status as an Empress of the Roman Empire, her reverence as a saint in both Orthodox and Roman Catholic traditions, her bravery in making the journey from Rome to Jerusalem, and her quest for truth were all characteristics that may have made her a favorable option as a prominent woman to feature. However, the later dates of her life (c. 246/248–c. 330) removed her from the scene of the Crucifixion by almost three centuries. If the Franciscans were choosing between Helena and Veronica, the latter, although not a documented historical character like the former, was still closer to Christ as a first-century woman who personally witnessed his suffering. She had seen and even touched him. Moreover, Veronica's actions reflected compassion toward others, a consistent theme in Jesus's preaching. Veronica's deed mirrored those of Christ himself, and she embodied the core message of his public ministry.

Another contributing factor to the selection of Veronica as a woman to include in the Stations of the Cross may have been a desire to balance spiritual experiences as differentiated by gender during the Early Modern period. Coakley (2006) has explored the relationship between the informal power of holy women and the official power of ecclesiastical men.[13] In examining the gender dynamics of these two realms of religious life, Coakley describes characteristics of female sanctity during the Early Modern period. Although sometimes regarded with suspicion, holy women were considered visionaries known for their penitence and closeness to Christ. They were largely viewed as prophetesses who received revelations, experienced ecstasies, and claimed their own authority to be heard.[14] Women's spiritual authority was often regarded as coming directly from God rather than through clerical office. Ultimately, the tenuous overlap of women's and men's respective spheres of religious life yielded a balance of authority within the Church's organizational structure, which encompassed the duality of unofficial/official, spiritual/clerical, and ecstatic/ecclesiastical experiences, respectively.[15] It is plausible that an interest in depicting a balance of religious life as experienced differently by the genders played a role in Veronica's eventual placement among the Stations of the Cross.

Furthermore, Veronica can be viewed in relationship to the foundation of the Order of Saint Clare (Poor Clares) in 1212 by its first abbess, Clare of Assisi (1194–1253) and Francis of Assisi.[16] Both the Order of Friars Minor (First Order of Saint Francis) and the Poor Clares (the Second Order) were known for their Marian devotions, with the Virgin a frequent, prominent subject in works of art that they commissioned.[17] Their collective interest in the iconography of Veronica may be related to, or stem from, their devotion to Mary. The Franciscans also may have highlighted Veronica in the Stations with the aim of her character serving as a pious model for this Second Franciscan order, which comprised women. Atkinson (2001) has written about women who, in renouncing roles as wives and mothers, looked to both historical female saints and contemporary religious women as spiritual models during the Early Modern era, both within and outside the context of convents. Atkinson describes the English pilgrim Margery Kempe's reverence for Birgitta of Sweden and Julian of Norwich, among other religious women, as pious role models for her spiritual life.[18] Although not a Poor Clare, Kempe's documented reverence for historical, pious women demonstrates that women with spiritually rich lives often looked to earlier female saints for inspiration and affirmation. Evidence for a Clarissan affinity for Veronica can be found in an early facsimile of the veronica, an icon in the Matilda Chapel at the Vatican (Figure 2.5). This copy was kept by nuns of the Order of Saint Clare in the convent of San Silvestro in Capite,[19] thereby demonstrating the order's virtual ownership of and devotion to the veronica in Rome. Passion imagery had been popular among both Franciscan friars and the Poor Clares.[20] In the fifteenth century, a Poor Clare named Eustochia constructed a set of Stations in her convent at Messina.[21] Such images and events indicate a devotion to the veronica and an affinity for the Stations of the Cross by followers of Saint Clare.

In a similar vein, we can consider the life of Saint Margaret of Cortona (b. 1247 Laviano–d. 1297 Cortona; canonized 1728), who was a member of the Third Order of the Franciscans.[22] Margaret was among the first female followers of Saint Francis to view her own *comune* (township) as a New Jerusalem during the thirteenth century. Within that theological framework or mindset, she was among the first female Franciscans to commemorate the Passion of Christ on Fridays. Margaret's life and actions are important because Cortona was also the home of Fra Elia (Assisi 1178–Cortona 1253), one of the closest and most significant followers of Francis. According to Margaret's confessor and biographer, the Franciscan Fra Giunta Bevegnati (c. 1240–c. 1312),[23] Margaret's inner life was notable for her penitence and intense devotion for Christ, and her external works were memorable for her charitable acts toward the poor and sick.[24] As noted by Morris (2005) and Renna (2012), Margaret considered her adopted Tuscan town of Cortona (she arrived in the city c. 1272) a New Jerusalem and lived near the church of San Francesco, where she protected the hilltop town.[25] In his *Legenda Margaritae*, Bevegnati recounts: "Although Margaret daily re-created in her mind the Passion of Christ, she commemorated Fridays in a special way. (She used to say that Christians should not be joyful on Fridays)."[26] Although it is not clear that Margaret or Fra Elia ever constructed or designated places as a Stations of the Cross, the combination of Margaret's view of Cortona as a New Jerusalem, her demonstrative devotion to Christ's Passion, and her focus on commemorating Fridays are notable developments in Franciscan practice in rural, central Italy during the thirteenth century. Bevegnati's purpose in writing her biography may have been to pose Margaret as an exemplar of the Third Order, in the way that Francis was to the First and Clare was to the Second. If Bevegnati's aim in part was to have Margaret's life serve as a model for Franciscan women who could not join convents, his recording of her practices may have been didactic with the goal of encouraging others to follow her pious example.[27]

To understand spiritual foundations within women's religious communities for the eventual merging of the Veronica legend with the Passion cycle, we can examine the

Meditationes vitae Christi (Meditations on the Life of Christ). As mentioned in Chapter 3 and as is well known, the *Meditationes vitae Christi* were composed in Tuscany in the mid-fourteenth century, c.1336–1364,[28] for a Poor Clare as a prayer guide.[29] Its authorship, attributed first to Bonaventure and then to a Pseudo-Bonaventure, remains uncertain. This text is important to the study of Veronica imagery from a gendered perspective[30] because its emphasis on affective forms of piety shaped religious iconography during the late Middle Ages. It exists in two versions, one short in Italian and one long in Latin, with the latter including an extensive section on the active and contemplative lives. The purpose of the text seems to have been to instruct novitiates on the foundational vows of a Franciscan life (obedience, poverty, and chastity) and to generate compassion among its readers toward events in the lives of Christ and the Virgin. The manuscript is known for its presentation of the narratives from a uniquely female perspective.[31]

In a new monograph on the *Meditationes*, McNamer (2018)[32] argues that the short Italian version is the original text. Moreover, and germane to this discussion, McNamer asserts that the text was originally composed by a Poor Clare nun living in Pisa, whose authorship was overshadowed by a Franciscan friar who later augmented and expanded the manuscript. Although the legend of Veronica is not included in the Passion story as recounted in the *Meditationes*, the emergence of this text within the milieu of women living in religious communities may have contributed to an increased devotion to the Passion by means of an emphasis on affective piety. In many ways, this fourteenth-century manuscript laid the social and spiritual foundation for the eventual merging of the Veronica legend with the Passion cycle, and thereby eventually into the Stations of the Cross.

As Hamburger (1998) has presented, women living in religious communities were among the initial viewers, owners, and patrons of copies of images of Veronica.[33] Julian of Norwich (English, c. 1346–after 1416), among other female mystics and writers,[34] pinned theological discussions about images and specifically Christ's face on the veronica, thereby offering a glimpse into the development of the relic's cult.[35] The nuns' collective interest in the character of Veronica, however, did not seem to stem solely from identification with her as a woman. Instead, they held her in high esteem because she had been an eyewitness to the Passion.[36] The character of Veronica embodied an innate, human desire to come *facie ad faciem* with the divine, a spiritual quest with which many nuns identified.

Religious women living in communities also collected mass-produced, miniature (small enough to fit in one's hand) reproductions of the *sudarium*, which bore the frontal face of Christ with the tripartite hair and beard shapes at the lower edge. Many of these emblems were produced in sheets (eight or ten to a sheet) that were not separated individually, perhaps implying that duplication increased the image's potency[37] or indicating an intent to distribute them among many worshipers. Souvenirs often obtained in Rome (although not necessarily produced in Rome), pilgrims' badges were commonly made of leather, parchment, or metal (Figure 1.4).[38] The commemorative tokens could be used in private devotion, as evidenced by the fact that some veronicas were rubbed with fingers and/or kissed, or they could be given as gifts. Frequently, the badges were inserted, stitched with needle and thread,[39] or glued into missals or psalters. Furthermore, veronicas were sometimes painted illusionistically as marginalia in manuscript illuminations in imitation of inserting actual badges in psalters or Books of Hours.[40] As an example, a folio in the French *Horae Secundum Usum Romanum* (MS 77, fol. 30r), datable to the fifteenth century and in the Musée Condé, Chantilly, features pilgrims' badges painted in the margins with a possible veronica in the upper right corner (Figure 5.2).

In the absence of priests in many women's religious communities, miniature copies of the veronica could serve as stand-ins for the Eucharist.[41] Some women also painted images of the Holy Face, as exemplified in two illuminations from *Des cleres et nobles femmes*, the French translation of Giovanni Bocaccio's *De Mulieribus Claris* (Latin for "About Famous Women"), datable to 1361/1362. One illumination comes from a manuscript commissioned by Duke Philip the Bold of Burgundy in 1402, and the second manuscript was made for Duke Jean de Berry in 1403. Both images focus on a woman called Irene, who paints images of the Holy Face. Without the use of sketches or models in her studio, Irene paints the face of Christ directly onto a panel seemingly from memory or spontaneous inspiration, a method that both suggests the visionary nature of her work and alludes to the sacred nature of her subject.[42]

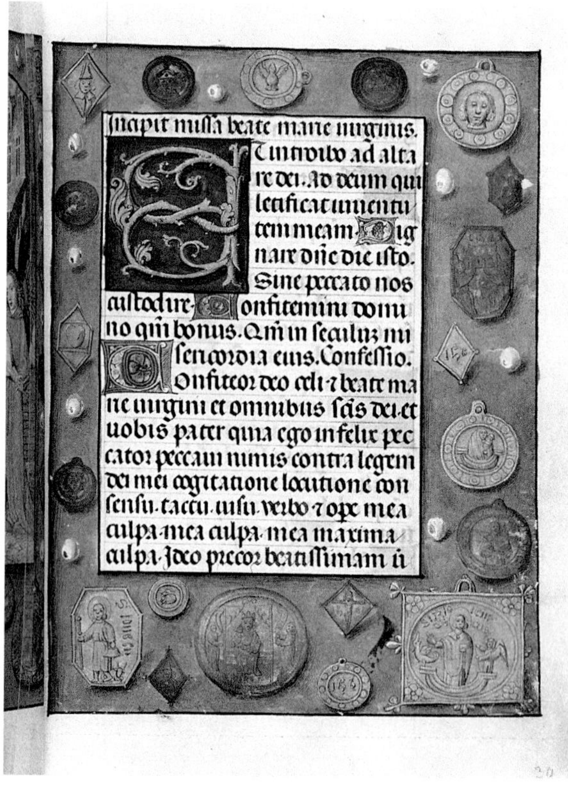
Incipit missa beate marie uirginis.
t introibo ad alta
re dei. Ad deum qui
letificat iuuentu
tem meam. Dig
nare dñe die isto.
Sine peccato nos
custodire. onfitemini domi
no qm̃ bonus. Qm̃ in seculum mi
sericordia eius. Confessio.
onfiteor deo celi 7 beate ma
rie uirgini et omnibus sc̃is dei et
uobis pater quia ego infelix pec
cator peccaui nimis contra legem
dei mei cogitatione locutione con
sensu. tactu. uisu. uerbo 7 ope mea
culpa. mea culpa. mea maxima
culpa. Ideo precor beatissimam u

Figure 5.2 Folio with historiated initial and painted pilgrims' badges as marginalia. *Horae Secundum Usum Romanum*. MS 77, fol. 30r. Fifteenth century. Parchment, 18 x 12.5 cm. Musée Condé, Chantilly, France.

Image credit: © RMN-Grand Palais/Art Resource, NY. Photo: René-Gabriel Ojéda

Regarding female interest in journeys to the Holy Land, Saint Jerome (Dalmatia, c. 347–419/420), who was writing in the late fourth and early fifth centuries, mentioned that many noble, married women had made a pilgrimage to Jerusalem, even naming them as Melania, Marcella, and Eustochia. He described the pilgrimage itinerary of Saint Paula as well.[43] We can also recall the noteworthy travel journals of Egeria in the fourth century and Margery Kempe at the turn of the fifteenth century as two examples among many female pilgrims to the Holy Land. However, alternative forms of Passion devotion developed in convents as a means of virtual pilgrimage because nuns were seldom allowed to travel to Rome or Jerusalem, despite intense desires to visit relics and holy sites.[44] Series of prints, book illustrations, or other reproductions of the Stations in Jerusalem or churches in Rome with maps and descriptions provided women opportunities to pray and meditate on events and objects associated with the Passion, including the veronica. They could even continue to receive the requisite indulgences from within the walls of their convents.[45] Such vicarious journeys, or spiritual pilgrimages, were often created for and by females whose social and religious circumstances prevented actual travel. Works of art depicting scenes from the Passion that were accompanied by prayers may have served as visual aids for nuns. The images could have inspired reconciliation with God and provided an opportunity for religious women to implore intercession, especially in preparation for their own deaths.[46]

Clark (2007) has explored the appeal of Veronica imagery to lay women, especially in regard to the correlation of venerating Veronica with women's education in manners and comportment.[47] The attraction to Veronica as a subject in art by women viewers (both lay and religious) can be considered in relationship to a few other iconographic themes that depicted female lead characters and engaged the senses with the aim of curbing doubt. As a key example, a triptych in the Seminario Patriarcale in Venice (Plate 10), datable from the end of the fifteenth to the beginning of the sixteenth centuries, features a Northern-European image of Veronica's cloth held by two angels in the center panel, flanked by outer wings painted by Filippino Lippi (Florence, 1457–1504): *Christ with the Samaritan Woman* on the left and the *Noli Me Tangere* on the right. The scenes on the wings reinforce Christ's role as Messiah through interactions with women, with a similar tension drawn between the genders and plots comparable to the Veronica legend. The Samaritan woman and Mary Magdalene touch and see Christ, offering testimony to his historical being, even as he reveals his mystical nature to them. However, only Veronica's cloth bearing the Holy Face (a product first of touch, then sight) held enduring, tangible proof of his dual nature as human and divine. The veronica's central placement in the triptych likely served to assuage any hesitancy on the part of the beholders to believe.

Mary Magdalene's role in the *Noli Me Tangere* (John 20:1–18),[48] in which she appears as the first eyewitness of Christ after the Resurrection, aligns her with the apocryphal character of Veronica because both female characters testify to Christ's identity and state of being by using the senses of touch and vision as proof. After attempting but not succeeding in touching Christ, Mary Magdalene spoke to the apostles and offered visual testimony: "I have seen the Lord."[49] As evident in the *Noli Me Tangere* story, sight was often given a preferential status over touch in comparisons among the senses and therefore in the *paragone* of painting versus sculpture.[50] Frank (2000) expounded on the primacy of sight and the secondary role of touch as senses employed by pilgrims, including groups of female ascetics to Jerusalem since the fourth century, as ways of experiencing and then preserving the memory of pious journeys.[51] As Rafanelli (2012) has argued, an emphasis on the primacy of vision (and therefore the image) was often used to rationalize and justify belief.[52] The same could be said for Veronica, whose role in the production of the *image* of Christ's face is granted higher status than her having touched his hand while giving him the linen cloth or having pressed the cloth to his brow.

Artists during the Early Modern period interpreted these stories, or *istorie*, using a visual vocabulary of pose, gesture, and gaze, which together exhibit multiple parallelisms. Although the Magdalene does not actually come into physical contact with Jesus at his imperative, the story hinges on her stretching her arm toward him in a manner similar to that of the woman with the hemorrhage, who reaches her hand out for Christ's cloak, and to Veronica, who extends her hand outward toward Christ to offer him a towel. In fact, the woman with the hemorrhage and the *Noli Me Tangere* as subjects of works of art share many compositional traits, such as the woman's crouched pose and the standing Christ, as well as demonstrative arm gestures, exchanged gazes, and curvilinear passages of negative space between the figures (compare Plate 2 and the right wing of Plate 10). Artists' compositions of the Veronica legend are so varied that it is hard to make the same connections. Often Veronica's pose can be reversed with Christ's as the one crouching under the weight of the cross while Veronica stands. But the iconography and similar compositions in artworks of all three narratives (the woman with the hemorrhage who touches Christ's garment, Veronica's offering him the *sudarium*, and the *Noli Me Tangere* in which Mary Magdalene reaches for Christ) share more commonalities than differences. As each story features an isolated scene of a woman interacting alone with Christ, the subjects are dramatic narratives that resonate with dialectical tension between the genders. Also noteworthy, these three stories each represent a significant phase in Christ's existence: his public ministry, the Passion, and his Resurrection, respectively. Each female character expresses affection, grief, and empathy toward Christ while seeking to understand – and prove – his dual nature as a divine human.

In concluding this section on looking at works of art with Veronica from a gendered perspective, we can recall the central role of a woman in the Western version of the legend from its outset. Bernice/Veronica as female protagonist in the Western interpretation of the story was likely a significant contributing factor to its eventual merging with the Gospel account of the woman with a hemorrhage. Thematic connections of blood (as a symbol of suffering that can be related to women's bodies) and cloth (as an emblem of salve) may have readily linked these stories to the Passion. In the Stations of the Cross, Veronica's role as a supportive woman aligned her with the Virgin Mary, Mary Magdalene, and the other grieving women in Jerusalem who were present at the Passion, all the while serving as a foil to the violence of the Roman soldiers. For the Franciscans, Veronica may have appealed as a role model for nuns in the Order of Saint Clare (the Poor Clares, or Second Order of Saint Francis) and women in the Third Order of Saint Francis; thus, she may have been highlighted to bring first-century women of the church forward during the fourteenth century when women's roles in the church were being reorganized. Appeals to religious women's emotions can be found in the *Meditationes vitae Christi*, a fourteenth-century Tuscan text written by and for female readers, which laid the social and spiritual foundations for the development of images of Veronica through an emphasis on affective piety. We know that religious women in communities had a special reverence for Veronica from their writings, collections of pilgrims' badges that featured images of the veronica, and ownership of works of art that included Veronica. Women's interest in the Stations of the Cross largely stemmed from Passion devotions by means of vicarious pilgrimage from the confines of convents, for which they could still obtain indulgences. Finally, the story of Veronica can be compared to and viewed *vis-à-vis* other salient themes in art that appealed to women viewers, especially the *Noli Me Tangere* because of a shared focus on sensorial experiences between a woman and Christ with the purpose of testifying to his nature. As the holder of a "true image" of Christ, the apocryphal figure of Veronica may have attracted the patronage and viewership of women during the Early Modern period because of the character's proximity to Christ during the liminal episodes of his walk toward death. Nuns could identify with Veronica's eyewitness to the living Christ in her *facie ad faciem* encounter, which relied on haptic perception but to a greater extent vision as proof of his dual human and divine nature. Inherent in the legend of Veronica was physical evidence of Christ's historical life and suffering, and moreover, a tangible promise of his everlasting presence through the miraculous imprint of his living face.

Notes

1 Sherry C. M. Lindquist, "The Iconography of Gender," in *The Routledge Companion to Medieval Iconography*, ed. Colum Hourihane, 412–424 (New York: Routledge, 2017). The earlier foundational reference on the topic is Margaret Schaus, ed., *Women and Gender in Medieval Europe: An Encyclopedia* (New York: Routledge, 2006).
2 Martha Easton, "Feminist Art History and Medieval Iconography," in *The Routledge Companion to Medieval Iconography*, ed. Colum Hourihane, 425–436 (New York: Routledge, 2017). For an introduction to a feminist approach to looking at works of art made by women during the sixteenth through nineteenth centuries, see Whitney Chadwick, "Women Artists and the Politics of Representation," in *Feminist Art Criticism: An Anthology*, eds. Arlene Raven, Cassandra L. Langer, and Joanna Frueh, 167–185 (New York: HarperCollins Publishers, 1988).
3 Wolf, "From Mandylion to Veronica," 174.
4 Coogan, et al., eds., *The New Oxford Annotated Bible*, 1759.
5 Ibid., 165.
6 Ibid.
7 For additional feminist interpretations of both the Leviticus passage and the Gospel story of the woman with the hemorrhage, see Elisabeth Schüssler Fiorenza, *In Memory of Her: A Feminist Theological Reconstruction of Christian Origins* (New York: The Crossroad Publishing Company, 1983), 124.
8 On the iconography of Mary Magdalene, see the collection of essays in *Mary Magdalene, Iconographic Studies from the Middle Ages to the Baroque*, eds. Michelle A. Erhardt and Amy M. Morris (Boston: Brill, 2012).
9 Coogan, et al., eds., *The New Oxford Annotated Bible,* 1789.
10 See Schüssler Fiorenza, *In Memory of Her*.

11 Rudy, "A Guide to Mental Pilgrimage," 495–496.
12 Peters, "The Procession That Never Was," 35–36.
13 John W. Coakley, *Women, Men, and Spiritual Power: Female Saints and their Male Collaborators* (New York: Columbia University Press, 2006).
14 Ibid., 213.
15 Ibid., 226–227.
16 On Clare, see Jeryldene Wood, *Women, Art, and Spirituality: The Poor Clares of Early Modern Italy* (Cambridge: Cambridge University Press, 1996); Joan Mueller, *The Privilege of Poverty: Clare of Assisi, Agnes of Prague, and the Struggle for a Franciscan Rule for Women* (University Park, PA: The Pennsylvania State University Press, 2006); Lezlie S. Knox, *Creating Clare of Assisi: Female Franciscan Identities in Later Medieval Italy* (Leiden: Brill, 2008); Joan Mueller, *A Companion to Clare of Assisi: Life, Writings, and Spirituality* (Leiden: Brill, 2010); Debby Ben-Aryeh, *The Cult of St Clare of Assisi in Early Modern Italy*; and most recently, Catherine M. Mooney, *Clare of Assisi and the Thirteenth-Century Church: Religious Women, Rules, and Resistance* (Philadelphia: University of Pennsylvania Press, 2016).
17 Derbes, *Picturing the Passion*, 167–168.
18 Clarissa W. Atkinson, "Female Sanctity in the Late Middle Ages," in *The Book of Margery Kempe: A New Translation, Contexts, and Criticism*, trans. and ed. Lynn Staley, 225–236 (New York: Norton & Company, 2001).
19 Belting, *Likeness and Presence*, 210.
20 Derbes, *Picturing the Passion*, 160.
21 Alston, "Way of the Cross."
22 Also called the Tertiary Order or Secular Order, the Third Order of Saint Francis was comprised of men and women who, due to marriage or other secular responsibilities, could not enter monastic life.
23 Although Fra Giunta Bevegnati and Saint Margaret were contemporaries, his biography of Margaret, written c. 1305–1308, post-dates her death.
24 For literary and hagiographical analyses of Fra Giunta Bevegnati's *Legenda Margaritae*, see Coakley, *Women, Men, and Spiritual Power*, 130–148. See also Thomas Renna, introduction to *The Life and Miracles of Saint Margaret of Cortona (1247–1297)* by Fra Giunta Bevegnati (Saint Bonaventure, NY: Franciscan Institute Publications, 2012), 9–42.
25 Morris, *The Sepulchre of Christ*, 293; and Renna, introduction to *The Life and Miracles of Saint Margaret of Cortona*, 24.
26 Fra Giunta Bevegnati, *The Life and Miracles of Saint Margaret of Cortona (1247–1297)*, transl. Thomas Renna, ed. Shannon Larson (Saint Bonaventure, NY: Franciscan Institute Publications, 2012), 114; and Fra Giunta Bevegnati, *Leggenda della vita e dei miracoli di Santa Margherita da Cortona*, trans. and ed. Eliodoro Mariani (Vicenza: L.I.E.F., 1978), 84.
27 Fra Giunta Bevegnati, *The Life and Miracles of Saint Margaret of Cortona (1247–1297)*, 26–27.
28 For further discussion on the date of the manuscript, see Flora and Cignoni, "Requirements of Devout Contemplation, 61–76. See also Holly Flora, *The Devout Belief of the Imagination: The Paris* Meditationes Vitae Christi *and Female Franciscan Spirituality in Trecento Italy* (Turnhout, Belgium: Brepols Publishers, 2009), 30.
29 The basic bibliography on the *Meditationes vitae Christi* includes: Isa Ragusa, trans., and Rosalie B. Green, ed., *Meditations on the Life of Christ: An Illustrated Manuscript of the Fourteenth Century* (Princeton, NJ: Princeton University Press, 1977); John of Caulibus, *Meditations on the Life of Christ*, trans. and ed. F. Taney, A. Miller, and C. M. Stallings-Taney (Asheville, NC: Pegasus Press, 2000); Flora, *The Devout Belief*; Sarah McNamer, "The Origins of the *Meditationes Vitae Christi*," *Speculum* 84 (2009): 905–955, www.jstor.org/stable/40593681; and most recently, McNamer, *Meditations on the Life of Christ: The Short Italian Text*, 2018.
30 See Holly Flora, "Gender, Image, and Devotion in Illustrated Manuscripts of the *Meditationes Vitae Christi*," in *Beyond the Text: Franciscan Art and the Construction of*

Religion, eds. Xavier Seubert and Oleg Bychov, 160–176 (Saint Bonaventure, NY: Franciscan Institute Publications, 2013).

31 Flora and Pecorini Cignoni, "Requirements of Devout Contemplation," 61. Specific characteristics about the text indicate female patronage, such as female-gendered commands.

32 McNamer, *Meditations on the Life of Christ,* 2018. This recent scholarship provides a critical edition of the text and an English translation with commentary.

33 Hamburger, *The Visual and the Visionary*, 322.

34 Ibid., 350–370. Hamburger examines writings that mention the veronica by two additional Early Modern female writers: Gertrude of Helfta (1256–1301/2) and Mechthild of Hackeborn (1241/42–1299).

35 Ibid.

36 Ibid.

37 Ibid.

38 For more on the provenance and materiality of *veronicae* as pilgrims' badges, see Hanneke Van Asperen, "'*Où il y a une Veronique attachiée dedens'*. Images of the Veronica in Religious Manuscripts, with Special Attention for the Dukes of Burgundy and their Family," in *The European Fortune of the Roman Veronica in the Middle Ages, Convivium Supplementum*, eds. A. Murphy, H. L. Kessler, M. Petoletti, E. Duffy, and G. Milanese, 232–249 (Turnhout, Belgium: Brepols Publishers, 2017).

39 See Hanneke van Asperen, "Praying, Threading, and Adorning: Sewn-in Prints in a Rosary Prayer Book (London, British Library, Add. MS 14042)," in *Weaving, Veiling, and Dressing: Textiles and their metaphors in the Late Middle Ages*, eds. Kathryn M. Rudy and Barbara Baert, 81–120, 82 (Turnhout, Belgium: Brepols Publishers, 2007).

40 See Megan H. Foster-Campbell, "Pilgrimage through the Pages: Pilgrims' Badges in Late Medieval Devotion," in *Push Me, Pull You: Imaginative, Emotional, Physical, and Spatial Interactions in Late Medieval and Renaissance Art*, edited by Sarah Blick and Laura Gelfand (Leiden: Brill Publishers, 2011) https://doi.org/10.1163/9789004215139_008.

41 Hamburger, *The Visual and the Visionary,* 333, 345. Kathryn M. Rudy has even proposed a possibility that the top paint layers on some veronicas were scraped and ingested for medicinal purposes, tying the purpose of the copies to the curative qualities of the original. See Rudy, "Eating the Face of Christ. Philip the Good and his Physical Relationship with Veronicas," in *The European Fortune of the Roman Veronica in the Middle Ages, Convivium Supplementum*, eds. A. Murphy, H. L. Kessler, M. Petoletti, E. Duffy, and G. Milanese, 168–179 (Turnhout, Belgium: Brepols Publishers, 2017).

42 Both illuminated manuscripts are in the Bibliothèque nationale de France, Paris: MS fr. 12420, fol. 92v and MS fr. 598, fol. 92. See Stephen Perkinson, "Rethinking the Origins of Portraiture," *Gesta* 46 (2008): 135–157, especially 142–145 and Figures 6–7.

43 Da Zedelgem, *Saggio Storico sulla Devozione alla Via Crucis,* 69. See Titus Tobler, *Itinera hierosolymitana Crucesignatorum* (Geneva: J. G. Fick, 1877), 27–40.

44 Miedema, "Following in the Footsteps of Christ," 85.

45 Ibid., 86.

46 Ibid., 91.

47 Anne L. Clark, "Venerating the Veronica: Varieties of Passion Piety in the later Middle Ages," *Material Religion* 3 (2007): 164–189, doi: 10.2752/175183407X219732.

48 Bibliography on the role of the senses in artists' depictions of the *Noli Me Tangere* includes: Erin E. Benay and Lisa M. Rafanelli, *Faith, Gender and the Senses in Italian Renaissance and Baroque Art: Interpreting the* Noli me tangere *and Doubting Thomas* (Burlington, VT: Ashgate Publishing Company, 2015); Lisa M. Rafanelli, "Thematizing Vision in the Renaissance: The *Noli Me Tangere* as a Metaphor for Art Making," in *Sense and the Senses in Early Modern Art and Cultural Practice*, eds. Alice E. Sanger and Siv Tove Kulbrandstad Walker, 149–168 (Burlington, VT: Ashgate Publishing Company, 2012); and Barbara Baert, "The Gaze in the Garden: Mary Magdalene in *Noli Me Tangere*," in *Mary Magdalene, Iconographic Studies from the Middle Ages to the Baroque*, eds. Michelle A. Erhardt and Amy M. Morris, 189–221 (Boston: Brill, 2012).

49 John 20:18. Coogan, et al., eds., *The New Oxford Annotated Bible*, 1915. The *Noli Me Tangere* does not appear in the synoptic Gospels.

50 On the *paragone*, see Geraldine A. Johnson, "The Art of Touch in Early Modern Italy," in *Art and the Senses*, eds. Francesca Bacci and David Melcher, 59–84 (Oxford: Oxford University Press, 2011).
51 Georgia Frank, "The Pilgrim's gaze in the age before icons," in *Visuality Before and Beyond the Renaissance: Seeing as Others Saw*, ed. Robert S. Nelson, 98–115 (Cambridge: Cambridge University Press, 2000).
52 Rafanelli, "Thematizing Vision in the Renaissance," 149.

6 The Iconography of Veronica in Western European Art

This final chapter looks beyond the history of the veronica relic and its early replicas, which have been extensively studied and illustrated elsewhere, to the Early Modern period. As a complement to extant literature, the goal of this section is to explore how the legend of Veronica and the *sudarium* as a physical object were interpreted by artists from the late Middle Ages through the Baroque period. Essentially, the subject of Veronica with the Holy Face in works of art is an image within an image, in a similar way that representations of Saint Luke painting the Virgin and some types of self-portraiture gave artists opportunities to render paintings within paintings.[1] More specifically, as effigies of holy figures,[2] works of art depicting Veronica and her cloth give visible form to a woman widely perceived to be a saint and to Christ as a deity not normally visible. Interpretations of Veronica and her relic in the visual arts largely indicate what some Christians imagined they would see when standing before Christ at the hour of judgment. In this sense, the Holy Face on the veronica can be described as an end-of-time vision. In approaching the development of this iconography, I will provide a brief chronology and point out some consistent themes before clustering the images into five roles at the end.

The iconographic study of Veronica in Early Modern art begins in the mid-thirteenth century in England[3] with Matthew Paris, who was the first known Western chronicler to produce illuminations of the veronica relic. The artist-scribe depicted the Holy Face in a psalter (British Library MS Arundel 157, folio 2r), datable c. 1240 (Figure 6.1).[4] In the *Chronica Majora* (c. 1240–1259), Matthew Paris rendered another Holy Face, a tinted drawing on vellum that was pasted onto the page, dated c. 1240–1250 (Figure 1.3). Plus, he represented the *sudarium* on a folio that juxtaposed three images: *Madonna and Child, Man of Sorrows, and the Veronica* (Figure 6.2).[5] Notably, all three foundational drawings of the veronica by Matthew Paris feature Christ with neck, collar, and shoulders. Although this design largely stems from Western bust-length portraiture, we can also notice a neck and shoulders on the image of Christ's face on a cloth in the painted icon from Mount Sinai that dates to the tenth century as a possible precedent (Plate 3).

Suzanne Lewis, whose monograph on Matthew Paris (1987) remains the foremost study on the *Chronica Majora*, judged it unlikely that Matthew saw the veronica relic in person in Rome; his source was more likely textual than visual.[6] As mentioned in Chapter 2, the first extant description of the relic by the pilgrim Gervase of Tilbury in his *Otia Imperialia* (Recreation for an Emperor), datable c. 1210–1215, refers to

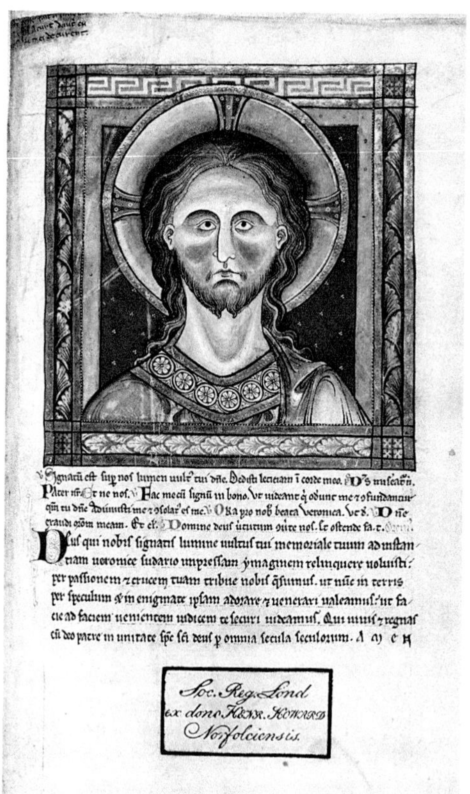

Figure 6.1 Matthew Paris, O.S.B. (English, c. 1200–1259), *The Veronica*, MS Arundel 157, fol. 2r., c. 1240. 145 × 130 mm. The British Library, London.
Image credit: © The British Library Board

the face of Christ as a bust (a face with neck, collar, and shoulders), which is how Matthew Paris depicted it.[7] The style in which the artist rendered Christ's face in the *Chronica Majora* – in color, in a larger scale than other drawings in the manuscript, with the use of firm contours rather than sketchy lines, and with an iconic stare that meets the gaze of the viewer – heightens the visage's dramatic effect, perhaps to emphasize an impression of the icon's power.[8] Matthew Paris's use of small, black pupils with the head surrounded by a broad halo (a feature also found in Byzantine and Norman images) intensified the effect of a piercing stare, a characteristic that yielded a distinctive artistic legacy in images of both God the Father and Christ. For example, similar visual effects can be found in heads of God the Father in thirteenth-century manuscript illuminations depicting *The Tree of Bigamy* in The Art Institute of Chicago and the *Arbor Consanguinitatis* (Tree of Blood Relationships) in the Cleveland Museum of Art.[9]

Pächt (1961),[10] who first had noticed a discrepancy between Matthew Paris's mid-thirteenth century depictions of the veronica (featuring the neck, collar, and shoulders) and later fourteenth- and fifteenth-century renditions (which did not),

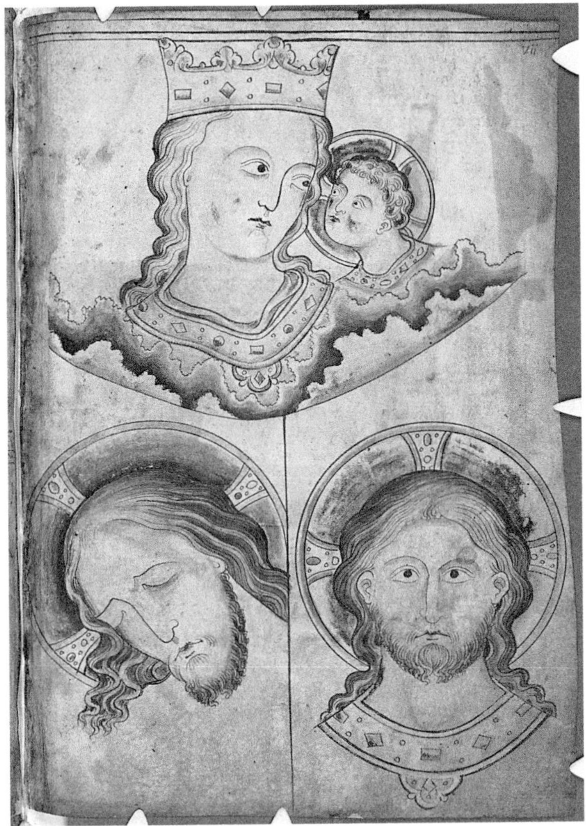

Figure 6.2 Matthew Paris, O.S.B. (English, c. 1200–1259), *Madonna and Child, Man of Sorrows, and the Veronica*, from the *Chronica Majora I*, MS 26, fol. viir, c. 1240–1250. Corpus Christi College, University of Cambridge.

Image credit: The Parker Library, Corpus Christi College, Cambridge

offered three possible scenarios to explain the difference. First, Pächt proposed the possibility that Matthew Paris did not depict the veronica relic at Old Saint Peter's basilica and that he had mistakenly drawn the likeness from another icon. Secondly, later artistic versions of the veronica could have been modernizations of the original type, which demonstrated an effort to align the image with the legend. Or thirdly, the English chronicler's drawing showed the Roman relic in a different, earlier stage.[11] Although I do not find any of these possibilities satisfying, Pächt did also suggest that a likely model for the eventual thirteenth-century form of the veronica was the *acheiropoieton* at the Lateran palace (Figure 1.2), which would have been a familiar image of Christ in Rome at the time.[12] The Lateran model, datable to the fifth or sixth centuries, was distinct from the Eastern *Mandylion* type and yet predated the suffering Christ imagery, which appears on the veronica by the mid-fifteenth century.[13] This final interpretation, with which I concur, agrees with the description written by Gervase of Tilbury ("from the chest upwards"). Morgan

(2017) has proposed further that Matthew Paris derived his version of the veronica and its associated text of the Office from the Lateran icon by means of a copy held at Westminster Abbey or the Palace in London.[14]

After Matthew Paris's colored drawings, the veronica in works of art largely shows Christ's face *without* the neck and shoulders, as exemplified in our initial example by the Master of Saint Veronica in London (Plate 1), among many others (Plates 5, 7a, 8, 9, 10, 14, and Figures 2.1, 3.6, 3.7, 4.3b, 4.4b, 4.5, 4.6, 4.8, 4.9, 6.5, 6.6, 6.11, 6.12, 6.13, 6.14, 6.17, 6.18, 6.20, 6.26, 6.27). Possible visual sources for the round shape of Christ's face on Veronica's veil, as suggested by Ann Van Dijk (2013), include medallions with portrait busts in them (*imago clipeata*), which were common on Roman imperial sarcophagi and triumphal arches. The design of a head within a roundel had been adapted by Christians by the fourth and fifth centuries, as evident in series of papal effigies at Old Saint Peter's basilica (no longer extant) and the basilica of *San Paolo fuori le mura* (Saint Paul outside the Walls), among other early Christian monuments in Rome.[15] The Holy Face floating on Veronica's swathe of cloth may have resonated with Western viewers because its form was similar to motifs in Late Antique portraiture rendered in relief. Secondly, the circular form evokes, and was perhaps derived in part from, the *clipeus*: a round, protective shield encapsulating the Christ child, which Mary sometimes holds on her chest in Byzantine icons that depict the Virgin of the Sign. A third source of influence for later paintings and sculptures of Veronica was likely the pilgrim's badge, a mass-produced, metal token with an image of Veronica and/or her cloth, created using the techniques of casting or die-stamping (Figure 1.4).[16] Called *veronicae* in Latin and Italian and *vernycles* or *vernicles* in English,[17] the badges were believed to protect wearers against sudden death without confession.[18] Images of the veronica also appeared on late medieval Roman coins c. 1350 (a Jubilee year), such as a gold ducat, indicating that the round form of the imprint of the veronica relic had become so renowned by the mid-fourteenth century that the emblem served as an unofficial symbol of the city of Rome.[19]

An increase in the number of works of art depicting Veronica holding the veil coincided with the popularity of the *Meditationes vitae Christi* in the mid-fourteenth century, as discussed in Chapters 3 and 5. The year 1300 marked a Jubilee, during which Pope Boniface VIII (papacy 1294–1303) named the relic among the *Mirabilia urbis Romae* (Marvels of the city of Rome). This decree increased interest in the iconography of Veronica, as evident in the inclusion of a woodcut depicting the exposition of the cloth to pilgrims in the editions of 1400 and subsequent years of the *Mirabilia Romae, Historia et Descriptio Urbis Romae*, for example this version datable c. 1485–1489 (Figure 6.3).[20] In addition, circa 1400 and through the fifteenth century, the Holy Face on the veronica was included in a collection of objects known as the *Arma Christi*, or Instruments of the Passion, signifying a further merging of the legend of Veronica with relics associated with Christ's Crucifixion, as evident in a South Netherlandish tapestry, begun c. 1475, in The Metropolitan Museum of Art, New York (Figure 6.4). Also occurring about 1400 and continuing through the end of the fifteenth century, a period that demonstrated a full flourishing of Veronica imagery, the Holy Face on the *sudarium* in art featured Christ wearing the crown of thorns, as evident in a second painting by the Master of Saint Veronica, datable c. 1420, in

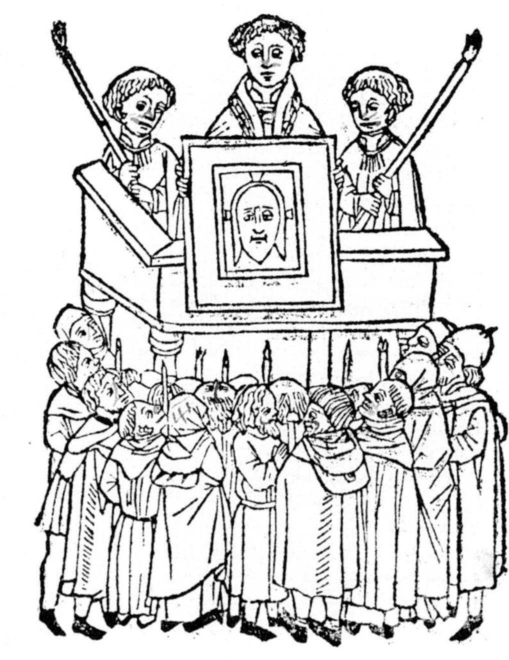

Figure 6.3 Italian, *Ostension of the Veronica for Pilgrims in Rome*. Page from *Mirabilia Romae, Historia et Descriptio Urbis Romae* by Pseudo-Aegidius Romanus. Published by Andreas Freitag, Rome. Datable not before 1485 and not after 1489. Woodcut on paper.

Image credit: Bridgeman Images, New York

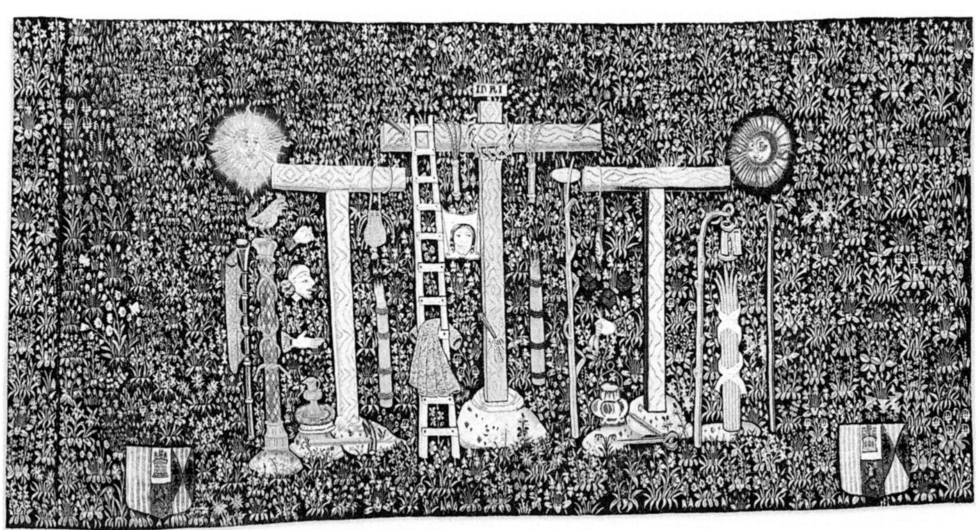

Figure 6.4 South Netherlandish, *Arma Christi*, 1475–1550. Woven tapestry made of wool, silk, gilt and silver threads. The Metropolitan Museum of Art, New York (53.34). The Cloisters Collection, 1952.

Image credit: The Metropolitan Museum of Art, New York

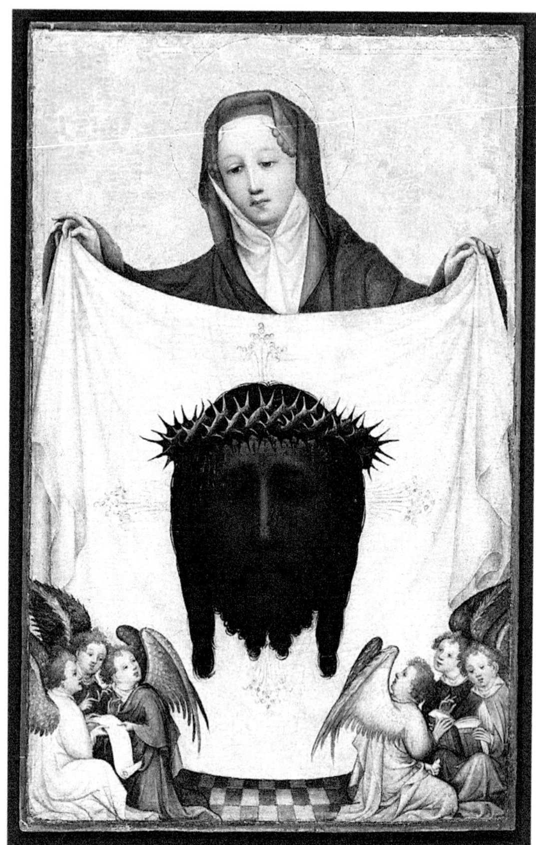

Figure 6.5 Master of Saint Veronica (Cologne, fl. 1400–1420), *Saint Veronica with the Holy Kerchief*, c. 1420. Bayerische Staatsgemäldesammlungen, Munich, Alte Pinakothek.
Image credit: © Bayerische Staatsgemäldesammlungen München, Alte Pinakothek. Photo: Sibylle Forster

Munich (Figure 6.5 and front cover), as well as a Flemish illumination by Lieven van Lathem, c. 1471 (Figure 3.6). A terra-cotta impression of the veronica from fifteenth-century Germany even has holes at the top for the attachment of actual thorns, a feature that, together with polychromy, would have heightened the illusion of the veracity of Christ's face (Figure 6.6). About 1450, according to Pearson (1887),[21] Christ's visage is depicted dramatically with blood and an expression of pain and anguish, as evident in *The Veil of Veronica*, a tempera on panel of 1450 by Wilhelm Kalteysen (from Aachen, active in Wroclaw, c. 1420–1496) in the National Museum in Wroclaw, Poland.

As Kessler (2017) has pointed out, works of art that showcase Veronica from the Early Modern period do not repeat a single model. Instead, these later works of art are creative depictions of a young woman holding a facial imprint of a man with a dual historical and divine nature. Artistic renditions of Veronica and her cloth were varied with a wide range of adaptations permissible.[22] Nevertheless, below I expound upon a few consistent leitmotifs of Veronica[23] before grouping them

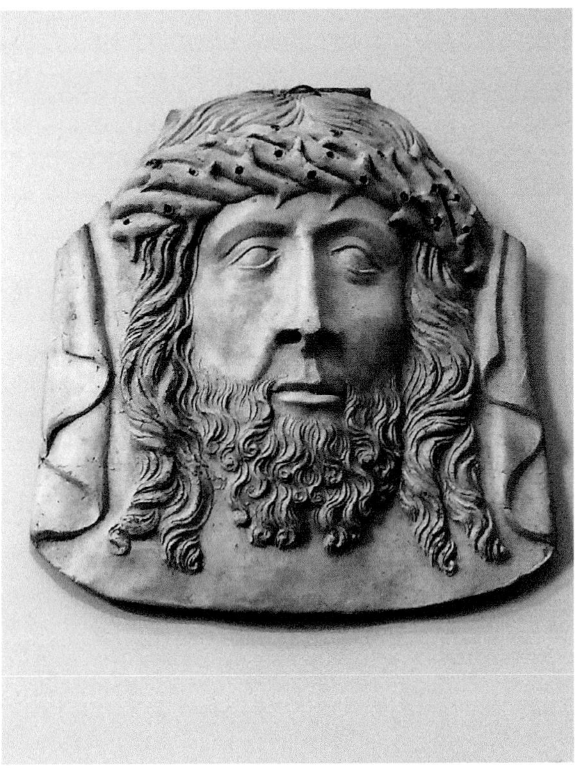

Figure 6.6 German, *Impression of a veronica with holes for the attachment of thorns*, fifteenth century. Terra-cotta. Staatliche Museen zu Berlin, Skulpturensammlung und Museum für Byzantinische Kunst.

Image credit: Author

into five roles. My focus on the attributes of the female character and her *sudarium* is in part because iconographic studies of the Holy Face on the veil have already been conducted by Pearson (1887),[24] with a re-evaluation of his work by Zardoni, Bossi, and Murphy (2017).[25] Themes in the latter study include links with the *Mandylion* or cut-out shape of Christ's face, the light versus dark colored face, the transfigured versus sorrowful face, and the transparent veil. I weave some of these themes into the subsequent paragraphs although these aspects are more thoroughly discussed in the prior study.

Regarding pose, Veronica is typically depicted standing or kneeling, positions that pilgrims were likely intended to imitate. In fact, the woodcut from the *Mirabilia urbis Romae*, datable c. 1485–1489 (Figure 6.3), shows worshipers kneeling and standing in adoration of the veronica, which is held above their heads. Memling (Plate 7a) places his figure of Veronica kneeling on the ground in a pose of humility. The gesture of Veronica's outstretched arms carries manifold connotations, among them ostension, almsgiving, and generosity. It also signals magnanimity, as she "gives" the living Christ to mankind. A similar connotation with the gesture can be found in images of the *Madonna della Misericordia*, in which Mary is shown with arms extended as the dispenser of Christ's mercy.[26] Veronica's arms positioned upward and outward, albeit not high, while displaying the *sudarium* are reminiscent of a priest's elevation of the host during Mass. The placement of the arms likens the function of Veronica to that of a monstrance. Veronica's gesture also recalls the reach of the woman with the hemorrhage who lunges toward Christ, longing for salve and healing, in attempts to touch the hem of his garment (Plate 2). Unassuming in dress, Veronica's head is typically covered with a veil (Plates 1, 12 and Figures 3.7, 6.5, 6.10, 6.14, 6.15). However, frequently she wears a turban, an attribute that may indicate beliefs in her character having Eastern origins,[27] as exemplified in Plate 7a and Figures 3.6, 4.6, 6.11, 6.12, 6.23.

In terms of gaze, Veronica is usually portrayed with eyes downcast (Plates 1, 7a, 12 and Figures 3.6, 4.5, 4.9, 6.5, 6.14, 6.19, 6.20). As an expression with connotations of feminine modesty, the downward gaze was also common in images of the Virgin. But in the case of Veronica, the downcast glance may have functioned further to prevent distraction from the viewer's opportunity to peer directly into the eyes of Christ.

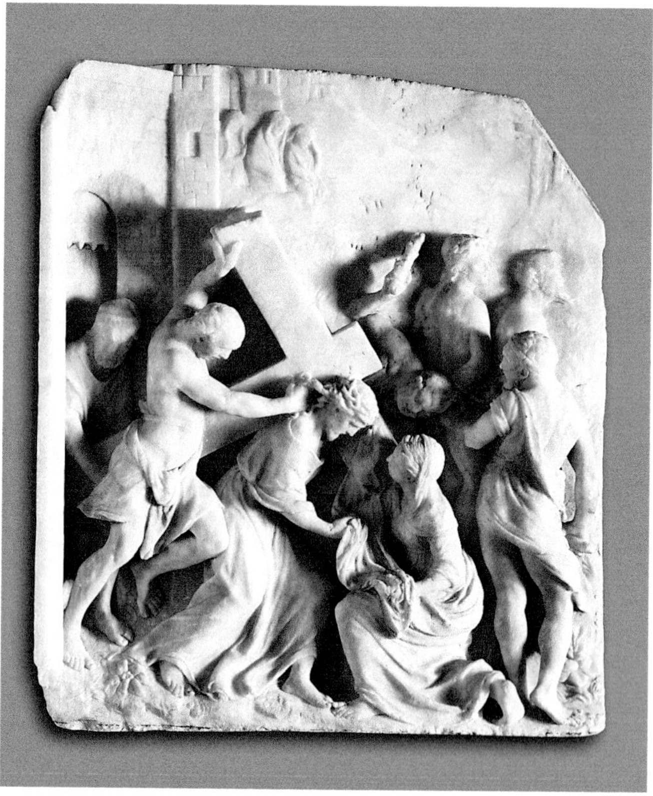

Figure 6.7 Workshop of Jacques Dubroeucq (South Netherlandish, c. 1500/10–c. 1584), *Christ Carrying the Cross with Saints Simon and Veronica,* c. 1545. Alabaster; overall 61.6 × 54 × 11.5 cm. The Cleveland Museum of Art, Purchase from the J. H. Wade Fund, 1971.5.

Image credit: Courtesy of The Cleveland Museum of Art

To reinforce this intention, the direction of Veronica's glance led to her cloth. In Stations of the Cross series, however, Veronica more commonly looks intensely into the eyes of Christ as he carries the cross, as exemplified in an alabaster relief from the workshop of Jacques Dubroeucq, datable to c. 1545, in the Cleveland Museum of Art (Figure 6.7). Occasionally, her eyes meet those of the viewer (Figures 6.11, 6.15).

Usually the figure of Veronica is shown in her youth (Plates 1, 7a and Figures 2.1, 3.6, 4.5, 4.9, 6.5, 6.15, 6.20), with the painting by the Master of Flémalle (Workshop of Robert Campin) (Figure 4.6) as an exception. Although the figure of Veronica is regularly portrayed in works of art with a Northern-European complexion, the face of Christ on her veil is sometimes characterized by dark skin, as for example in the Master of Saint Veronica's *Saint Veronica with the Holy Kerchief*, c. 1420, in Munich (Figure 6.5 and front cover). Flora Lewis (1985) brought forth some thought-provoking observations about the brown skin tones of some images of the Holy Face.[28] Lewis noted that blackness as an indication of race was a characteristic in some Eastern copies of the *Mandylion*. Some versions of the legend included reference to this trait about the icon from Edessa, as well as about the Arab Christian King Abgar Uchama "the Black," who originated from northern Syria. Moreover, Lewis noticed that the black veronicas reflected an aspect of the relic more closely related to Byzantine copies, such as the Holy Face of Laon, a Serbian *Mandylion* in which Christ has a dark skin tone (Figure 6.8).[29] Holy Faces with dark complexions were unconnected with the Way of the Cross legend, even though Christ's torture,

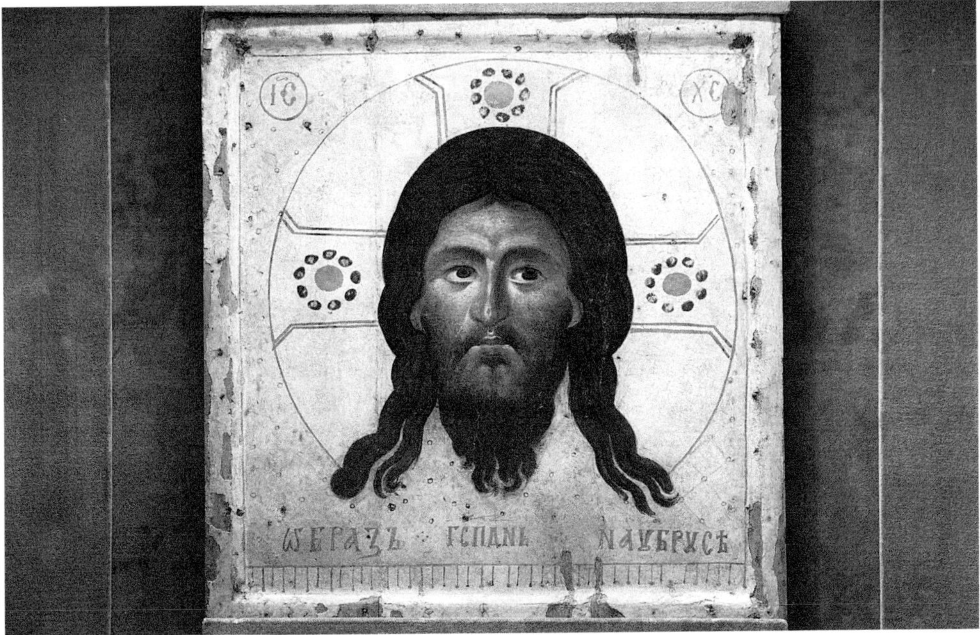

Figure 6.8 Serbian, *Holy Face*, late twelfth or early thirteenth centuries. Panel. From the Cathedral of Laon, Aisne, France.

Image credit: Art Resource, NY. Photo: Manuel Cohen

physical exertion, and bloodshed during the Passion were often used to explain dark skin tones. In 1249, Jacques Pantaléon, the eventual Pope Urban IV (papacy 1261–1264), sent the Laon copy to his sister, who was abbess at a convent in France, for the nuns' use in prayer.[30] In a letter to her, he explained that the dark skin was a result of Christ's Passion.[31] The subject was broached the following century by Julian of Norwich (English, c. 1346–after 1416). In the second of her *Revelations of Divine Love* (written in Middle English 1373, published 1395), the Christian mystic likened the darkness of the Holy Face to human sin and attributed his skin tone to suffering. She also pointed out variations in the expressions and coloring of Christ's visage on veronicas, a testament to the image's malleability and to variations in works of art:

> It was an emblem and likeness of our foul, black, mortal covering, which our fair, bright, blessed Lord bore for our sins. It made me think of the holy Vernicle in Rome, which he imprinted with his own blessed face while he was in his cruel Passion, willingly going to his death, and often changing colour. Many marvel how it could be – the brownness and blackness, the pitifulness and leanness of this image – considering that he imprinted it with his blessed face, which is the fairness of heaven, the flower of earth, and the fruit of the Virgin's womb. Then how could this image be so discoloured and so far from fair? I would like to say what I have understood by the grace of God. [...] This is the meaning of what was said before: it was the image and likeness of our foul, black, mortal covering, within which our fair, bright, blessed Lord God is hidden. But I dare say most confidently, and we ought to believe, that there was never so fair a man as he, until the time when his fair colour was changed by trouble and sorrow, and suffering and dying. This is spoken of in the eighth revelation, where more is said about the same likeness. And as concerns the Vernicle in Rome, it moves through various changes in colour and expression, sometimes more comfortingly and animated, and sometimes more pitiful and deathly, as may be seen in the eighth revelation.[32]

Renderings of Christ's face on Veronica's veil in Early Modern works of art were varied and accommodated a broad range of skin tones. Zardoni, Bossi, and Murphy (2017) concluded in their important iconographic study, with which I concur, that there is not a clear connection between a dark face and a suffering Christ and that both light and dark faces can be found in Holy Face imagery.[33]

Especially in earlier works of art, the *sudarium* is most often envisioned as a predominantly smooth cloth, stretched parallel to the picture plane (Plate 10 and Figures 6.15, 6.20), or slightly askew (Plates 5, 7a, 12 and Figures 2.1, 3.6, 6.13, 6.25). The flatness of the cloth provides a backdrop for a direct, frontal encounter between the viewer and the face of Christ. In some ways, the veil acts as a cloth of honor that isolates Christ's head in order to increase its visual impact. Yet, Veronica's cloth is frequently white or another light, solid color against which the Holy Face is silhouetted, unlike cloths of honor, which are typically ornamented with intricate patterns and brocades. More commonly in later works of art, the cloth is rendered as drapery that appears to fall naturalistically, gently pulled down by gravity, and characterized by folds in *chiaroscuro* (a technique in which highlights and shadows give the illusion of three-dimensionality) (Plates 1, 5, 7a, 8, 9, 14 and Figures 3.7, 4.3b, 4.8, 6.5, 6.11,

6.27). Sometimes the cloth is conceived as transparent and folded or creased, perhaps to indicate the thin membrane that separates earthly existence and eternity, as evident in the paintings by the Flemish artist (Figure 4.5) and the Master of Flémalle (Workshop of Robert Campin) (Figure 4.6).[34]

Both the creation of an image of Veronica as a work of art and participation in a dramatic reenactment of the scene of Christ meeting Veronica in a Passion play were considered pious acts, which fostered a cross-pollination of artistic ideas.[35] Réau (1959), in his exploration of the connections between religious drama and the iconography of Early Modern art in the Christian West, distinguished two forms: liturgical drama and theater of the mysteries, with the latter performed outdoors for lay audiences in the vernacular.[36] The theater of the mysteries, which was most popular during the fifteenth century, comprised performances characterized by spectacle and pageantry; these were accompanied by a sermon or other dialogue.[37] Although the most common themes of the productions were the Incarnation, Passion, and Resurrection, the lives of saints were also featured, among them the episode of Veronica's encounter with Christ Carrying the Cross.[38] Such reenactments at their apogee during the fifteenth century influenced the development of the plastic arts, especially as many painters were also commissioned to decorate stage sets.[39] Without proposing which influence was greater or came first, Réau sees the relationship as a two-way street and states that many parallels and thematic exchanges can be drawn between public, liturgical dramas and the development of themes in the visual arts during the late Middle Ages and through the Renaissance.[40]

Mâle (1925) earlier had proposed that religious theatrical performances had provided the initial stimulus for certain iconographic scenes, including Veronica's meeting with Christ, which flourished in the visual arts during the late medieval period.[41] Mâle proposed that only under the influence of religious plays did the legend of Veronica become associated with the Passion of Christ.[42] Although religious drama may have renewed or augmented interest in Veronica as a subject for painting and sculpture, I would concur with Réau that there was a fluid, idiomatic exchange between the two art forms.

Furthering this discussion, Weigert (2015) elucidated the relationship between Vengeance plays (dramatic productions about events that follow the Passion and death of Christ) and images about Veronica on painted cloths and woven tapestries in France and Northern Europe.[43] In particular, she studied a series of seven painted cloths at the Reims Museum of Fine Arts, datable to the sixteenth century, which depict the destruction of Jerusalem, based on a play performed in Reims in 1531.[44] The series of painted cloths are related to a script of the play printed in Paris in 1491, possibly made for a performance in honor of a visit to Reims by King Charles VIII. Yet, the printed text and painted cloths diverged from the performance of the Vengeance play in their focus on the punishment of the Jews, including the destruction of Jerusalem and the enslavement of its citizens.[45] Weigert argues that the painted and printed versions of the script provided an alternative to the viewpoints and events depicted in the performance. However, all forms depicted the pivotal event of Veronica's bringing her *sudarium* to Vespasian in Spain to cure him of disease, which allegedly led to his conversion to Christianity.[46]

Additional correlations between religious drama and images of the Veronica legend in France can be found in a three-day Passion play script called *La Vengeance de Nostre-Seigneur par personnages*, a manuscript attributed to Eustache Marcadé (b.

Artois, date unknown, d. 1440), in which the Vengeance play followed the Passion play.[47] Such scripts had a textual basis in *La Vengeance de Nostre-Seigneur* (The Vengeance of our Lord), the twelfth-century epic poem with prose versions in Old and Middle French.[48] Production documentation (diagrams of stage directions) attests to the complicated scene changes, which indicated various locations, with the scene of Veronica meeting Vespasian largely located in Spain.[49] This pair of characters and their interaction were featured in tapestries that served as part of stage sets for Vengeance plays. The Flemish tapestry, datable c. 1510, in The Metropolitan Museum of Art in New York is an example of this type (Figure 2.1).

Franciscan interest in sacred theater and the reenactment of events in the lives of Christ and Francis can be exemplified by the institution of the Crib of Greccio, an event in which Francis recreated Bethlehem in the small village of Greccio outside of Assisi in a *tableau vivant,* complete with animals and a manger in a natural cave. Francis's display, as recounted by his biographer Bonaventure,[50] was depicted in fresco among the 28 scenes, painted c. 1297–1300 in the Upper Church of the Basilica of San Francesco at Assisi (Figure 6.9). A Franciscan penchant for religious *tableaux vivants* may have been a factor in the friars' attraction to Veronica's gesture, or action of compassion, as one to emulate and reenact as part of their program of evangelization, which emphasized compassion as one of the core tenets of Jesus's teachings. We can now turn to the five roles in which Veronica and/or her relic appear in Early Modern art.

The Five Roles

1. *Veronica as female protagonist who holds the cloth, sometimes accompanied by saints*

Painting and sculpture from North and South of the Alps, ranging in date from the end of the thirteenth to the first quarter of the eighteenth centuries, typically represent Veronica in one of five iconographic roles. Foremost, Veronica is depicted alone as a female protagonist who holds a cloth with Christ's visage as her hallmark attribute. As a woman with the suffering Christ, Veronica with her veil can be compared to the *Pietà* (Italian for pity or compassion), a subject traditionally comprised of Mary alone holding the body of the dead Christ. Both Veronica and the *Pietà* are iconic subjects that were used for devotional purposes, even though each theme embodies a narrative element. Both pairs of figures (Veronica with the Holy Face and Mary holding the dead Christ) are stills that have been extracted from more complex scenes for close, focused contemplation. The characters of Mary and Veronica align in similar roles. Yet, Christ's divergent states of being are foils to one another. Whereas in the *Pietà*, Christ's body is in early stages of *rigor mortis* (the stiffening of a body shortly after death), Veronica holds the imprint of the *Christus vivans* (the living Christ). Each woman displays Christ, albeit in contrasting states of death and everlasting life. Salient examples of Veronica in this category, in approximate chronological order, include:

- Artist unknown, *Saint Veronica holding the veil with the Face of Christ*, end of the thirteenth century. Fresco. Santa Veronica Church, Santa Maria Hoè, Lecco[51]
- French (Normandy or Ile-de-France), *Sainte Véronique*, c. 1311–1313. Stone with traces of polychromy. Church of Nôtre-Dame, Écouis (Eure) (Figure 6.10)[52]

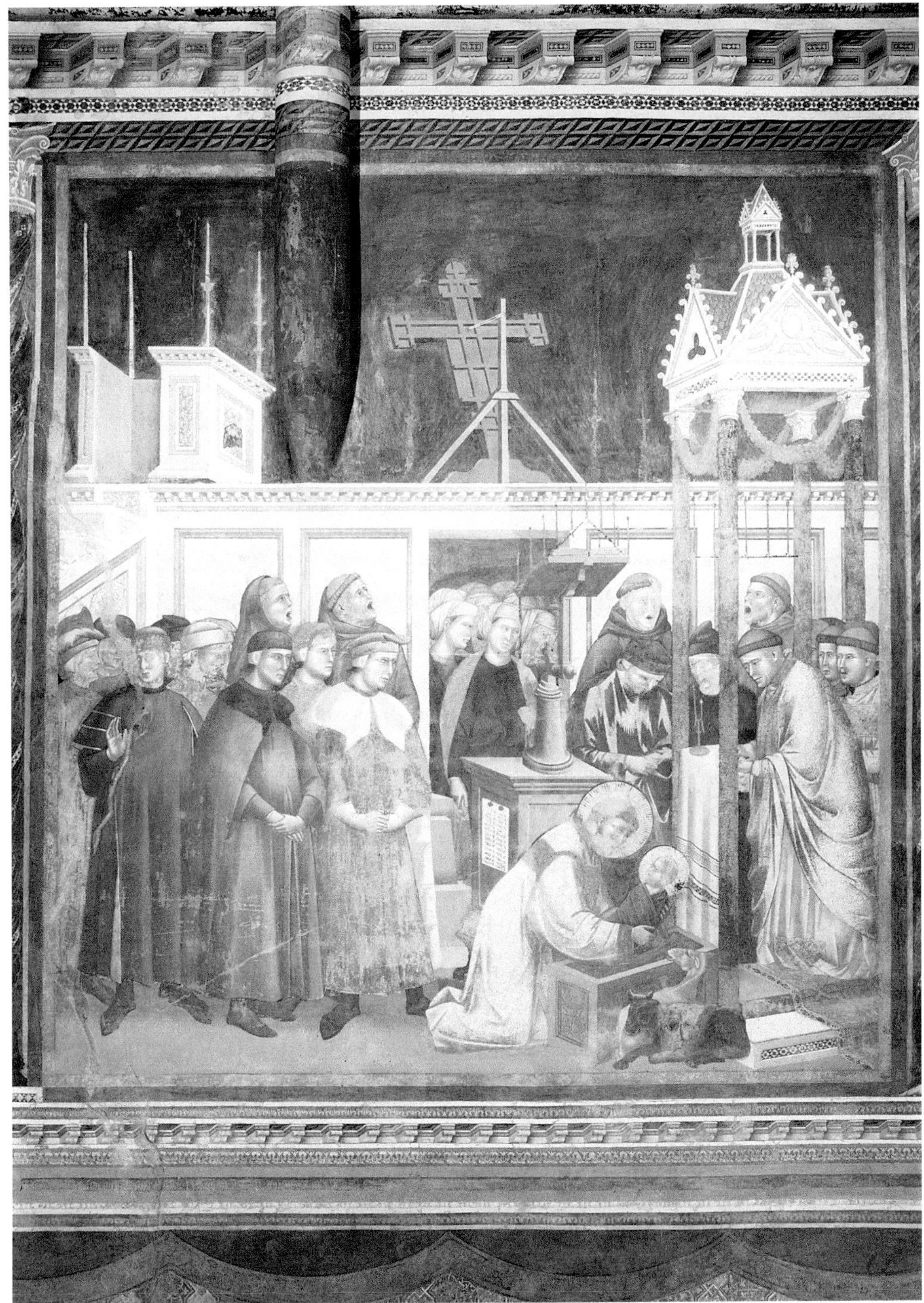

Figure 6.9 Italian, *Francis Instituting the Crib at Greccio*, 1297–1300. Fresco; 270 × 230 cm. Upper Church, Basilica of San Francesco, Assisi.

Image credit: Scala/Art Resource, NY

- Master of Saint Veronica (Cologne, fl. 1395–1420), *Saint Veronica with the Sudarium*, c. 1420. The National Gallery, London (Plate 1)
- Master of Saint Veronica (Cologne, fl. 1395–1420), *Saint Veronica with the Holy Kerchief*, c. 1420. Alte Pinakothek, Munich (Figure 6.5 and front cover)
- Master of Flémalle (Workshop of Robert Campin, Netherlandish, c. 1375–1444), *Veronica displaying the Sudarium*, c. 1430. Städel Museum, Frankfurt (Figure 4.6)
- Master of Guillebert de Mets (Flemish, fl. 1410–1450), *Saint Veronica Displaying the Sudarium*, MS 2 (84.ML.67), fol. 13v. 1450–1455. The J. Paul Getty Museum, Los Angeles (Figure 6.11)
- Hans Memling, *Veronica*, 1470–1475. National Gallery of Art, Washington. Samuel H. Kress Collection (Plate 7 a–b)
- Master of Saint Ursula Legend, *Veronica*, 1475–1500. Private collection
- Martin Schongauer, *Saint Veronica with the Veil*, c. 1480. Engraving. The Metropolitan Museum of Art, New York (Figure 6.12)
- Piero di Cosimo, *Saint Veronica*, c. 1510. Private collection
- Netherlandish, *Saint Veronica*, c. 1525. Woven tapestry made of wool, silk, and gilded silver threads. The Metropolitan Museum of Art, New York (Figure 6.13)
- El Greco (Greek, 1541–1614), *Saint Veronica with the Sudarium*, c. 1577–1578. Oil on canvas, 84 x 91 cm. Museo de Santa Cruz, Toledo

As a variation on this role, Veronica holding her cloth with the Holy Face is sometimes flanked by Saints Peter and Paul, the two principal apostles in the Roman Catholic Church, on whose feast day the veronica was displayed at Old Saint Peter's basilica. The presence of the saints singles out this relic as one of the Church's most sacred possessions. As two examples of this iconography from the sixteenth century, one from each the North and South, we can compare Albrecht Dürer (German, 1471–1528)'s woodcut of 1510 (Figure 6.14) with Ugo da Carpi (Bologna, c. 1480–-1532)'s tempera on panel, datable c. 1524–1527 (Figure 6.15). Both artists employed a similar composition with Peter on the viewer's left and Paul on the viewer's right as compositional brackets around Veronica in the center. Peter and Paul hold readily recognizable attributes of the keys and sword, respectively. Additionally, Ugo da Carpi's figure of Paul also holds a codex as a reference to his letters and writings. Both pairs of titular saints don halos and are represented as aged, bearded, dressed in voluminous drapery, and barefoot, perhaps to imply that they are standing on sacred ground. Whereas Dürer's figures are roughly isocephalic, that is, aligned at the same height, Ugo da Carpi has placed Veronica on the uppermost of three steps, creating a subtle, pyramidal composition. The two male saints are turned in three-quarter poses, which guide viewers' attention toward Veronica and the Holy Face in the center. In both works of art, the figures do not engage with each other, implying an iconic rather than narrative function. Only Ugo da Carpi's Veronica looks outward toward the viewer. Furthermore, each artist has placed the figure group in a fictive architectural space. Dürer set the trio in a cubical room, drafted in perspective, whereas Ugo da Carpi situated his group in an abstract, architectural space with a large window or doorway, in front of which Veronica is silhouetted. Both artists used directional light and cast shadows to convey a sense of continuity between the space of the images and that of the viewers. The primary points of distinction, apart from the differences inherent in the two mediums, are the styles of the Holy Face.

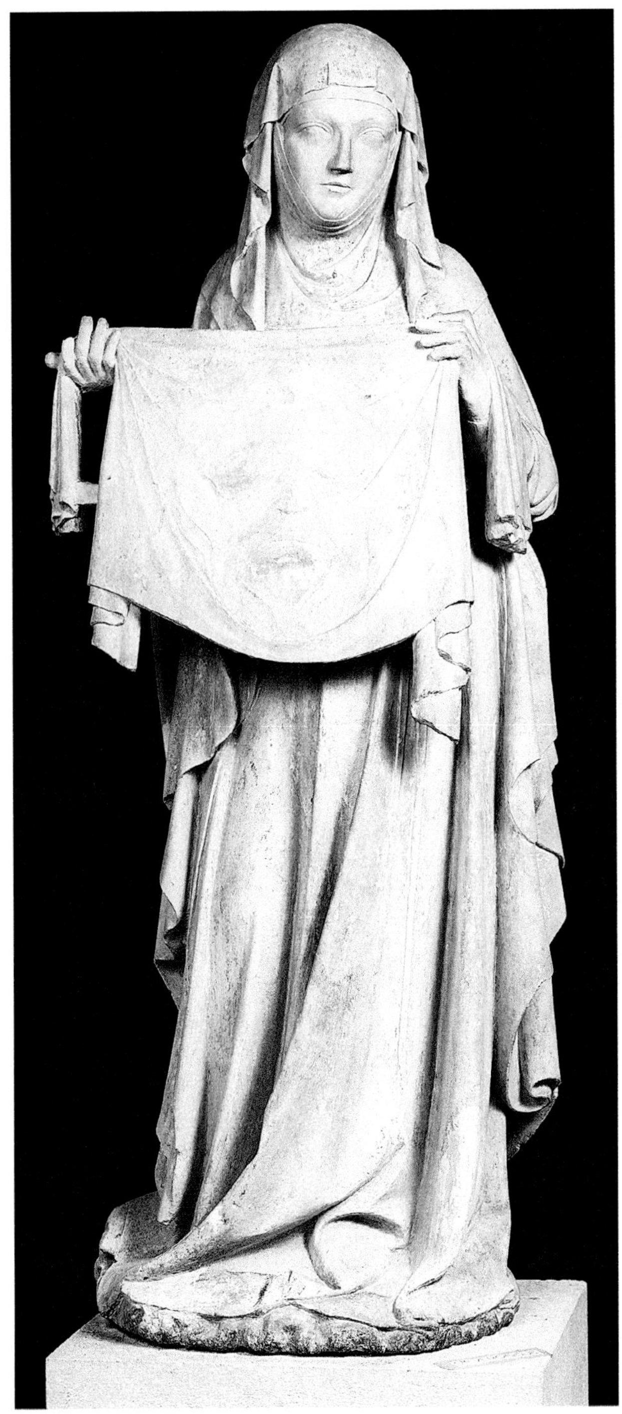

Figure 6.10 French (Normandy or Ile-de-France), *Sainte Véronique*, c. 1311–1313. Stone with traces of polychromy. Church of Nôtre-Dame, Écouis (Eure), France.

Image credit: Bridgeman Images

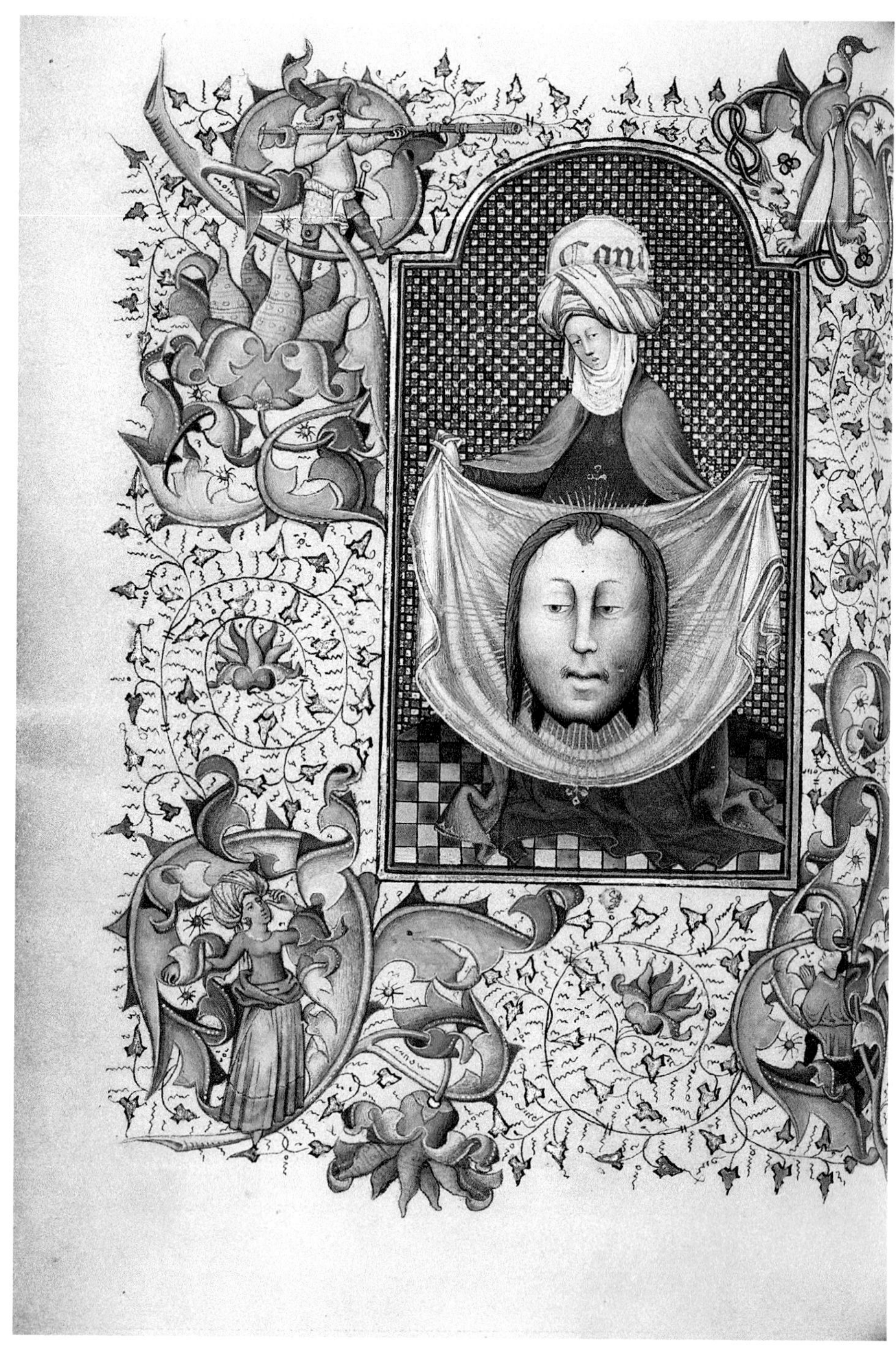

Figure 6.11 Master of Guillebert de Mets (Flemish, fl. 1410–1450), *Saint Veronica Displaying the Sudarium*, MS 2 (84.ML.67), fol. 13v., c. 1450–1455. Tempera colors, gold leaf, and ink on parchment; 19.4 × 14 cm (leaf). The J. Paul Getty Museum, Los Angeles.

Image credit: The J. Paul Getty Museum, Los Angeles/Open Content Program

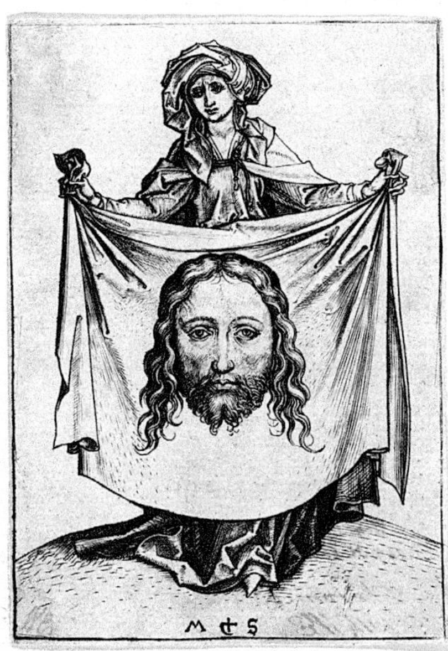

Figure 6.12 Martin Schongauer (Colmar, c. 1450/53–1491), *Saint Veronica with the Veil*, c. 1480. Engraving; 8.7 × 6.1 cm (sheet). The Metropolitan Museum of Art, New York (32.64.3). Harris Brisbane Dick Fund, 1932.

Image credit: The Metropolitan Museum of Art, New York

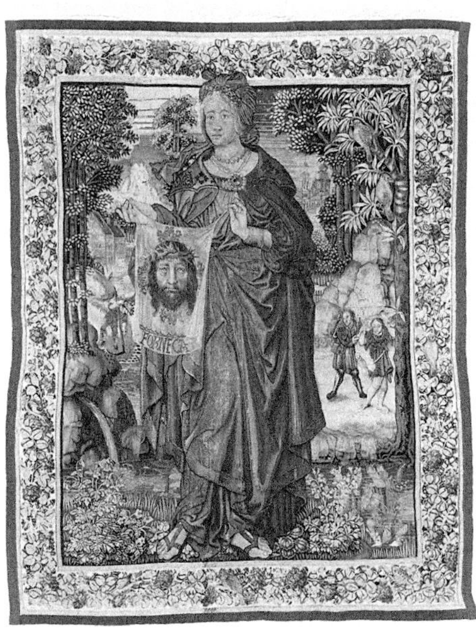

Figure 6.13 Netherlandish, possibly after a design by Bernard van Orley (Brussels, c. 1492–1541/42), *Saint Veronica*, c. 1525. Woven tapestry made of wool, silk, and gilded silver threads. The Metropolitan Museum of Art, New York (41.190.80). Bequest of George Blumenthal, 1941.

Image credit: The Metropolitan Museum of Art, New York

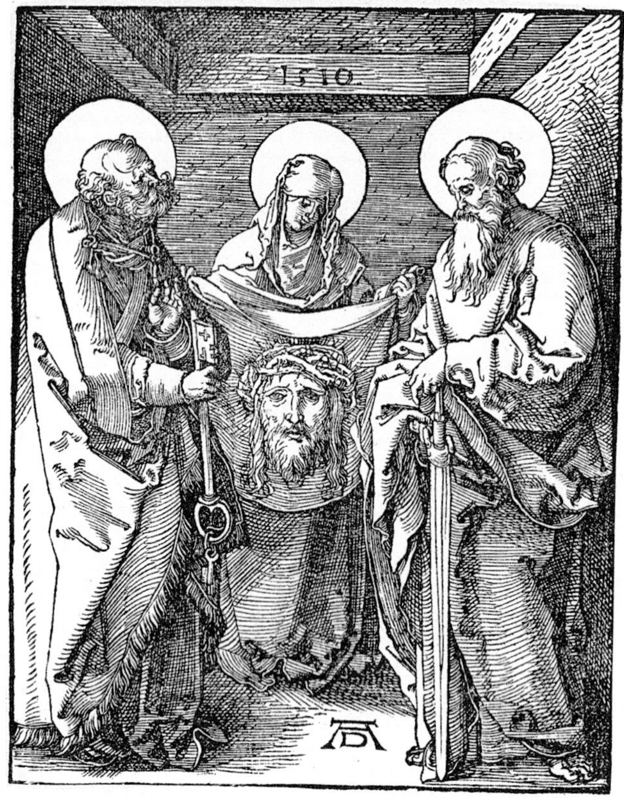

Figure 6.14 Albrecht Dürer (German, 1471–1528), *Saint Veronica between Saints Peter and Paul* from *The Small Passion*, 1510. Woodcut; 12.8 × 9.8 cm. The Metropolitan Museum of Art, New York (19.73.192). Gift of Junius Spencer Morgan 1919.
Image credit: The Metropolitan Museum of Art, New York

Whereas Dürer's face of Jesus is naturalistic, with his suffering implied by the crown of thorns, Ugo da Carpi's head with the tripartite hair and beard cut-out shape at the bottom edge derived from the *Mandylion* type.

The painting by Ugo da Carpi was placed near the ciborium of Pope Celestine III in New Saint Peter's basilica during the Jubilee Year of 1525, which was likely the occasion for the commission. In a clever reference to the veronica's status as an *acheiropoieton*, the artist signed the painting with the phrase: "*Per Vgo/da Carpi Intaiatore/ fata senza/penello*" (For Ugo da Carpi, woodcut engraver, made without a brush). Paradoxically, although signing the work with his name, he distanced himself as maker by identifying himself as a printmaker rather than a painter. Ugo da Carpi's claim that he made the work, which is his only extant painting, without a brush implied a miraculous production that paralleled the veronica's having been made without human hands.[53] Although Giorgio Vasari in his 1568 edition of his *Vite* had interpreted the signature phrase to mean that the artist had used his fingers rather than

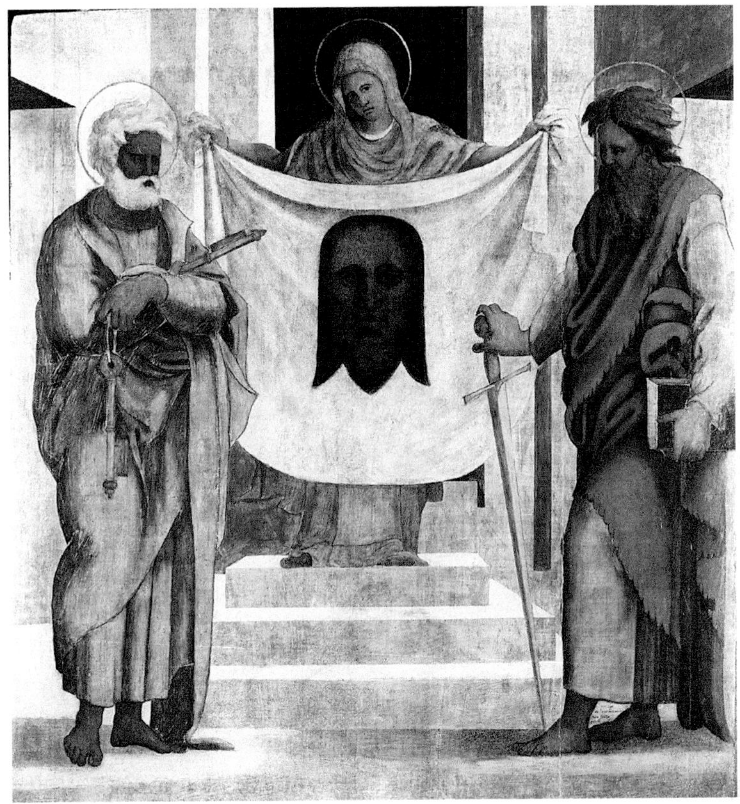

Figure 6.15 Ugo da Carpi (Bologna, c. 1480–1532), *Veronica with Saints Peter and Paul*, 1524–1527. Tempera on panel. Archivio della Fabbrica di San Pietro, Vatican.

Image credit: World Archive/Alamy Stock Photo

a brush to apply paint,[54] Blackwood (2013)'s study indicates that instead Ugo da Carpi relied on his skills as a wood engraver to create the design. Ugo da Carpi's painting is based on a *chiaroscuro* ink drawing by Parmigianino (Parma, 1503–1540), datable to 1524. The preparatory sketch, in the Gabinetto dei disegni e delle stampe at the Galleria degli Uffizi in Florence, is gridded for transfer and appears to be the compositional source for Ugo da Carpi's painting. In this regard, perhaps the elusive meaning of his signature furthermore alludes to a collaborative process with Parmigianino. Dürer, a printmaker and painter, also signed his woodcut with his hallmark AD monogram at the bottom. His placement of 1510 on a beam at the top implied the date was incised into the wood, also a clever play on the work's technique.

Another variation in this first category is Veronica within the broader subject of the *Sacra Conversazione* (Sacred Conversation), or holy gathering of saints, as for example Francesco Bissolo (Venetian, fl. 1492, d. 1554)'s *The Virgin and Child with Saints Michael and Veronica and Two Donors*, an oil on wood datable c. 1500–1525) in The National Gallery in London. The inclusion of Veronica in the *Sacra Conversazione* continued through the early eighteenth century, as exemplified by an oil on canvas of *Saints*

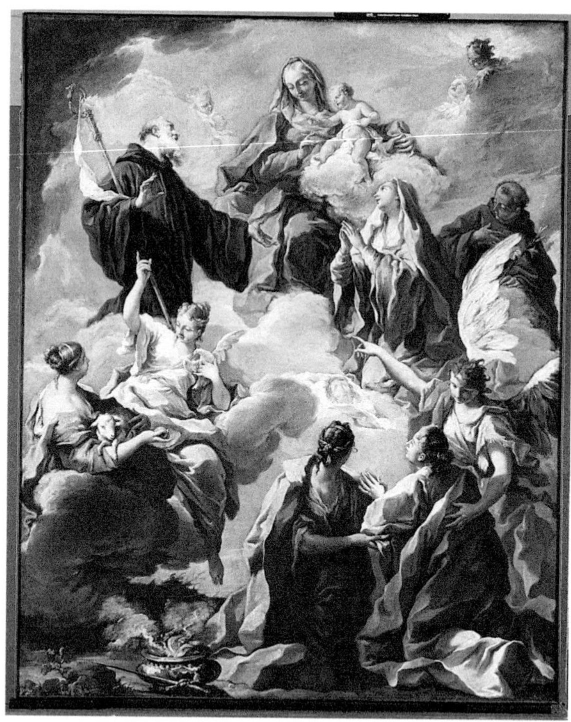

Figure 6.16 Giovanni Battista Pittoni (Venice, 1687–1767), *Saints Presenting a Devout Woman to the Virgin and Child*, c. 1720s. Oil on canvas; framed: 185 × 149 × 6.5 cm; unframed 172 x 135.5 cm. The Cleveland Museum of Art, Leonard C. Hanna, Jr. Fund, 1982.36.

Image credit: Courtesy of The Cleveland Museum of Art

Presenting a Devout Woman to the Virgin and Child by Giovanni Battista Pittoni (Venetian, 1687–1767), datable c. 1720s and in the Cleveland Museum of Art (Figure 6.16). An angel in the lower right corner presents a female donor, whose identity remains uncertain, to the Virgin and Child. Rendered *di sotto in su* (from below looking upwards) in a Rococo style, Mary is seated on billowing, cumulus clouds with several angels' heads peeking above them, features that indicate Mary's role as *Regina Coeli* (Queen of Heaven). Joining Mary to the donor in a circular pattern are Saints Lucy, Agnes, Scholastica, Benedict, Anthony of Padua, and Veronica (upper right).[55] Positioned directly under Mary's gaze and Christ's gesture of blessing, Veronica kneels in adoration with hands clasped in prayer, in a *locus* and pose that emphasize her role as intercessor. Her attribute of the *sudarium* that lays on a cloud visually connects the donor to Mary.

2. *The veronica within the context of other devotional imagery, such as the Man of Sorrows, Instruments of the Passion, and Mass of Saint Gregory*

In a second context, we can find the veronica inserted in (or juxtaposed with) imagery of the Man of Sorrows, the *Arma Christi*, and/or the Mass of Saint Gregory. The veronica placed behind or near a Man of Sorrows in a sepulcher indicates a pairing of image types that are both primarily devotional in function. Works of art with the veronica relic as subject had an early affiliation with Man of Sorrows imagery, as evident in the third colored drawing by Matthew Paris, which features the Holy Face alongside a Madonna and Child, plus an early version of the Man of Sorrows (Figure 6.2). Imagery that joined the veronica with the Man of Sorrows remained a favorite theme of the Franciscans, as exemplified in a fifteenth-century painting by Jacopo del Sellaio in the Hermitage in Saint Petersburg (Figure 6.17).

By 1400, the veronica had been incorporated into the *Arma Christi* (Instruments of Christ's Passion) in works of art. The impetus to depict the collective *Arma Christi* likely originated from the movement of relics from the Holy Land to the West, beginning in the sixth century and continuing through the end of the Crusades, as well as an interest in any indulgences associated with devotion to them.[56] The *Arma Christi* had initially appeared in Western art about 1100, without Byzantine precedents, as a limited number of essential objects (cross, crown of thorns, nails, and hammer) associated with the Crucifixion.[57] Depictions of these objects became particularly popular in French art during the twelfth and thirteenth centuries.[58] In the early fourteenth century, the *Arma Christi* remained limited in the number of objects included within the group, and their meaning focused on Christ's triumph over these obstacles (and thus over death). In the second half of the fourteenth century, however, there is a marked expansion of the *Arma Christi*, not only in the number of objects but moreover in

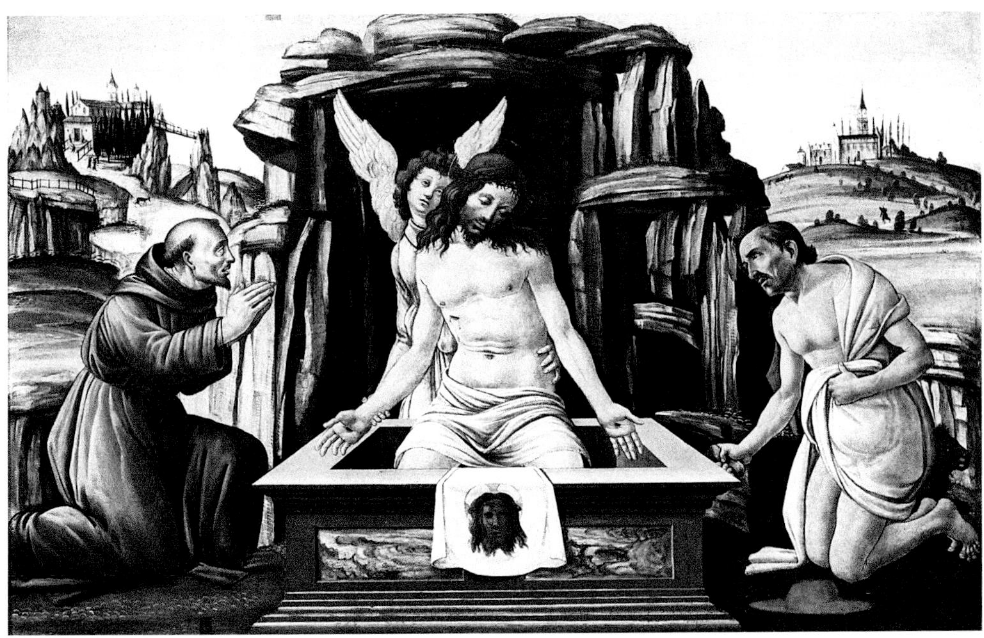

Figure 6.17 Jacopo del Sellaio (Florence, c. 1441–1493), *Lamentation over the Dead Christ with Saints Francis and Jerome*, fifteenth century. Tempera on panel. The State Hermitage Museum, Saint Petersburg.

Image credit: Prisma Archivo/Alamy Stock Photo

their role in the torture and suffering of Christ.[59] It is within this later expansion in scope of the *Arma Christi* that we find the beginning of the association of the veronica with the Instruments of the Passion, perhaps as a reminder of Christ's transcendence over death in spite of the use of these accessories to harm him.

From the thirteenth century forward, the Franciscans in Italy and the Levant encouraged viewing of the *Arma Christi* as a method of meditating on the suffering of Christ, a practice that may have paralleled or contributed to the development of the Stations of the Cross.[60] During the fifteenth and continuing through the seventeenth centuries, the Holy Face on a cloth had become a recurring object amidst a broad collection of artefacts aside from the cross: nails, hammer, pliers, ladder, rope,[61] whips, blindfold, column, rooster, spears, Judas's bag of coins, discarded and ripped garments, dice, spitting heads, ear of Malchus sometimes with a knife attached to it, the hands of Pilate in a basin with a ewer of water above it, horns or shofars, the superscription with INRI,[62] and various jeering and gesturing hands (Figure 6.4 is a previously mentioned example). The Holy Face among these objects associated with the Passion initially appears with eyes open and a placid mouth. But circa 1450, the visage changes to a state of anguish, with the suffering Christ bleeding and wearing a crown of thorns.

On the *Arma Christi*, the principal bibliography is Berliner (1955),[63] Schiller (1971–1972),[64] and more recently, Cooper and Denny-Brown (2014), who have edited a volume of critical essays dedicated to interpreting the *Arma Christi* as a group of items for devotion that indicates a fascination with the materiality of objects used during Christ's Passion.[65] The tools associated with the Crucifixion in art are typically spaced slightly apart from each other (without overlapping) and separated from any narrative context. The equipment is usually represented parallel to the picture plane in the form of a hovering vision or floating assemblage.[66] The *Arma* are shown grouped together as an invitation for viewers to meditate upon them collectively. The plethora of Early Modern works of art depicting the instruments indicates a belief in the power of objects to serve as intercessors.[67] A corollary poem about the *Arma Christi*, the Middle English "O Vernicle," datable to the early fifteenth century, employed individual images of each item to guide the devotional lyric poem that commenced with Veronica's veil, hence the title.[68] The purpose of the poem, which is in the format of a prayer roll, was likely to encourage readers to consider their own transgressions in relationship to specific instruments of the Passion as a sensorial approach to penitence, even as a kind of virtual pilgrimage.[69] Significantly, Newhauser and Russell (2014) tie the prayer roll and its depiction of the *Arma Christi* to liturgical Hours of the Cross and thus with prayer times throughout the day from Matins to Compline.[70]

The veronica among the Instruments of the Passion can be found frequently within the iconography of the Mass of Saint Gregory.[71] In this subject, which was common c. 1400–1550 in Germany, the Netherlands, France, and England,[72] the veronica can sometimes be found in place of (or near) the host on an altar. The Mass of Saint Gregory has been traditionally interpreted as a visual exposition of the doctrine of Transubstantiation, the transformation during the Eucharist of wine and bread into the blood and body of Christ. The Man of Sorrows appears in a vision to Pope Gregory I (called "Gregory the Great," papacy 590–604), frequently but not exclusively during the consecration of the host. When the subject was used for altarpieces, the theme may have been employed in part to assert the True Presence of Christ during the Eucharist. However, Bynum (2006) has noted that this subject evoked spiritual responses from the laity and clergy alike, in both private devotional settings (as in manuscript illuminations) and in places of communal worship (as on altarpieces). Works of art depicting the Mass of Saint Gregory were not solely didactic in purpose, nor were they intended to alleviate doubt or illustrate doctrine.[73] The primary intent was more likely to give visible form to holy objects, persons, deities, and events that otherwise could not be seen.[74] The inclusion of the Holy Face within the broader context of the Mass of Saint Gregory underscored the overarching purpose of the subject as largely to testify to the enduring presence of Christ, even, and perhaps especially, when invisible. Such themes were inherent in the imagery of Veronica and her *sudarium* as well.

Examples of works of art featuring the veronica in this category include:

- Master of Saint Veronica (fl. 1395–1415), *The Man of Sorrows between the Virgin and Saint Catherine of Alexandria*, 1400–1420. The Royal Museum of Fine Arts, Antwerp (Figure 3.5)
- Anonymous Flemish, *The Mass of Saint Gregory*, fifteenth century. Musée des Beaux-Arts de Tours (Figure 6.18)
- Spanish, perhaps Burgos or Segovia, *Mass of Saint Gregory* from a *Book of Hours* (Hours of Infante Don Alfonso of Castile), MS M. 854, fol. 225v., 1465–1480. The Morgan Library & Museum, New York (Plate 11)
- Workshop of the Master of the Augustine Altar, *Mass of Saint Gregory with Saints Catherine, Thomas Aquinas, Francis, and Vincent Ferrer*, c. 1490. Germanisches Nationalmuseum, Nuremberg.[75] This example shows a proximity of Saint Francis of Assisi to a veronica hanging on the sepulcher of Christ
- Flemish, from Antwerp, *Mass of Saint Gregory*, exterior panel of the *Passion Altar*, c. 1510–15. Lambertikirche, Aurich[76]
- Master of the Saint Bartholomew Altar, *Mass of Saint Gregory*, c. 1480–1495. Wallraf-Richartz-Museum, Cologne, on loan from Bischöflisches Museum, Trier[77]
- Master of the Aachen Altar, *Mass of Saint Gregory*, c. 1500. Rijksmuseum het Catharijneconvent, Utrecht[78]

3. *As a corollary scene within a larger narrative from the Passion*

Third, we can find Veronica depicted as a corollary figure within a larger narrative episode from the Passion cycle. Veronica's introduction into art of the Passion occurs about 1400 and continues through the fifteenth and sixteenth centuries.[79] The Carrying of the Cross and the Crucifixion are the most common scenes in which Veronica is included as a subordinate character, yet she also appears occasionally in a Deposition or Entombment. In relationship to the central narrative scene with Christ as protagonist, Veronica is usually shown smaller in scale and placed to one side of the main action.

Derbes's seminal book (1996) correlates Franciscan ideologies with changes in the iconography of the Passion in Italian works of art during the mid-thirteenth century. Her study convincingly presents reasons why the Franciscans embraced and promoted the Way to Calvary as a principal subject for panels and frescoes.[80] Duecento artists redesigned certain events in the Passion by choosing idioms from Northern-European and Byzantine prototypes that underscored the Franciscan mission.[81] For example, a new motif in the art of the mid-thirteenth century is an enlarged cross; a continuation of this theme is apparent in Plates 5, 13 and Figures 6.7, 6.23. Secondly, there is

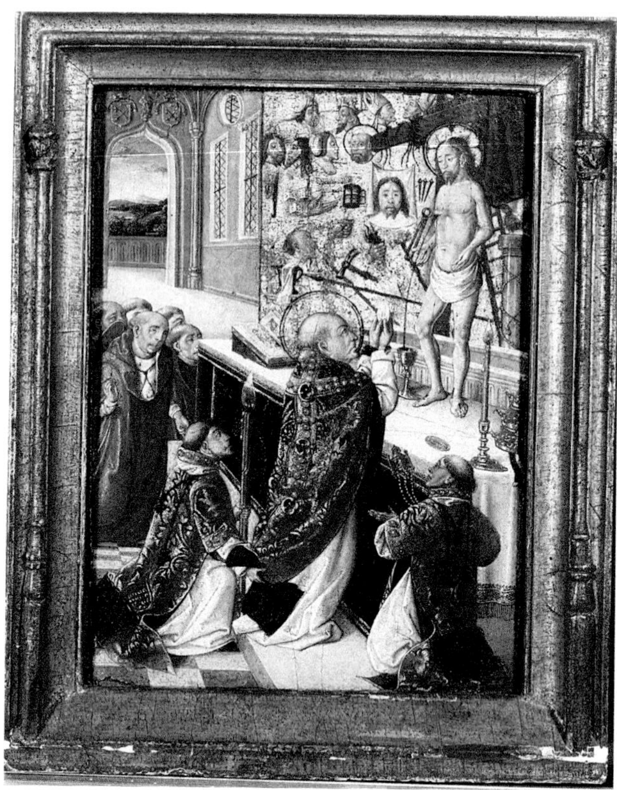

Figure 6.18 Anonymous Flemish, *The Mass of Saint Gregory*, fifteenth century. Tempera and gold leaf on wood. Musée des Beaux-Arts de Tours.

Image credit: © Musée des Beaux-Arts de Tours

a demonstrative emphasis on Christ's frailty and fatigue, as evident in his faltering stance.[82] The stumbling pose can be found in late Byzantine art, but the choice to focus on this aspect of his suffering in the visual arts dates to the mid-thirteenth century. The shift to a more expressive style for the subject of Christ Carrying the Cross cannot be attributed to a single source; rather, it reflects an eclectic blend of eastern and western motifs.[83] In general, the rise of Franciscan cultural hegemony resulted in a heightened pathos in images of Christ.[84] Bonaventure, the thirteenth-century Franciscan theologian, philosopher, and biographer of Francis, in his *Lignum vitae* (Wood of Life),[85] had emphasized the theme of Christ Carrying the Cross.[86] The Franciscans frequently commissioned, made, or promoted works of art depicting this subject because it underscored his humanity and suffering. Moreover, the iconography evoked the verse on which the Franciscan Rule of the Order was founded,[87] Matthew 16:24: "Then Jesus told his disciples, 'If any want to become my followers, let them deny themselves and take up their cross and follow me.'"[88] Beginning with Pope Urban II (papacy 1088–1099), this verse was used to justify those who participated in the Crusades, and the passage contributed to a culture of crusader fervor and rhetoric.[89]

Selected examples in this category in approximate chronological order include:

- Lorch in the Rhine Valley, *Christ bearing the Cross*, c. 1425. Terra-cotta with remnants of polychromy. Staatliche Museen zu Berlin, Skulpturensammlung und Museum für Byzantinische Kunst (Figure 6.19 and Plate 12)
- Rogier Van der Weyden, *Crucifixion Triptych with Mary Magdalene, Veronica, and donors*, 1440–1445. Kunsthistorisches Museum, Vienna (Figure 6.20)
- Biagio d'Antonio, *Christ Carrying the Cross*, 1466. Musée du Louvre, Paris
- Bavarian, *Veronica* (left) *in a fragment from an altarpiece of the Crucifixion*, c. 1480, lindenwood. Staatliche Museen zu Berlin, Skulpturensammlung und Museum für Byzantinische Kunst (Figure 6.21)
- Martin Schongauer, *The Bearing of the Cross with Saint Veronica*, late fifteenth century. Engraving. The Metropolitan Museum of Art, New York. This one is interesting because the image of the cross-carrying Christ wears a crown of thorns, but the Holy Face on Veronica's cloth does not.[90] (Figure 6.22)
- Netherlandish, *Baluster Column with Veronica meeting Christ during the Carrying of the Cross*, c. 1500. Staatliche Museen zu Berlin, Skulpturensammlung und Museum für Byzantinische Kunst (Figure 6.23)
- Albrecht Dürer, *Christ Carrying the Cross* from *The Passion*, 1512. Engraving. The Metropolitan Museum of Art (Figure 6.24)
- Giovanni Francesco Caroto, *The Entombment of Christ*, 1510. Samuel H. Kress Collection, Portland Art Museum, Portland, Oregon

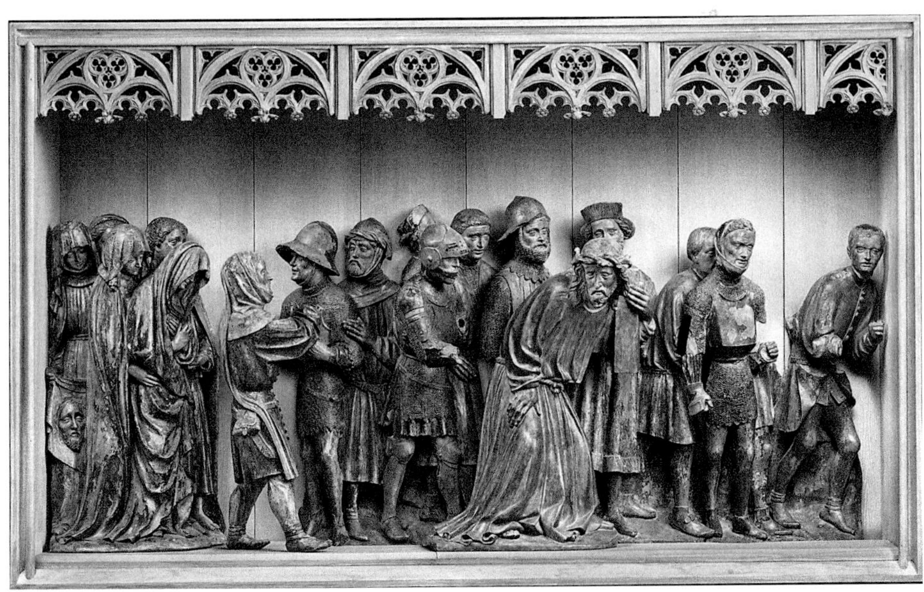

Figure 6.19 Lorch in the Rhine Valley, *Christ bearing the Cross*, c. 1425. Terra-cotta with remnants of polychromy. Staatliche Museen zu Berlin, Skulpturensammlung und Museum für Byzantinische Kunst (Inv. 8499). For a detail of Veronica, see Plate 12.

Image credit: Staatliche Museen zu Berlin – Preußischer Kulturbesitz. Skulpturensammlung und Museum für Byzantinische Kunst. Photos: A. Voigt, Berlin

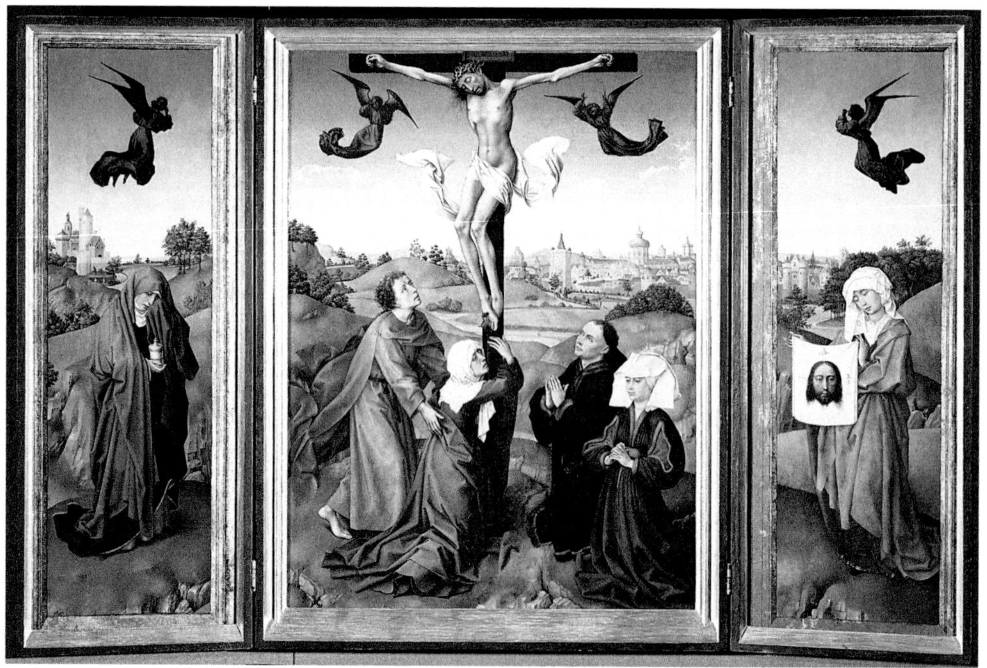

Figure 6.20 Rogier Van der Weyden (Netherlandish, c. 1399/1400–1464), *Crucifixion Triptych with Mary Magdalene, Veronica, and donors*, 1440–1445. Kunsthistorisches Museum, Vienna.

Image credit: Erich Lessing/Art Resource, NY

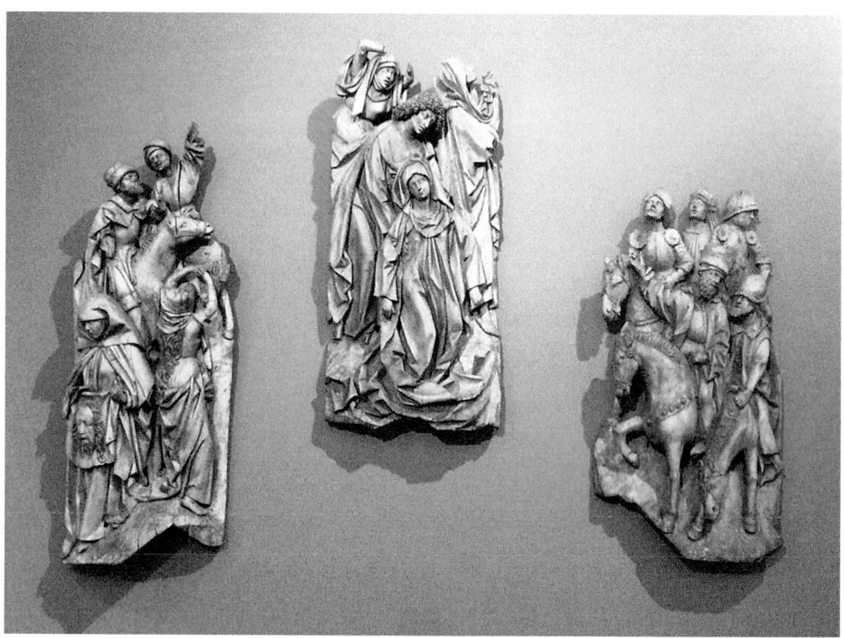

Figure 6.21 Bavarian, *Veronica (left) in a fragment from an altarpiece of the Crucifixion*, c. 1480. Lindenwood. Staatliche Museen zu Berlin, Skulpturensammlung und Museum für Byzantinische Kunst.

Image credit: Author

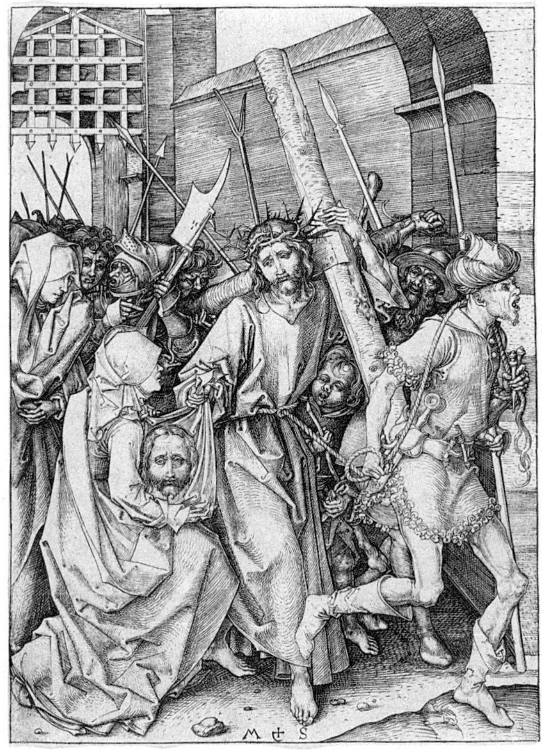

Figure 6.22 Martin Schongauer (Colmar, c. 1450/53–1491), *The Bearing of the Cross with Saint Veronica*, late fifteenth century. Engraving; 16.3 x 11.5 cm (sheet). The Metropolitan Museum of Art, New York. Harris Brisbane Dick Fund, 1928.

Image credit: The Metropolitan Museum of Art, New York

- Master of Antwerp, *Christ Carrying the Cross*, beginning of the sixteenth century. Strahov Gallery, Prague
- Follower of Hieronymus Bosch, *Christ Carrying the Cross*, 1510–1535. Oil on panel. Museum of Fine Arts, Ghent
- Giovanni de' Busi Cariani, *Carrying of the Cross with Saint Veronica*, c. 1523–1525. Private Collection
- Pontormo, *Deposition*, 1528. Santa Felicità, Florence
- Girolamo Muziano, *Veronica*, 1557. Oil on canvas. Altar of the Immaculate Conception, Duomo of Orvieto, Museo dell'Opera del Duomo, Orvieto
- Jacopo Bassano, *The Way to Calvary*, 1544–1545. Oil on canvas. The National Gallery, London
- Jan Collaert II (Flemish), *Christ Carrying the Cross and the Miracle of Veronica's Sudarium*, Plate 23 from the series *The Passion, Death, and Resurrection of our Lord Jesus Christ*, 1580–1587. Engraving. The British Museum, London
- Federico Zuccari, *The Encounter of Christ and Veronica on the Way to Calvary*, 1594. Oil on panel. Basilica of S. Prassede, Rome[91]

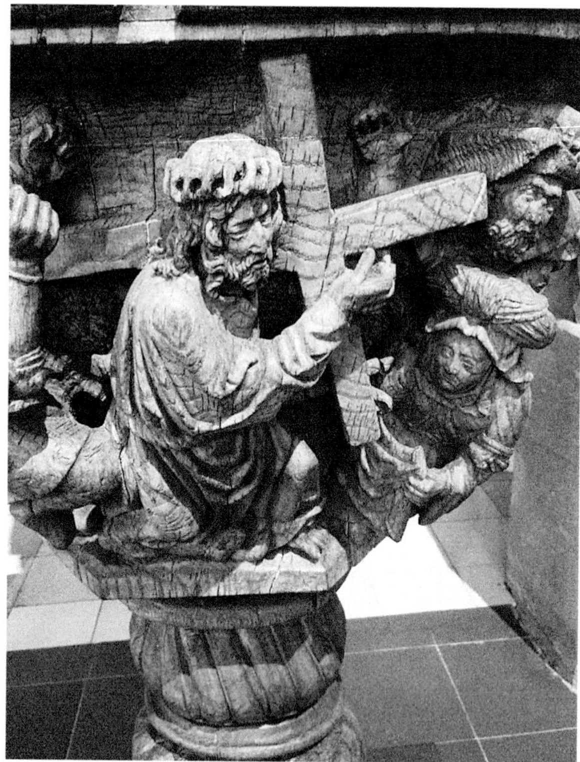

Figure 6.23 Netherlandish, *Baluster Column with Veronica meeting Christ during the Carrying of the Cross*, c. 1500. Staatliche Museen zu Berlin, Skulpturensammlung und Museum für Byzantinische Kunst.

Image credit: Author

- Pieter Brueghel the Younger (1564–1838), *Carrying of the Cross*, 1606. Gemäldegalerie, Berlin (Plate 13)
- Peter Paul Rubens, *Carrying of the Cross*, 1537. Oil on canvas
- Jacob Jordaens, *Christ Carrying the Cross*, 1660. Oil on canvas. Rijksmuseum, Amsterdam

4. *Within the Stations of the Cross*

In this fourth context, Veronica offering her cloth becomes incorporated into the Stations of the Cross, as discussed at length in Chapters 3 and 4. At its core, the Stations of the Cross derive from an expansion of the theme of Christ Carrying the Cross. As the protagonist of an independent Sixth Station, Veronica serves as an eyewitness to Christ's last hours of suffering, offers him a token of comfort, and reinforces the sympathetic roles of other women in the Passion series. A few noteworthy examples, in addition to the ones mentioned prior, include:

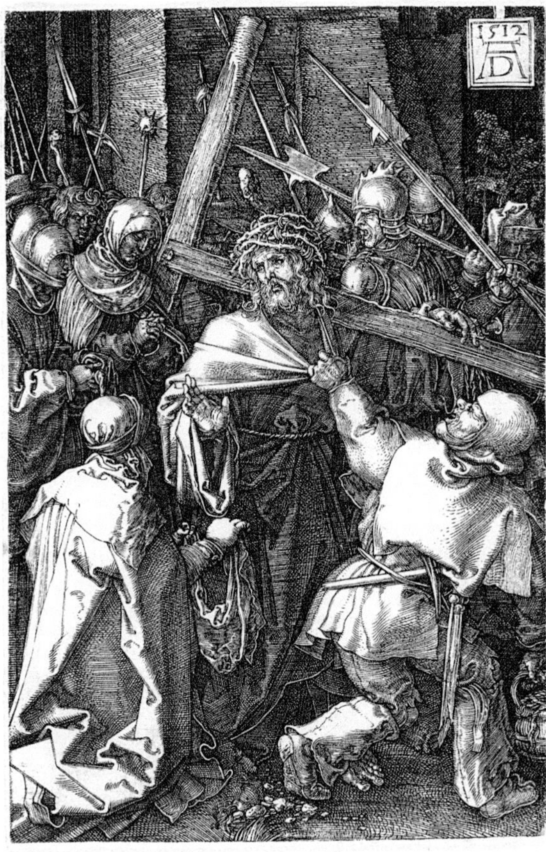

Figure 6.24 Albrecht Dürer (German, 1471–1528), *Christ Carrying the Cross* from *The Passion*, 1512. Engraving; 11.6 x 7.4 cm (sheet). The Metropolitan Museum of Art, New York (59.534.49). Bequest of Alexandrine Sinsheimer, 1959.

Image credit: The Metropolitan Museum of Art, New York

- *Veronica*, Station VI of the *Bamberger Kreuzweg*, 1503. Bavaria, Germany
- South Netherlandish (Brussels), *The Way to Calvary with Saint Veronica Receiving the Veil Imprinted with the Face of Christ*, c. 1510. Walnut, paint, and gilding. The Metropolitan Museum of Art, New York (Figure 6.25)
- Workshop of Jacques Dubroeucq, *Christ Carrying the Cross with Saints Simon and Veronica,* c. 1545. Alabaster. Cleveland Museum of Art (Figure 6.7)

5. *The relic of the Holy Face as an independent focus of devotion*

In a fifth and final role, the relic is exhibited alone, with a focus on the Holy Face and without the accompanying female character. The upper corners of the cloth are sometimes held up by a pair of angels; if present, they are usually rendered in symmetrical, mirror-image poses that flank the central relic and guide

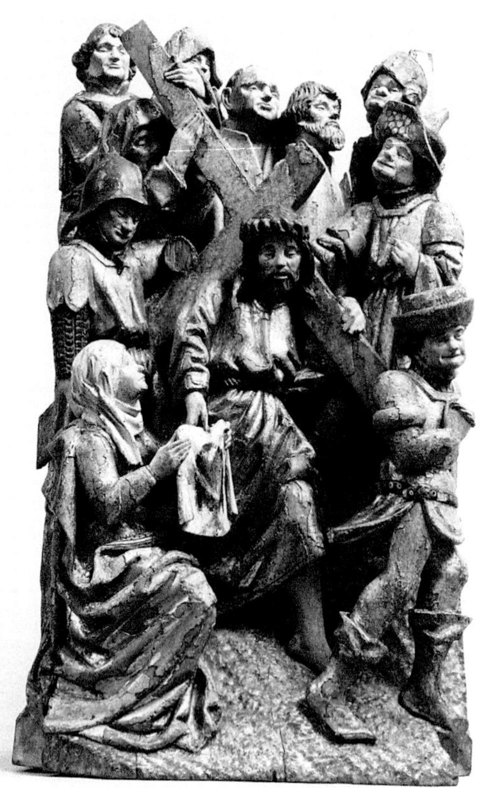

Figure 6.25 South Netherlandish (Brussels), *The Way to Calvary with Saint Veronica Receiving the Veil Imprinted with the Face of Christ*, c. 1510. Walnut, paint, and gilding; 49.5 x 26.4 x 20 cm. The Metropolitan Museum of Art, New York (15.12). Rogers Fund, 1915.

Image credit: The Metropolitan Museum of Art, New York

viewers' attention toward it. However, late renditions of this type are more likely to represent the holy cloth completely alone such that the image of Christ's visage is the sole point of devotion. In this context, the veil as *vera icon* was often placed on the *predella* or the reverse of freestanding retables. By the mid-seventeenth century, renditions of the Holy Face had become particularly expressive, with an aim toward hyperrealism, as evident in late versions by Domenico Fetti (Rome, c. 1589–1623) (Plate 14) and Claude Mellan (French, 1598–1688) (Figure 6.26).

Fetti's *The Veil of Veronica*, datable c. 1618–1622 and in the National Gallery of Art, Washington, catches viewers' attention immediately with the tactile quality of the cloth, which hangs from a bar at the top. Implied light from the left sharply models Christ's face such that it seems to protrude from the cloth. The earth tones of the head lend a human quality to Christ's otherwise spectral countenance, an effect heightened by the head's superimposition onto the icy hues of the cloth. The combined use of highlights and shadows on the folds, as well as the frayed selvages of the fabric, demonstrates a *trompe l'oeil* (fool the eye) effect. Fetti was in Rome in 1606 when the veronica relic

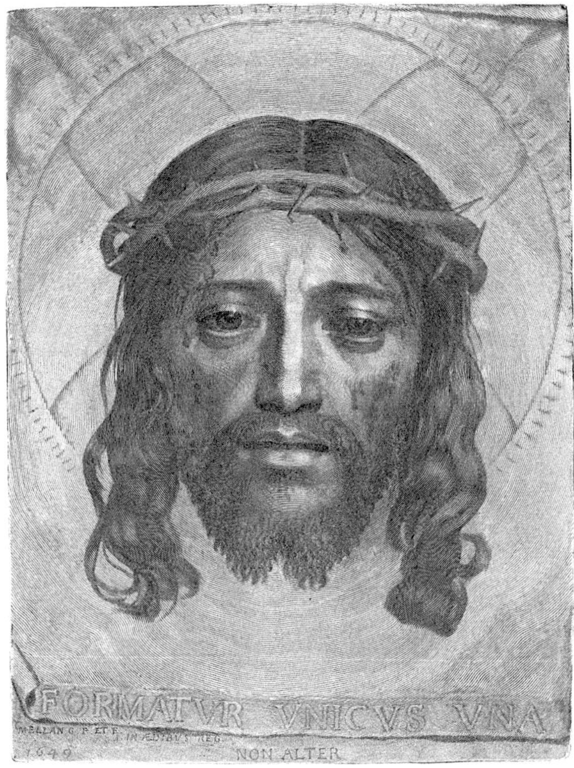

Figure 6.26 Claude Mellan (French, 1598–1688), *The Sudarium of Saint Veronica*, 1649. Engraving. National Gallery of Art, Washington (1943.3.6144). Rosenwald Collection.

Image credit: National Gallery of Art, Washington

was on view in the crossing of New Saint Peter's basilica. The painter's sensitivity to this subject may be a result of his own experiences. Fetti's acute attention to details in the face and *sudarium* resulted in a painting that could be perceived as a "true image of a true image." In this manner, the votive image mirrors the role of the painter.[92]

In Mellan's engraving, *The Sudarium of Saint Veronica* of 1649 in the National Gallery of Art, Washington, the artist deftly incised the image, using a single line. The artist's painstaking care in delineating each lock of hair, the heavily lidded eyes, and even the halo and background, points to an interest in realism also, yet in a more restrained style than that of Fetti. Mellan's technical mastery entices viewers to peer closely at the surface and to marvel at his controlled line that models the head in a way that conjures responses of compassion.

Additional examples in this category in approximate chronological order include:

- North Italian (Veneto?), *Capital with Angels holding the Veil of Saint Veronica*, c. 1325–1375. The Metropolitan Museum of Art, New York
- Wilhelm Kalteysen (from Aachen, active in Wroclaw, c. 1420–1496), *The Veil of Veronica (Vera Icon)*, c. 1450. Tempera on silver plate on spruce wood, 72 x 52 cm. National Museum in Wroclaw, Poland

- Bartholomäus Zeitblom (German, 1455/60–1518/22), *Veronica's Veil Held by Two Angels*, 1496. Staatliche Museen zu Berlin, Gemäldegalerie (Figure 4.8)
- Italian (Milan), *Veronica's Veil*, late fifteenth century, gold and enamel medallion, diameter 5.7 cm. The Metropolitan Museum of Art, New York
- German, *Veil of Veronica Held by Two Angels* (part of a *predella*?), c. 1500. Staatliche Museen zu Berlin, Skulpturensammlung und Museum für Byzantinische Kunst (Plate 9)
- French, *Angel with a Veil of Veronica*, c. 1500, oak with traces of paint. The Metropolitan Museum of Art, New York
- Albrecht Dürer, *The Sudarium displayed by two Angels*, 1513. Engraving. The Metropolitan Museum of Art, New York (Figure 6.27)
- Francisco de Zurbarán (Spanish, 1598–1664), *The Veil of Saint Veronica*, c. 1635. Oil on canvas, 69.9 x 51.1 cm. National Museum, Stockholm
- Philippe de Champaigne (1602–1674), *Le Voile de Véronique*, mid-seventeenth century. Musée des Beaux-Arts, Caen[93]

The legacy of this last role is evident in the iconography of the Head (or Face) of Christ. This genre shares more with portraiture than with representations of sacred

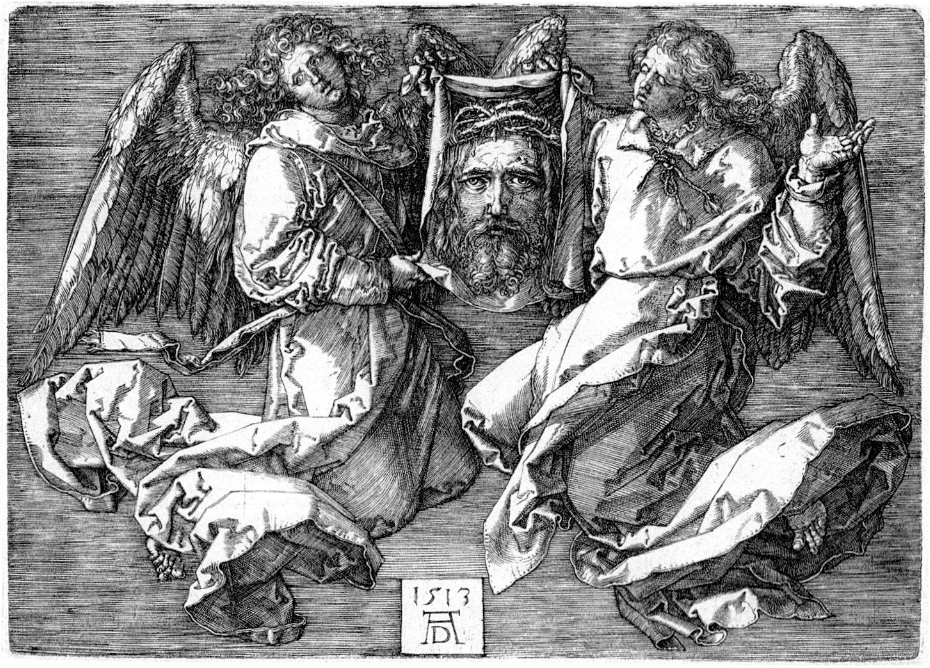

Figure 6.27 Albrecht Dürer, *Sudarium displayed by two Angels,* 1513. Engraving; 9.8 x 13.8 cm (plate). The Metropolitan Museum of Art, New York (19.73.31), Fletcher Fund, 1919.

Image credit: The Metropolitan Museum of Art, New York

artefacts. Northern-European paintings in oil especially tend toward a realism meant to heighten the veracity of the Holy Face as a focal point of devotion. Two key works called *Head of Christ* that exemplify this legacy of images of the veronica include a painting attributed to the workshop of Rogier van der Weyden (Netherlandish, c. 1399/1400–1464) in the National Gallery in London and a painting by Petrus Christus (active by 1444–d. 1472/73), datable to the mid-fifteenth century, in the Metropolitan Museum of Art in New York.[94] In a singular twist to this theme, Petrus Christus also painted a *Portrait of a Young Man* that includes in the upper right corner, as if affixed to a wall in a room, a Holy Face with the *Salve sancta facies* prayer underneath it.[95] With the Holy Face and prayer serving as the unidentified sitter's attributes, Christus portrayed the man as a devout Christian who is spiritually prepared to meet his maker.

In reviewing the five roles in which Veronica and her cloth are depicted in works of art during the Early Modern period, we notice several leitmotifs, such as her youth, standing or kneeling pose, extension of the arms, downward gaze, modest dress with a veil or turban, pale complexion, and the two-dimensionality of the cloth. One salient attribute that changed over time is the shape of Christ's face. Initially shown as a bust, it evolved into a disc. Likewise, the addition of a crown of thorns, blood, and an expression of pain and anguish to Christ's face on Veronica's veil occurs around 1450. Images of Veronica and her relic generally fall into one of these five contexts, each of which emphasized different theological or sacramental connotations. Sources for the various guises of Veronica and her veil stem from other known icons of Christ in Rome, a fluid exchange of ideas with religious theater, and the Franciscans' interest in promoting affective piety among pilgrims to the Levant and urban populations in the West.

Notes

1 On types of self-portraiture in the Renaissance, see Katherine T. Brown, *The Painter's Reflection: Self-portraiture in Renaissance Venice, 1458–1625* (Florence: Leo S. Olschki Press, 2000). On paintings within paintings, see Ian Verstegen, "Between Presence and Perspective: The Portrait-in-a-Picture in Early Modern Painting," in *Zeitschrift für Kunstgeschichte* 71 (2008): 513–526.

2 On images of saints and their purposes, see Teodoro De Giorgio, "Le Icone archetipiche dei santi nell'alto Medioevo: origine, funzione e percezione di una specifica tipologia di ritratto 'dal vero' e 'a somiglianza' dell'effigiato," in *Intorno al ritratto: origini, sviluppi e trasformazioni*, eds. Fabrizio Crivello and Laura Zamparo in collaboration with Federica Boràgina, 93–98 (Torino: Accademia University Press, 2019).

3 For a condensed history of Veronica and the veronica in English art and the writings of English pilgrims to Rome, see Barry Windeatt, "'Vera Icon'? The Variable Veronica of Medieval England," in *The European Fortune of the Roman Veronica in the Middle Ages, Convivium Supplementum*, eds. A. Murphy, H. L. Kessler, M. Petoletti, E. Duffy, and G. Milanese, 58–71 (Turnhout, Belgium: Brepols Publishers, 2017).

4 Suzanne Lewis, *The Art of Matthew Paris*, 127.

5 Ibid., 126.

6 Ibid., 128. See also Connolly, "Imagined Pilgrimage," 598–622.

7 Gervase of Tilbury, *Otia* Imperialia, 604–607. Suzanne Lewis, *The Art of Matthew Paris,* 129.

8 Suzanne Lewis, *The Art of Matthew Paris*, 126–127, 130.

9 For more on the legacy of Matthew Paris's rendition of the Holy Face, see Edgar Breitenbach, "The Tree of Bigamy and the Veronica Image of St. Peter's," *Art Institute of Chicago Museum Studies* 9 (1978): 30–38, Figures 1, 3, and 6.

10 Otto Pächt, "The 'Avignon Diptych' and Its Eastern Ancestry," in *De Artibus Opuscula XL: Essays in Honor of Erwin Panofsky*, vol. I, edited by Millard Meiss, 402–421 (New York: New York University Press, 1961).
11 Ibid., 406.
12 Ibid., 407–409.
13 Ibid., 409.
14 Nigel Morgan, "'Veronica' Images and the Office of the Holy Face in Thirteenth-Century England," in *The European Fortune of the Roman Veronica in the Middle Ages, Convivium Supplementum*, eds. A. Murphy, H. L. Kessler, M. Petoletti, E. Duffy, and G. Milanese, 84–99 (Turnhout, Belgium: Brepols Publishers, 2017).
15 Ann Van Dijk,"The Veronica, the *Vultus Christi* and the veneration of icons in medieval Rome," 250.
16 For an in-depth presentation of the use of relief and impressions to disseminate images of the veronica, see Aden Kumler, "*Signatis ... vultus tui*: (Re) impressing the Holy Face before and after the European Cult of the Veronica," in *The European Fortune of the Roman Veronica in the Middle Ages, Convivium Supplementum*, eds. A. Murphy, H. L. Kessler, M. Petoletti, E. Duffy, and G. Milanese, 102–113 (Turnhout, Belgium: Brepols Publishers, 2017).
17 Goodwin, *The Anglo-Saxon Legends,* viii.
18 Hand, *Hans Memling's Saint John the Baptist and Saint Veronica*. About Veronica on pilgrims' badges, see also André Chastel, "La Véronique," *Revue de l'art*, 40–41 (1978).
19 The gold ducat features the papal arms on the obverse and Veronica with cloth on the reverse. A photograph of both sides is published in Arthur L. Friedberg and Ira S. Friedberg, *Gold Coins of the World from Ancient Times to the Present*, 9th ed. (Williston, VT: Coin and Currency Institute, 2017), 773, Figure 20. I wish to thank Robert D. Leonard, Jr. for sharing with me his knowledge of numismatics and of this ducat in particular.
20 The *Mirabilia urbis Romae* was written c. 1143 by Master Benedict, a canon at Saint Peter's basilica. For the Latin with English translation, see Master Benedict, *The Marvels of Rome: Mirabilia urbis Romae*, 2nd ed., trans. and ed. Francis Morgan Nichols with introduction by Eileen Gardiner (New York: Italica Press, Inc., 1986). See also Dale Kinney, "Fact and Fiction in the *Mirabilia urbis Romae*," in *Roma Felix–Formation and Reflection of Medieval Rome*, eds. Éamonn Ó Carragain and Carol L. Neuman de Vegvar, 235–252 (Burlington, VT: Ashgate Publishing Company, 2007). For a later version, *The Ostension of the Sudarium*, a woodcut from the 1511 edition, see Scott, "Seeing the Shroud," 628, Figure 23.
21 Pearson, *Die Fronica*, 74.
22 Herbert L. Kessler, "Introduction: The Literary Warp and Artistic Weft of Veronica's Cloth," in *The European Fortune of the Roman Veronica in the Middle Ages, Convivium Supplementum*, eds. A. Murphy, H. L. Kessler, M. Petoletti, E. Duffy, and G. Milanese, 12–30, 22 (Turnhout, Belgium: Brepols Publishers, 2017).
23 For a comprehensive online database of images of Veronica searchable by iconographic feature, location with map, and century, see Il Volto Ritrovato (association), *Veronica Route*, accessed July 18, 2018, www.veronicaroute.com.
24 Pearson, *Die Fronica*.
25 Raffaella Zardoni, Emanuela Bossi, and Amanda Murphy, "The Iconography of the Roman Veronica. From the Repertoires of Karl Pearson to Veronica Route," in *The European Fortune of the Roman Veronica in the Middle Ages, Convivium Supplementum*, eds. A. Murphy, H. L. Kessler, M. Petoletti, E. Duffy, and G. Milanese, 286–301 (Turnhout, Belgium: Brepols Publishers, 2017).
26 Katherine T. Brown, *Mary of Mercy in Medieval and Renaissance Italian Art,* 21–47 (Chapter 1 on pose and gesture).
27 Kamal Boullata, "To Measure Jerusalem: Explorations of the Square," *Journal of Palestine Studies* 28 (1999): 83–91, 87.
28 Flora Lewis, "The Veronica: Image, Legend and Viewer," 100.
29 Ibid., 101.
30 Alexa Sand, *Vision, Devotion, and Self-Representation in Late Medieval Art* (New York: Cambridge University Press, 2014): 36–38. Sand expounds upon this narrative at length.
31 Flora Lewis, "The Veronica: Image, Legend and Viewer," 104.

32 Julian of Norwich, *Revelations of Divine Love*, trans. Barry Windeatt (Oxford: Oxford University Press, 2016), 53–54.
33 Zardoni, Bossi, and Murphy, "The Iconography of the Roman Veronica," 288–289.
34 Ibid., 299.
35 N. H. J. Zwijnenburg, *Die Veronicagestalt in den deutschen Passionsspielen des 15. und 16. Jahrhunderts* (Amsterdam: Rodopi, 1988).
36 Réau, *Iconographie,* vol. 1, 258–259. Réau clarifies that the word *mysteries* used in reference to religious drama does not derive from the Latin *mysterium*, meaning mystery, but rather from a confusion with the word *ministerium*, meaning ministry or ceremony.
37 Ibid., 259.
38 Ibid., 261.
39 Ibid., 261, 264.
40 Ibid., 264.
41 Émile Mâle, *L'Art Religieux de la Fin du Moyen Age en France* (Paris: Librairie Armand Colin, 1925), http://archive.org. See Chapter 2: "L'Art et le Theatre Religieux," especially 64. Other scenes in the life of Christ depicted in works of art that were inspired or influenced by liturgical theater, according to Mâle, include the Nativity, Adoration of the Shepherds, Passion, Last Supper, Resurrection, among others, 509.
42 Réau, vol. 3, 1314. Réau offers this opinion in his rebuttal to Mâle.
43 Laura Weigert, *French Visual Culture and the Making of Medieval Theater* (New York: Cambridge University Press, 2015), 161–164.
44 Ibid., 161.
45 Ibid., 163.
46 Ibid.
47 Ibid., 131–132.
48 Ford, ed., *La Vengeance de Nostre-Seigneur.*
49 Weigert, *French Visual Culture and the Making of Medieval Theater*, 133–135, and Figures 91–92.
50 Bonaventure, *The Life of Saint Francis,* 110–111. See also Hammond, Hellmann, and Goff, *A Companion to Bonaventure*; and Cullen, *Bonaventure.*
51 This fresco, one of the earliest representations of Veronica holding the cloth, is a key example from the region of Lombardy, which is particularly rich in Veronica iconography. See Stefano Candiani, "The Iconography of the Veronica in the Region of Lombardy: Thirteenth- fourteenth Centuries," in *The European Fortune of the Roman Veronica in the Middle Ages, Convivium Supplementum*, eds. A. Murphy, H. L. Kessler, M. Petoletti, E. Duffy, and G. Milanese, 260–273 (Turnhout, Belgium: Brepols Publishers, 2017).
52 Galeries nationales du Grand Palais, Paris, *L'Art au temps des rois maudits: Philippe le Bel et ses fils, 1285–1328* (Paris: Réunion des Musées Nationaux, 1998), 104–107, Cat. 53.
53 Nicole Blackwood, "Printmaker as Painter: Looking Closely at Ugo da Carpi's *Saint Veronica Altarpiece*," *Oxford Art Journal* 36 (2013): 167–184.
54 Vasari's description of the painting and its inscription is as follows: "Now since, as I have said, he [Ugo da Carpi] was a painter, I must not omit to tell that he painted in oils, without using a brush, but with his fingers, and partly, also, with other bizarre instruments of his own, an altar-piece which is on the altar of the Volto Santo in Rome. Upon this altar-piece, being one morning with Michelangelo at that altar to hear Mass, I saw an inscription saying that Ugo da Carpi had painted it without a brush; and I laughed and showed the inscription to Michelangelo, who answered, also with a laugh, that it would have been better if he had used a brush, for then he might have done it in a better manner." Giorgio Vasari, *Lives of the Painters, Sculptors and Architects*, vol. 2, trans. Gaston du C. de Vere (New York: Alfred A. Knopf, 1996), 89.
55 Cleveland Museum of Art, wall text, visited May 5, 2019.
56 Gertrud Schiller, *Iconography of Christian Art*, vol. 2, trans. Janet Seligman (Greenwich, CT: New York Graphic Society, 1971–1972), 184–230.
57 Derbes, *Picturing the Passion,* 121.
58 Ibid.
59 Richard G. Newhauser and Arthur J. Russell, "Mapping Virtual Pilgrimage in an Early Fifteenth-Century *Arma Christi* Roll," in *The Arma Christi in Medieval and Early Modern*

Material Culture: with a critical edition of "O Vernicle," eds. Lisa H. Cooper and Andrea Denny-Brown, 83–112 (Burlington, VT: Ashgate Publishing Company, 2014), 86.

60 Schiller, *Iconography of Christian Art*, vol. 2, 190–191; Lisa H. Cooper, and Andrea Denny-Brown, introduction to *The Arma Christi in Medieval and Early Modern Material Culture: with a critical edition of "O Vernicle,"* eds. Lisa H. Cooper and Andrea Denny-Brown (Burlington, VT: Ashgate Publishing Company, 2014), 6; and Newhauser and Russell, "Mapping Virtual Pilgrimage," 84.

61 On the addition and significance of the ladder and rope to the *Arma Christi*, see Derbes, *Picturing the Passion,* Chapter 5 on "The Way to Calvary," especially 123.

62 INRI is an acronym for the Latin phrase: *Iesus Nazarenus, Rex Iudaeorum* (Jesus of Nazareth, the King of the Jews). According to John 19:20–21, Pilate had put this inscription, written in Hebrew, Latin and Greek, on Jesus's cross during his execution.

63 Rudolf Berliner, "Arma Christi," *Münchner Jahrbuch der bildenden Kunst* 6 (1955): 35–116.

64 Schiller, *Iconography of Christian Art*, vol. 2, 184–230.

65 Lisa H. Cooper and Andrea Denny-Brown, eds., *The Arma Christi in Medieval and Early Modern Material Culture: with a critical edition of "O Vernicle"* (Burlington, VT: Ashgate Publishing Company, 2014), with additional bibliography.

66 Ibid., 4. Newhauser and Russell, "Mapping Virtual Pilgrimage," 87; and Schiller, *Iconography of Christian Art*, vol. 1, 184.

67 Cooper and Denny-Brown, introduction to *The Arma Christi in Medieval and Early Modern Material Culture*, 2.

68 See Ann Eljenholm Nichols, "O Vernicle: A Critical Edition," in *The Arma Christi in Medieval and Early Modern Material Culture: with a critical edition of "O Vernicle,"* eds. Lisa H. Cooper and Andrea Denny-Brown (Burlington, VT: Ashgate Publishing Company, 2014): 354–355.

69 Cooper and Denny Brown, introduction to *The Arma Christi in Medieval and Early Modern Material Culture*, 13; and Newhauser and Russell, "Mapping Virtual Pilgrimage," 83–112, especially 99–101.

70 Newhauser and Russell, "Mapping Virtual Pilgrimage," 88–90. The authors parallel the sequence of the text of the roll with the Stations of the Cross, the liturgical Hours of the Cross, and a Middle English poem, "The Stations of Jerusalem," 107.

71 Caroline Walker Bynum, "Seeing and Seeing Beyond: The Mass of St. Gregory in the fifteenth Century," in *The Mind's Eye: Art and Theological Argument in the Middle Ages*, eds. Jeffrey Hamburger and Anne-Marie Bouché, 208–240 (Princeton, NJ: Princeton University Press, 2006).

72 Ibid., 208.

73 Ibid., 208–209.

74 Ibid., 231.

75 Ibid., Fig 1.

76 Ibid., Fig. 6.

77 Ibid., Fig. 7.

78 Ibid., Fig. 11.

79 Kessler, "Introduction: The Literary Warp and Artistic Weft of Veronica's Cloth," 16. The author discusses and reproduces the earliest known works that show Veronica in the context of the Passion, including Jacquemart de Hesdin's *Christ of the Way to Calvary*, c. 1400–1410 in the Musée du Louvre, Paris, 13, Fig. 1.

80 Derbes, *Picturing the Passion,* Chapter 5 on "The Way to Calvary."

81 Ibid., 113.

82 Ibid., 117, 126.

83 Ibid., 118, 128–129.

84 Ibid., 129.

85 See Catherine Innes-Parker, "Bonaventure's *Lignum vitae*: The Evolution of a Text," in *The Pseudo-Bonaventuran Lives of Christ: Exploring the Middle English Tradition*, eds. Ian Johnson and Allan F. Westphall, 425–456 (Turnout, Belgium: Brepols, 2013).

86 Derbes, *Picturing the Passion,* 129.

87 Ibid., 129, 136–137.

88 Coogan, et al., eds., *The New Oxford Annotated Bible,* 1771.
89 Derbes, *Picturing the Passion,* 122, 130.
90 Hand, "*Salve sancta facies*," 14, 16.
91 Livia Stoenescu, "Ancient Prototypes Reinstantiated: Zuccari's *Encounter of Christ and Veronica* of 1594," *The Art Bulletin* 93 (2011): 423–448.
92 National Gallery of Art, Washington, accessed July 3, 2019, www.nga.gov.
93 On this Baroque painting, see Louis Marin and Marie Maclean, "The Figurability of the Visual: The Veronica or the Question of the Portrait at Port-Royal," *New Literary History* 22 (1991): 261–296.
94 The work by Petrus Christus is a tempera and oil on parchment, mounted on wood, measuring 14.9 x 10.8 cm. See Hand, "*Salve sancta facies*," 7–18, Figure 1.
95 The painting is in The National Gallery, London. Ibid., Figures 4–5.

Epilogue

> Hear, O Lord, when I cry aloud, be gracious to me and answer me! "Come," my heart says, "seek his face!" Your face, Lord, do I seek. Do not hide your face from me.
>
> Psalm 27:7–9[1]

The desire to see God's countenance[2] was and remains a potent human impulse that, I proffer, drove the development of the Veronica character, the veneration of her relic, and the subsequent production of works of art, including as part of the Stations of the Cross. As a legendary eyewitness to Christ's walk to Calvary, Veronica was an ordinary woman who participated in an extraordinary event. As a character with whom Holy Land pilgrims and Western Christians could identify, she fulfilled some of their deepest spiritual needs. Veronica and her image-bearing cloth gave tangible form to the visage of Christ, which helped to satiate worshippers' desires to meet the gaze of their maker and redeemer. Ultimately, the veronica advanced heated conversations about what was seeable or unseeable, knowable or unknowable. Veronica and her cloth signified the spiritual presence of Christ despite his physical absence. The *sudarium* functioned as a dual symbol for his temporal incarnation and his eternal presence. As such, the Holy Face could serve as a stand-in for the host elevated during Mass and/or a proxy for the flag of the Resurrection as a promise of eternal life.

The Franciscans capitalized on these overlapping themes and converging circumstances – literary, material, topographical, theological, social, and artistic – by inserting a woman, Veronica with her veil, into the *Via Crucis*. In doing so, the friars both adapted the legend and intervened in the urban centers of Jerusalem and Western European cities in order to elicit compassion from those whom they sought to evangelize. Veronica proved an effective choice because she represented the "true image" of Christ less by her relic than by her actions: her gesture of compassion mirrored Christ's call to love one another. The Franciscans' purpose was to connect the lives of Christ and Francis to the lives of pilgrims and religious women in communities at a time when women's roles in the church and auxiliary activities were being reformulated in the fourteenth century. Furthermore, Veronica, as a symbol of the relic of the living Christ, offered a promise of the Resurrection to Christians in Europe and Jerusalem. The legacy of this choice is evident in the numerous works of art featuring Veronica as subject matter from North and South of the Alps, created from the early fifteenth through the mid-seventeenth centuries, in a variety of compelling iconographic roles.

Notes

1 Coogan, et al., eds., *The New Oxford Annotated Bible,* 794.
2 Milanese finds and offers exegesis on additional passages in the Hebrew scriptures that elucidate a dual desire and fear to meet God *facie ad faciem*. See Guido Milanese, "*Quaesivi vultum tuum*. Liturgy, figura and Christ's Presence," in *The European Fortune of the Roman Veronica in the Middle Ages, Convivium Supplementum*, eds. A. Murphy, H. L. Kessler, M. Petoletti, E. Duffy, and G. Milanese, 126–135 (Turnhout, Belgium: Brepols Publishers, Milanese, 2017), 128.

Bibliography

Primary Sources

Association des Amis de la Basilique Nôtre Dame de la Fin des Terres de Soulac-sur-Mer. *Nôtre Dame de la Fin des Terres*. Soulac, n.p., 1993.

Baugh, Nita Scudder, ed. *A Worcestershire Miscellany Compiled by John Northwood, c. 1400, edited from British Museum MS Add. 37.787*. Philadelphia, PA, n.p., 1956.

Bede. *The Complete Works of Venerable Bede, in the original Latin, collated with the Manuscripts and various printed editions, and accompanied by a new English translation of the Historical Works, and a Life of the Author*. 8 vols. Edited by Rev. J. A. Giles. London: Whittaker and Co., 1843.

Benedict (Master). *The Marvels of Rome: Mirabilia urbis Romae*. English and Latin edition. 2nd ed. Translated and edited by Francis Morgan Nichols. Introduction by Eileen Gardiner. New York: Italica Press, Inc., 1986.

Benedict XVI. "Pilgrimage to the Shrine of the Holy Face of Manoppello." September 1, 2006. Accessed March 25, 2018. http://w2.vatican.va/content/benedict-xvi/en/speeches/2006/september/documents/hf_ben-xvi_spe_20060901_manoppello.html.

Benedictus Canonicus. *Liber Censuum Romanae Ecclesiae*. Vol. II. Edited by P. Fabre and L. Duchesne. Paris: Fontemoing, 1910.

Bernard, Abbot of Clairvaux. *Life and Works of Saint Bernard*. 2 vols. 2nd ed. Edited by Dom. John Mabillon. Translated and edited by Samuel J. Eales. London: Burns & Oats, Ltd., 1889.

Bevegnati, Fra Giunta. *Leggenda della vita e dei miracoli di Santa Margherita da Cortona*. Translated and edited by Eliodoro Mariani. Vicenza: L.I.E.F., 1978.

—— *The Life and Miracles of Saint Margaret of Cortona (1247–1297)*. Translated by Thomas Renna. Edited by Shannon Larson. Saint Bonaventure, NY: Franciscan Institute Publications, 2012.

Bonaventure. *The Life of Saint Francis*. Translated by Ewert Cousins, with an introduction by Donna Tartt. New York: HarperCollins, 2005.

Braun, Frans, ed., and Georg Hogenberg, engravings. *Civitates Orbis Terrarum*. 6 vols. Cologne, 1572–1617. Library of Congress. Accessed May 31, 2019. www.loc.gov/resource.

Chaucer, Geoffrey. *The Canterbury Tales*. Translated by David Wright. Oxford: Oxford University Press, 1998. eBook Collection (EBSCOhost).

Coogan, Michael D., Marc Z. Brettler, and Carol Newsom, ed., with contributions by Pheme Perkins. *The New Oxford Annotated Bible with Apocrypha: New Revised Standard Edition*. 4th ed. Oxford: Oxford University Press, 2010.

Dante Alighieri. *The Divine Comedy*. Translated by C. H. Sisson. Oxford: Oxford University Press, 1980.

—— and Mark Musa. *Dante's* Vita Nuova, *New Edition: A Translation and an Essay*. Bloomington, IN: Indiana University Press, 1973.

De Boron, Robert. *Joseph d'Arimathie*. Edited by Richard O'Gorman. *Studies and Texts* 120. Toronto: Pontifical Institute for Mediaeval Studies, 1995.

De Rossi, Joh. Bapt., and Ludov. Duchesne, eds. *Martyrologium Hieronymianum: Ad Fidem Codicum, Adiectis Prolegomenis*. Brussels: Typis Polleunis et Ceuterick, 1894.

Ehrman, Bart D. *Lost Scriptures: Books that Did Not Make It into the New Testament*. Oxford: Oxford University Press, 2003.

—— and Zlatko Pleše. *The Apocryphal Gospels: Texts and Translations*. Oxford: Oxford University Press, 2011.

Ernoul. *Chronique d'Ernoul et de Bernard le Tresorier*. Edited by L. de Mas Latrie. Paris: Société de l'histoire de France, 1871.

Eusebius Pamphili. *Ecclesiastical History, Books 1–5*. Vol. 19. Translated by Roy J. Deferrari. In *The Fathers of the Church: A New Translation*. Washington, DC: Catholic University of America Press, 2005.

Ford, Alvin E., ed. *La Vengeance de Nostre-Seigneur: The Old and Middle French Prose Versions: The Cura Sanitatis Tiberii (The Mission of Volusian), the Nathanis Judaei Legatio (Vindicta Salvatoris), and the Versions found in the Bible en français of Roger d'Argenteuil or influenced by the Works of Flavius Josephus, Robert de Boron and Jacobus de Voragine*. Toronto: Pontifical Institute of Mediaeval Studies, 1984.

Fratris Felicis Fabri (Fra Felix Fabri). *Evagatorium in Terræ Sanctæ, Arabiæ et Egypti Peregrinationem*. Vol. 1, 1494. Edited by Konrad Dietrich Hassler. Stuttgardiæ: Societatis Litterariæ Stuttgardiensis, 1843. www.gutenberg.org.

Gervase of Tilbury. *Otia Imperialia*. Edited and translated by S. E. Banks and J. W. Binns. Oxford: Oxford University Press, 2002.

Giraldus Cambrensis. *Opera: Speculum Ecclesiae*. Edited by J. S. Brewer, M.A. London: Her Majesty's Stationery Office, 1873. Reprinted by Kraus Reprint, Ltd., 1964.

Goodwin, Charles Wycliff, trans. and ed. for the Cambridge Antiquarian Society. *The Anglo-Saxon Legends of St. Andrew and St. Veronica*. Cambridge: Deighton, MacMillan and Co., 1851.

Guylforde, Sir Richard. *The Pylgrymage of Sir Richard Guylforde to The Holy Land, A.D. 1506*. Edited by Sir Henry Ellis. London: Camden Society, 1851. Reprinted New York: AMS Press, 1968.

Horn, Elzear. *Ichnographiae Monumentorum Terrae Sanctae, 1724–1744*. Edited and translated by Eugene Hoade and Bellarmino Bagatti. Jerusalem: Franciscan Press, 1962.

Ignatius of Loyola. *The Spiritual Exercises of St. Ignatius based on Studies in the Language of the Autograph*. Translated by Louis J. Puhl. New York: Vintage Books, 2000.

Izydorczyk, Zbigniew. *The Medieval Gospel of Nicodemus: Texts, Intertexts, and Contexts in Western Europe*. Tempe, AZ: Medieval and Renaissance Texts and Studies, 1997.

Jacobus de Voragine. *The Golden Legend: Readings on the Saints*. Translated by William Granger Ryan. Introduction by Eamon Duffy. Princeton, NJ: Princeton University Press, 2012.

—— *The Golden Legend: Readings on the Saints*. Vol. 1. Translated by William Granger Ryan. Princeton, NJ: Princeton University Press, 1993.

James, M. R., trans. *The Gospel of Nicodemus, or Acts of Pilate*. Oxford: Clarendon Press, 1924.

John of Caulibus. *Meditations on the Life of Christ*. Translated and edited by Francis X. Taney, Anne Miller, and C. Mary Stallings-Taney. Asheville, NC: Pegasus Press, 2000.

Julian of Norwich. *Revelations of Divine Love*. Translated by Barry Windeatt. Oxford: Oxford University Press, 2016.

Kempe, Margery. *The Book of Margery Kempe*, c. 1440. MS 61823, British Library, London. www.bl.uk/manuscripts.

—— *The Book of Margery Kempe: A New Translation, Contexts, Criticism*. Translated and edited by Lynn Staley. New York: W. W. Norton & Company, 2001.

Levänen, Tuomas, trans. *Cura Sanitatis Tiberii*. www.academia.edu/15436621/Cura_Sanitatis_Tiberii_English_Translation.

Lewis, Agnes Smith, trans. and ed. *Apocrypha Syriaca: The Protoevengelium Jacobi and Transitus Mariae*. Cambridge: Cambridge University Press, 1902, reprinted 2012.

Luther, Martin. *Luther's Works: Church and Ministry III*. Vol. 41. Edited by Eric W. Gritsch and Helmut T. Lehmann. Philadelphia, PA: Fortress Press, 1966.

Matthæi Parisiensis, Monachi Sancti Albani (Matthew Paris). *Chronica Majora*. Vol. 3. Edited by Henry Richards Luard, M.A. London: Her Majesty's Stationery Office, 1872. Reprinted Weisbaden: Kraus Reprint Ltd., 1964. http://archive.org.

McNamer, Sarah. *Meditations on the Life of Christ: The Short Italian Text*. Notre Dame, IN: University of Notre Dame Press, 2018.

Mueller, Joan. *A Companion to Clare of Assisi: Life, Writings, and Spirituality*. Leiden: Brill, 2010.

Niccolò da Poggibonsi. *Libro d'Oltramare, pubblicato da Alberto Bacchi della Lega*. Bologna: Presso Gaetano Romagnoli, 1881. www.archive.org.

Petrarch, Francesco, and Mark Musa. *The Canzoniere, or Rerum Vulgarium Fragmenta*. Bloomington, IN: Indiana University Press, 1999.

Ragusa, Isa, trans., and Rosalie B. Green, ed. *Meditations on the Life of Christ: An Illustrated Manuscript of the Fourteenth Century*. Princeton, NJ: Princeton University Press, 1977.

Rosweyde, Heribert, and Jean Bolland. *Acta Sanctorum*. Antwerp and Brussels: Société des Bollandistes, 1643–1940. Accessed April 24, 2018. *ProQuest*. http://acta.chadwyck.co.uk.

Rufus, John. "'A Pilgrimage in Jerusalem,' in *The Life of Peter the Iberian*, c. 500." In *Jerusalem Pilgrims before the Crusades*, translated and edited by John Wilkinson, 99–102. Warminster, England: Aris & Phillips, 2002.

Schroeder, H. J., trans. *Canons and Decrees of the Council of Trent*. Charlotte, NC: Tan Books, 1978.

Suriano, Fra Francesco. *Treatise on The Holy Land*. Translated by Fr. Theophilus Bellorini and Fr. Eugene Hoade. Jerusalem: Franciscan Press, 1949.

Theodosius the Cenobiarch. "*The Topography of the Holy Land*, c. 518." In *Jerusalem Pilgrims before the Crusades*, translated and edited by John Wilkinson, 103–116. Warminster, England: Aris & Phillips, 2002.

Vasari, Giorgio. *Lives of the Painters, Sculptors and Architects*. 2 vols. Translated by Gaston du C. de Vere. New York: Alfred A. Knopf, 1996.

Wey, William. *The Itineraries of William Wey*. Edited and translated by Francis Davey. Oxford: The Bodleian Library, University of Oxford, 2010.

Wilkinson, John, trans. and ed. *Egeria's Travels*. 3rd ed. Oxford: Aris & Phillips, 1999.

Zuallart, Jean. *Il Devotissimo Viaggio di Gerusalemme*. Rome: F. Zanetti & Gia Ruffinelli, 1587. www.archive.org.

Secondary Sources

Ahl, Diane Cole. "Camposanto, *Terra Santa*: Picturing the Holy Land in Pisa." *Artibus Et Historiae* 24 (2003): 95–122.

Alston, George Cyprian. "Way of the Cross." In *The Catholic Encyclopedia*. Vol. 15. New York: Robert Appleton Company, 1912. Accessed May 21, 2019. www.newadvent.org.

Arad, Prima. "Pilgrimage, Cartography, and Devotion: William Wey's Map of the Holy Land." *Viator* 43 (2012): 301–322.

Atkinson, Clarissa W. "Female Sanctity in the Late Middle Ages." In *The Book of Margery Kempe: A New Translation, Contexts, and Criticism*, translated and edited by Lynn Staley, 225–236. New York: Norton & Company, 2001.

Aurélien, des Célestins de l'Ordre de Saint Benoit. *Sainte Véronique, apôtre de l'Aquitaine: son tombeau et son culte à Soulac, ou, Notre-Dame de Fin-des-Terres, Archidiocèse de Bordeaux*. Toulouse: L. Hébraile, 1877.

Bacci, Michele. "The *Volto Santo*'s Legendary and Physical Image." In *Envisioning Christ on the Cross: Ireland and the Early Medieval West*, edited by Juliet Mullins, Jenifer Ní Ghrádaigh, and Richard Hawtree, 214–233. Dublin, Ireland: Four Courts Press, 2013.

—— "Alla Ricerca del Volto di Cristo." In *Gesù: Il Corpo, Il Volto dell'Arte*, edited by Timothy Verdon, 90–95. Milan: Silvana Editoriale, 2010.

Baert, Barbara. "The Gaze in the Garden: Mary Magdalene in *Noli Me Tangere*." In *Mary Magdalene, Iconographic Studies from the Middle Ages to the Baroque*, edited by Michelle A. Erhardt and Amy M. Morris, 189–221. Boston: Brill, 2012.

—— (with the collaboration of Emma Sidgwick). "Touching the Hem: The Thread between Garment and Blood in the Story of the Woman with the Haemorrhage (Mark 5: 24b–34parr)." *Textile* 9 (2011): 308–352.

—— "Weaving." In *Weaving, Veiling, and Dressing: Textiles and Their Metaphors in the Late Middle Ages*, edited by Kathryn M. Rudy and Barbara Baert, 39–40. Turnhout, Belgium: Brepols Publishers, 2007.

Baldi, P. Donatus. *Enchiridion Locorum Sanctorum*. Jerusalem: Franciscan Printing Press, 1955, reprinted 1982.

Ballardini, Antonella, and Paola Pogliani. "A reconstruction of the oratory of John VII (705–707)." In *Old Saint Peter's, Rome*, edited by Rosamond McKitterick, John Osborne, Carol M. Richardson, and Joanna Story, 190–213. Cambridge: Cambridge University Press, 2013.

Barbier de Montault, Xavier. "Iconographie du chemin de la croix." *Annales Archaéologiques*, xxiii (1867).

Barnay, Sylvie. "Il Volto non fatto da mano d'uomo." In *Gesù: Il Corpo, Il Volto dell'Arte*, edited by Timothy Verdon, 96–103. Milan: Silvana Editoriale, 2010.

Beckett, The Rt. Rev. Michael, O. P. "Blessed Alvarez of Cordova." *The Order of Preachers Independent* (February 19, 2015). Accessed May 30, 2019. www.theorderofpreachersindependent.org.

Behind the Name. "Berenice." Accessed June 21, 2019. www.behindthename.com.

Belting, Hans. *Likeness and Presence: A History of the Image in the Age before Art*. Chicago, IL: University of Chicago Press, 1994.

Benay, Erin E., and Lisa M. Rafanelli. *Faith, Gender and the Senses in Italian Renaissance and Baroque Art: Interpreting the* Noli me tangere *and Doubting Thomas*. Burlington, VT: Ashgate Publishing Company, 2015.

Berliner, Rudolf. "Arma Christi." *Münchner Jahrbuch der bildenden Kunst* 6 (1955): 35–116.

Blackwood, Nicole. "Printmaker as Painter: Looking Closely at Ugo da Carpi's *Saint Veronica Altarpiece*." *Oxford Art Journal* 36 (2013): 167–184.

Blair Moore, Kathryn. *The Architecture of the Christian Holy Land: Reception from Late Antiquity through the Renaissance*. Cambridge: Cambridge University Press, 2017.

—— "The Disappearance of an Author and the Emergence of a Genre: Niccolò Da Poggibonsi and Pilgrimage Guidebooks between Manuscript and Print." *Renaissance Quarterly* 66 (2013): 357–411.

Bölling, Jörg. "Face to Face with Christ in Late Medieval Rome. The Veil of Veronica in Papal Liturgy and Ceremony." In *The European Fortune of the Roman Veronica in the Middle Ages, Convivium Supplementum*, edited by Amanda Murphy, Herbert L. Kessler, Marco Petoletti, Eamon Duffy, and Guido Milanese, 136–143. Turnhout, Belgium: Brepols Publishers, 2017.

Borrini, Matteo, and Luigi Garlaschelli. "A BPA Approach to the Shroud of Turin." *Journal of Forensic Sciences* (July 2018). doi:10.1111/1556-4029.13867.

Boullata, Kamal. "To Measure Jerusalem: Explorations of the Square." *Journal of Palestine Studies* 28 (1999): 83–91.

Bourrières, Michel. *Saint Amadour and Sainte Véronique*. Paris: Tolra, 1895.

Bowers, Terence N. "Margery Kempe as Traveler." *Studies in Philology* 97 (2000): 1–28.

Breitenbach, Edgar. "The Tree of Bigamy and the Veronica Image of St. Peter's." *Art Institute of Chicago Museum Studies* 9 (1978): 30–38.

Brockmann, Stephen. *Nuremberg: The Imaginary Capital*. Rochester, NY: Camden House, 2006.

Brown, Katherine T. *Mary of Mercy in Medieval and Renaissance Italian Art: Devotional Image and Civic Emblem*. New York: Routledge, 2017.

—— *The Painter's Reflection: Self-portraiture in Renaissance Venice, 1458–1625*. Florence: Leo S. Olschki Press, 2000.

Brown, Peter. *The Cult of the Saints. Its Rise and Function in Latin Christianity*. Chicago, IL: University of Chicago Press, 1982.

Bynum, Caroline Walker. *Christian Materiality: An Essay on Religion in Late Medieval Europe*. Cambridge, MA: Zone Books, 2011.

—— "Seeing and Seeing Beyond: The Mass of St. Gregory in the 15th Century." In *The Mind's Eye: Art and Theological Argument in the Middle Ages*, edited by Jeffrey Hamburger and Anne-Marie Bouché, 208–240. Princeton, NJ: Princeton University Press, 2006.

—— *The Resurrection of the Body in Western Christianity, 200–1336*. New York: Columbia University Press, 1995.

Candiani, Stefano. "The Iconography of the Veronica in the Region of Lombardy: 13th–14th Centuries." In *The European Fortune of the Roman Veronica in the Middle Ages, Convivium Supplementum*, edited by Amanda Murphy, Herbert L. Kessler, Marco Petoletti, Eamon Duffy, and Guido Milanese, 260–273. Turnhout, Belgium: Brepols Publishers, 2017.

Casper, Andrew R. "Display and Devotion: Exhibiting Icons and Their Copies in Counter-Reformation Italy." In *Religion and the Senses in Early Modern Europe*, edited by Wietse de Boer and Christine Göttler, 43–62. Leiden: Brill Publishing, 2013.

Carr, Annemarie Weyl. "The Face Relics of John the Baptist in Byzantium and the West." *Gesta* 46 (2007): 159–177.

Chadwick, Whitney. "Women Artists and the Politics of Representation." In *Feminist Art Criticism: An Anthology*, edited by Arlene Raven, Cassandra L. Langer, and Joanna Frueh, 167–185. New York: HarperCollins Publishers, 1988.

Chastel, André. "La Véronique," *Revue de l'art* 40–41 (1978).

Clark, Anne L. "Venerating the Veronica: Varieties of Passion Piety in the later Middle Ages." *Material Religion* 3 (2007): 164–189. doi: 10.2752/175183407X219732.

Cleveland Museum of Art. Accessed July 15, 2019. www.clevelandart.org.

—— Wall text. Visited May 5, 2019.

Collins, Adela Yarbro. *Crisis and Catharsis: The Power of the Apocalypse*. Philadelphia, PA: The Westminster Press, 1984.

Coakley, John W. *Women, Men, and Spiritual Power: Female Saints and their Male Collaborators*. New York: Columbia University Press, 2006.

Connolly, Daniel K. "Imagined Pilgrimage in the Itinerary Maps of Matthew Paris." *Art Bulletin* 81 (1999): 598–622.

Cooper, Lisa H., and Andrea Denny-Brown. "Introduction." In *The Arma Christi in Medieval and Early Modern Material Culture: With a Critical Edition of 'O Vernicle'*, edited by Lisa H. Cooper and Andrea Denny-Brown, 1–19. Burlington, VT: Ashgate Publishing Company, 2014.

Cross, J. E., ed., with contributions by Denis Brearley, Julia Crick, Thomas N. Hall, and Andy Orchard. *Two Old English apocrypha and their manuscript source: 'The Gospel of Nichodemus' and 'The Avenging of the Savior.'* Cambridge: Cambridge University Press, 1996.

Cullen, Christopher M. *Bonaventure*. Oxford: Oxford University Press, 2006.

Custodia Terræ Sanctæ: Franciscan Missionaries Serving the Holy Land. Accessed January 15, 2018. www.custodia.org.

Da Zedelgem, Amédée (Teetaert). *Saggio Storico sulla Devozione alla Via Crucis: Evocazione e rappresentazione degli episodi e dei luoghi della Passione di Cristo*. Bergamo: Atlas, 2004.

—— *Aperçu historique sur la dévotion au chemin de la croix*. In *Collectanea Franciscana* 19 (1949): 45–142.

Damon, P. E., D. J. Donahue, et al. "Radiocarbon dating of the Shroud of Turin." *Nature* 337 (1989): 611–615.

Darby, Peter, and Daniel Reynolds. "Reassessing the 'Jerusalem Pilgrims': The Case of Bede's *De locis sanctis*." *Bulletin for the Council for British Research in the Levant* 9 (2014): 27–31.

D'Arcy, David. "Custodians of the Holy Land: the Franciscans to Open New Museum in Jerusalem." *The Art Newspaper* (January 6, 2017). www.theartnewspaper.com.

Davey, Francis. "William Wey: An English Pilgrim's Journey to Jerusalem." In *Pilgrimage: The Sacred Journey*, edited by Ruth Barnes and Crispin Branfoot (Oxford: Ashmolean Museum, 2006): 80–95.

Debby Ben-Aryeh, Nirit. *The Cult of St Clare of Assisi in Early Modern Italy*. Burlington, VT: Ashgate Publishing Company, 2014.

Degert, Antoine. "Saint Veronica." In *The Catholic Encyclopedia: An International Work of Reference on the Constitution, Doctrine, Discipline, and History of the Catholic Church*, edited by Charles G. Herbermann, et al. New York: Robert Appleton Company, 1912.

De Giorgio, Teodoro. "Le Icone archetipiche dei santi nell'alto Medioevo: origine, funzione e percezione di una specifica tipologia di ritratto 'dal vero' e 'a somiglianza' dell'effigiato." In *Intorno al ritratto: origini, sviluppi e trasformazioni*, edited by Fabrizio Crivello and Laura Zamparo in collaboration with Federica Boràgina, 93–98. Torino: Accademia University Press, 2019.

Derbes, Anne. *Picturing the Passion in Late Medieval Italy*. Cambridge: Cambridge University Press, 1996.

Di Blasio, Tiziana Maria. *Veronica: il mistero del volto; itinerari iconografici, memoria e rappresentatzione*. Rome: Città Nuova Ed., 2000.

Di Fruscia, Chiara. "*Datum Avenioni*. The Avignon Papacy and the Custody of the Veronica." In *The European Fortune of the Roman Veronica in the Middle Ages, Convivium Supplementum*, edited by Amanda Murphy, Herbert L. Kessler, Marco Petoletti, Eamon Duffy, and Guido Milanese, 218–230. Turnhout, Belgium: Brepols Publishers, 2017.

Di Pippo, Gregory. "Passion Sunday: The Veil of St. Veronica and the Stational Liturgy at St. Peter's," with an embedded video by Lucas Viar, 2008. *New Liturgical Movement* (March 26, 2012). Accessed June 20, 2018. www.newliturgicalmovement.org.

Dobschütz, Ernst von. *Christusbilder; Untersuchungen zur christlichen Legende*. Leipzig: L. C. Hinrichs, 1899.

Doublier, Étienne. "*Sui pretiossisimi vultus Imago*: Veronica e prassi indulgenziale nel XIII e all'inizio del XIV secolo." In *The European Fortune of the Roman Veronica in the Middle Ages, Convivium Supplementum*, edited by Amanda Murphy, Herbert L. Kessler, Marco Petoletti, Eamon Duffy, and Guido Milanese, 180–193. Turnhout, Belgium: Brepols Publishers, 2017.

Drossbach, Gisela. "The Roman Hospital of Santo Spirito in Sassia and the Cult of the Vera Icon." In *The European Fortune of the Roman Veronica in the Middle Ages, Convivium Supplementum*, edited by Amanda Murphy, Herbert L. Kessler, Marco Petoletti, Eamon Duffy, and Guido Milanese, 158–167. Turnhout, Belgium: Brepols Publishers, 2017.

Easton, Martha. "Feminist Art History and Medieval Iconography." In *The Routledge Companion to Medieval Iconography*, edited by Colum Hourihane, 425–436. New York: Routledge, 2017.

Edson, Evelyn. *Mapping Time and Space: How Medieval Mapmakers Viewed their World*. London: British Library, 1999.

Eglash, Ruth. "Archaeologists find possible site of Jesus's trial in Jerusalem." *The Washington Post* (Washington, DC). January 4, 2015. Accessed July 11, 2018. www.washingtonpost.com.

Evans, Rev. John, M. A. *The Statutes of the Fourth General Council of Lateran, Recognized and Established by Subsequent Councils and Synods Down to the Council of Trent.* London: L. and G. Seeley, 1843.

Fein, Susanna. "Mary to Veronica: John Audelay's Sequence of Salutations to God-Bearing Women." *Speculum* 86 (2011): 964–1009.

Fiorenza, Elisabeth Schüssler. *In Memory of Her: A Feminist Theological Reconstruction of Christian Origins*. New York: The Crossroad Publishing Company, 1983.

Flora, Holly. "Gender, Image, and Devotion in Illustrated Manuscripts of the *Meditationes Vitae Christi*." In *Beyond the Text: Franciscan Art and the Construction of Religion*, edited by Xavier Seubert and Oleg Bychov, 160–176. Saint Bonaventure, NY: Franciscan Institute Publications, 2013.

—— *The Devout Belief of the Imagination: The Paris* Meditationes Vitae Christi *and Female Franciscan Spirituality in Trecento Italy*. Turnhout, Belgium: Brepols Publishers, 2009.

—— and Arianna Pecorini Cignoni. "Requirements of Devout Contemplation: Text and Image for the Poor Clares in Trecento Pisa." *Gesta* 45 (2006): 61–76.

Folda, Jaroslav. "Jerusalem and the Holy Sepulchre through the Eyes of Crusader Pilgrims." In *The Real and Ideal Jerusalem in Jewish, Christian and Islamic Art. Studies in Honor of Bezalel Narkiss on the Occasion of his Seventieth Birthday*, edited by Bianca Kühnel, 158–164. Jerusalem: *Jewish Art* 23/24, 1997–1998.

Foster-Campbell, Megan H. "Pilgrimage through the Pages: Pilgrims' Badges in Late Medieval Devotion." In *Push Me, Pull You: Imaginative, Emotional, Physical, and Spatial Interactions in Late Medieval and Renaissance Art*, edited by Sarah Blick and Laura Gelfand. Leiden: Brill Publishers, 2011. doi:10.1163/9789004215139_008.

Frank, Georgia. "The Pilgrim's gaze in the age before icons." In *Visuality Before and Beyond the Renaissance: Seeing as Others Saw*, edited by Robert S. Nelson, 98–115. Cambridge: Cambridge University Press, 2000.

French, Dorothea R. "Felix Fabri." In *Encyclopedia of Medieval Pilgrimage*, edited by Larissa J. Taylor, et al. Leiden: Brill Publishers, 2012. Accessed July 23, 2019. http://dx.doi.org/10.1163.

Friedberg, Arthur L., and Ira S. Friedberg. *Gold Coins of the World from Ancient Times to the Present*. 9th ed. Williston, VT: Coin and Currency Institute, 2017.

Frugoni, Chiara. "Una proposta per il *Volto Santo*." In *Il Volto Santo. Storia e culto*, edited by Clara Baracchini and Maria Teresa Filieri, 15–48. Lucca: Pacini Fazzi, 1982.

Galeries nationales du Grand Palais, Paris. *L'Art au temps des rois maudits: Philippe le Bel et ses fils, 1285–1328*. Paris: Réunion des Musées Nationaux, 1998.

Gallo, Federico. "*De sacrosanto sudario Veronicae* by Giacomo Grimaldi. Preliminary Investigations." In *The European Fortune of the Roman Veronica in the Middle Ages, Convivium Supplementum*, edited by Amanda Murphy, Herbert L. Kessler, Marco Petoletti, Eamon Duffy, and Guido Milanese, 72–83. Turnhout, Belgium: Brepols Publishers, 2017.

Ghiberti, Giuseppe. "Il Corpo della Sindone." In *Gesù: Il Corpo, Il Volto dell'Arte*, edited by Timothy Verdon, 116–123. Milan: Silvana Editoriale, 2010.

Godding, Robert, ed. *De Rosweyde aux Acta Sanctorum: La recherche hagiographique des Bollandistes à travers quatre siècles: actes du Colloque international, Brussels, 5 October 2007*. Brussels: Société des Bollandistes, 2009.

Gounelle, Rémi, and Céline Urlacher-Becht. "Veronica in the *Vindicta Salvatoris*." In *The European Fortune of the Roman Veronica in the Middle Ages, Convivium Supplementum*, edited by Amanda Murphy, Herbert L. Kessler, Marco Petoletti, Eamon Duffy, and Guido Milanese, 50–57. Turnhout, Belgium: Brepols Publishers, 2017.

Hamburger, Jeffrey. *The Visual and the Visionary: Art and Female Spirituality in Late Medieval Germany*. New York: Zone Books, 1998.

Hammond, Jay M., J. A. Wayne Hellmann, and Jared Goff. *A Companion to Bonaventure*. Boston: Brill, 2013.

Hand, John Oliver. *Hans Memling's Saint John the Baptist and Saint Veronica*. Washington, DC: National Gallery of Art, 1994.

—— "*Salve sancta facies*: Some Thoughts on the Iconography of the *Head of Christ* by Petrus Christus." *Metropolitan Museum Journal* 27 (1992): 7–18.

Holcomb, Melanie. "Matthew Paris's Map of the Holy Land" (catalogue entry 1). In *Jerusalem 1000–1400: Every People Under Heaven*, edited by Barbara Drake Boehm and Melanie Holcomb. New York: The Metropolitan Museum of Art, and New Haven: Yale University Press, 2016.

Hulbert, J. R. "Some Medieval Advertisements of Rome." *Modern Philology* 20 (1923): 403–424. www.jstor.org/stable/433697.

Innes-Parker, Catherine. "Bonaventure's *Lignum vitae*: The Evolution of a Text." In *The Pseudo-Bonaventuran Lives of Christ: Exploring the Middle English Tradition*, edited by Ian Johnson and Allan F. Westphall, 425–456. Turnout, Belgium: Brepols, 2013.

Izydorczyk, Zbigniew. "The *Cura Sanitatis Tiberii* a Century after Ernst von Dobschütz." In *The European Fortune of the Roman Veronica in the Middle Ages, Convivium Supplementum*, edited by Amanda Murphy, Herbert L. Kessler, Marco Petoletti, Eamon Duffy, and Guido Milanese, 32–49. Turnhout, Belgium: Brepols Publishers, 2017.

Johnson, Geraldine A. "The Art of Touch in Early Modern Italy." In *Art and the Senses*, edited by Francesca Bacci and David Melcher, 59–84. Oxford: Oxford University Press, 2011.

Keppler, Paul Wilhelm von. *Die XIV stationen des heiligen kreuzwegs eine geschichtliche und kunstgeschichtliche studie zugleich eine erklaerung der kreuzweg-vilder der malerschule von veuron*. Freiburg: Herder, 1904.

Kessler, Herbert L. "Introduction: The Literary Warp and Artistic Weft of Veronica's Cloth." In *The European Fortune of the Roman Veronica in the Middle Ages, Convivium Supplementum*, edited by Amanda Murphy, Herbert L. Kessler, Marco Petoletti, Eamon Duffy, and Guido Milanese, 12–30. Turnhout, Belgium: Brepols Publishers, 2017.

—— "Il *mandylion*." In *Il Volto di Cristo*, edited by Giovanni Morello and Gerhard Wolf, 64–99. Milan: Electa, 2000.

—— and Gerhard Wolf, eds. *The Holy Face and the Paradox of Representation: Papers from a Colloquium held at the Bibliotheca Hertziana, Rome and the Villa Spelman, Florence, 1996*. Bologna: Nuova Alfa, 1998.

Keyvanian, Carla. *Hospitals and Urbanism in Rome, 1200–1500*. Leiden: Brill, 2015.

Kinney, Dale. "Fact and Fiction in the *Mirabilia urbis Romae*." In *Roma Felix—Formation and Reflection of Medieval Rome*, edited by Éamonn Ó Carragain and Carol L. Neuman de Vegvar, 235–252. Burlington, VT: Ashgate Publishing Company, 2007.

Kirkland-Ives, Mitzi. "Alternate Routes: Variation in Early Modern Stational Devotions." *Viator* 40 (2009): 249–270.

Kleinbauer, W. Eugene. "The Anastasis Rotunda and Christian Architectural Invention." In *The Real and Ideal Jerusalem in Jewish, Christian, and Islamic Art. Studies in Honor of Bezalel Narkiss on the Occasion of his Seventieth Birthday*, edited by Bianca Kühnel, 140–146. Jerusalem: *Jewish Art* 23/24, 1997–1998.

Knox, Lezlie S. *Creating Clare of Assisi: Female Franciscan Identities in Later Medieval Italy*. Leiden: Brill, 2008.

Koerner, Joseph. *The Moment of Self-portraiture in German Renaissance Art*. Chicago, IL: University of Chicago Press, 1996.

Kumler, Aden. "*Signatis…vultus tui*: (Re) impressing the Holy Face before and after the European Cult of the Veronica." In *The European Fortune of the Roman Veronica in the Middle Ages, Convivium Supplementum*, edited by Amanda Murphy, Herbert L. Kessler, Marco Petoletti, Eamon Duffy, and Guido Milanese, 102–113. Turnhout, Belgium: Brepols Publishers, 2017.

Kuryluk, Ewa. *Veronica and Her Cloth: History, Symbolism, and Structure of a "True" Image*. Cambridge, MA: Basil Blackwell, Inc., 1991.

Lang, Uwe Michael. "Origins of the Liturgical Veneration of the Roman Veronica." In *The European Fortune of the Roman Veronica in the Middle Ages, Convivium Supplementum*, edited by Amanda Murphy, Herbert L. Kessler, Marco Petoletti, Eamon Duffy, and Guido Milanese, 144–155. Turnhout, Belgium: Brepols Publishers, 2017.

Lange, Judith. "Die Verslegende <<Veronica II>>: Hybridedition und Studien zur Überlieferung." PhD. diss., Aachen University, Germany, 2013.

Lenzi, Sarah. *The Stations of the Cross: The Placelessness of Medieval Christian Piety*. Turnhout, Belgium: Brepols Publishers, 2016.

Lewis, Flora. "The Veronica: Image, Legend and Viewer." In *England in the Thirteenth Century: Proceedings of the 1984 Harlaxton Symposium*, edited by W. M. Ormrod, 100–106. Woodbridge, England: Boyndell Press, 1985.

Lewis, Suzanne. *The Art of Matthew Paris in the Chronica Majora*. Berkeley and Los Angeles, CA: University of California Press, 1987.

Lindquist, Sherry C. M. "The Iconography of Gender." In *The Routledge Companion to Medieval Iconography*, edited by Colum Hourihane, 412–424. New York: Routledge, 2017.

Lingo, Estelle. "Mochi's Edge." *Oxford Art Journal* 32 (2009): 3–16.

Lord, Frank K. "Image, vision, and faith: Viewers' responses to the Mandylion, Veronica's Veil, and the Shroud of Turin." PhD. diss., University of North Carolina at Chapel Hill, 2003.

Machielsen, Jan. "Heretical Saints and Textual Discernment: The Polemical Origins of the *Acta Sanctorum* (1643–1940)." In *Angels of Light? Sanctity and the Discernment of Spirits in the Early Modern Period*, edited by Clare Copeland and Jan Machielsen, 103–141. Leiden: Brill, 2013.

Mâle, Émile. *L'Art Religieux de la Fin du Moyen Age en France*. Paris: Librairie Armand Colin, 1925. https://archive.org.

Maréchaux, Bernard-Marie. *Notre Dame de la Fin des Terres de Soulac*. Bordeaux: Imprimerie Nouvelle A. Bellier, 1893.

Marin, Louis, and Marie Maclean. "The Figurability of the Visual: The Veronica or the Question of the Portrait at Port-Royal." *New Literary History* 22 (1991): 261–296.

Maury, Alfred. "Lettres sur l'étymologie du nom de Véronique donné a la femme qui porte la sante face et sur l'origine de son culte." *Revue Archéologique* 2 (Paris: Presses Universitaires de France, 1851): 484–495.

McNamer, Sarah. "The Origins of the *Meditationes Vitae Christi*." *Speculum* 84 (2009): 905–955. www.jstor.org/stable/40593681.

Mezuret, M. l'abbé. *Notre-Dame de Soulac ou de la fin-des-terres: L'Apostolat de Sainte-Véronique en Aquitaine: le tombeau et le culte de Saine-Véronique a Soulac*. Lesparre: J. Rivet Imprimeur-Libraire, 1865.

Miedema, Nine. "Following in the Footsteps of Christ: Pilgrimage and Passion Devotion." In *The Broken Body: Passion Devotion in Late-Medieval Culture*, edited by A. A. MacDonald, H. N. B. Ridderbos, and R. M. Schlusemann, 73–92. Groningen: Egbert Forsten, 1998.

Milanese, Guido. "*Quaesivi* vultum tuum. Liturgy, *figura* and Christ's Presence." In *The European Fortune of the Roman Veronica in the Middle Ages, Convivium Supplementum*, edited by Amanda Murphy, Herbert L. Kessler, Marco Petoletti, Eamon Duffy, and Guido Milanese, 126–135. Turnhout, Belgium: Brepols Publishers, 2017.

Molinari, Andrea Lorenzo. "Saint Veronica: Evolution of a Sacred Legend." *Priscilla Papers* 28 (2014): 9–15.

Molteni, Ferdinando. "Storia e devozione della Sindone." In *Il Volto di Cristo*, edited by Giovanni Morello and Gerhard Wolf, 276–282. Milan: Electa, 2000.

Montagu, Jennifer. "A Model by Francesco Mochi for the 'Saint Veronica.'" *The Burlington Magazine* 124 (1982): 430–437.

Mooney, Catherine M. *Clare of Assisi and the Thirteenth-Century Church: Religious Women, Rules, and Resistance*. Philadelphia, PA: University of Pennsylvania Press, 2016.

Morgan, Nigel. "'Veronica' Images and the Office of the Holy Face in Thirteenth-Century England." In *The European Fortune of the Roman Veronica in the Middle Ages, Convivium Supplementum*, edited by Amanda Murphy, Herbert L. Kessler, Marco Petoletti, Eamon Duffy, and Guido Milanese, 84–99. Turnhout, Belgium: Brepols Publishers, 2017.

Morris, Colin. *The Sepulchre of Christ and the Medieval West: From the Beginning to 1600*. Oxford: Oxford University Press, 2005.

Mueller, Joan. *The Privilege of Poverty: Clare of Assisi, Agnes of Prague, and the Struggle for a Franciscan Rule for Women*. University Park, PA: The Pennsylvania State University Press, 2006.

The National Gallery, London. Accessed August 31, 2019. www.nationalgallery.org.uk.

National Gallery of Art, Washington. Accessed July 3, 2019. www.nga.gov.

Newhauser, Richard G., and Arthur J. Russell. "Mapping Virtual Pilgrimage in an Early Fifteenth-Century *Arma Christi* Roll." In *The Arma Christi in Medieval and Early Modern Material Culture: With a Critical Edition of 'O Vernicle'*, edited by Lisa H. Cooper and Andrea Denny-Brown, 83–112. Burlington, VT: Ashgate Publishing Company, 2014.

Nichols, Ann Eljenholm. "O Vernicle: A Critical Edition." In *The Arma Christi in Medieval and Early Modern Material Culture: With a Critical Edition of 'O Vernicle'*, edited by Lisa H. Cooper and Andrea Denny-Brown, 308–392. Burlington, VT: Ashgate Publishing Company, 2014.

Nisbet, Jim. *An Illustrated Stations of the Cross: The Devotion and Its History*. Mystic, CT: Twenty-Third Publications, 1982.

Noga-Banai, Galit. "*Places of Remembrance*: A Via Dolorosa in Berlin's Bavarian Quarter." In *Between Jerusalem and Europe: Essays in Honour of Bianca Kühnel*, edited by Renana Bartal and Hanna Vorholt, 173–196. Leiden: Brill Publishers, 2015.

Ousterhout, Robert. "Flexible Geography and Transportable Topography." In *The Real and Ideal Jerusalem in Jewish, Christian, and Islamic Art. Studies in Honor of Bezalel Narkiss on the Occasion of his Seventieth Birthday*, edited by Bianca Kühnel, 393–404. Jerusalem: *Jewish Art* 23/24, 1997–1998.

Pächt, Otto. "The 'Avignon Diptych' and Its Eastern Ancestry." In *De Artibus Opuscula XL: Essays in Honor of Erwin Panofsky*. Vol. I, edited by Millard Meiss, 402–421. New York: New York University Press, 1961.

Palme, Jos. *Die Deutschen Veronicalegenden des XII Jahr*. Prague: Verlag des K. K. Deutschen obergymnasiums der Kleinseite, 1892.

Pearson, Karl. *Die Fronica, Ein Beitrag zur Geschichte des Christusbildes in Mittelalter*. Strasbourg: Verlag von Karl J. Trübner, 1887.

Perkinson, Stephen. "Rethinking the Origins of Portraiture." *Gesta* 46 (2008): 135–157.

Perdrizet, Paul. "De La Véronique et De Seinte Véronique." In *Seminarium Kondakovianum* 5, 1–16. Prague: Institute: Kondakov, 1932.

Peters, F. E. "The Procession That Never Was: The Painful Way in Jerusalem." *The Drama Review* 29 (1985a): 31–41.

—— *Jerusalem: The Holy City in the Eyes of Chroniclers, Visitors, Pilgrims, and Prophets from the Days of Abraham to the Beginnings of Modern Times*. Princeton, NJ: Princeton University Press, 1985b.

Petoletti, Marco, and Angelo Piacentini. "The *Veronica* of Boniface of Verona." In *The European Fortune of the Roman Veronica in the Middle Ages, Convivium Supplementum*, edited by Amanda Murphy, Herbert L. Kessler, Marco Petoletti, Eamon Duffy, and Guido Milanese, 250–259. Turnhout, Belgium: Brepols Publishers, 2017.

Pringle, Denys. *Pilgrimage to Jerusalem and the Holy Land, 1187–1291*. New York: Routledge, 2016.

—— "The Planning of Some Pilgrimage Churches in Crusader Palestine." *World Archaeology* 18 (1987): 341–362. www.jstor.org/stable/124590.

Rafanelli, Lisa M. "Thematizing Vision in the Renaissance: The *Noli Me Tangere* as a Metaphor for Art Making." In *Sense and the Senses in Early Modern Art and Cultural Practice*, edited by Alice E. Sanger and Siv Tove Kulbrandstad Walker, 149–168. Burlington, VT: Ashgate Publishing Company, 2012.

Réau, Louis. *Iconographie de L'Art Chrétien*. 3 vols. Paris: Presses Universitaires de France, 1959. Millwood, NY: Kraus Reprint, 1983.

Renna, Thomas. Introduction to *The Life and Miracles of Saint Margaret of Cortona (1247–1297)* by Fra Giunta Bevegnati, 9–42. Saint Bonaventure, NY: Franciscan Institute Publications, 2012.

Rhodes, James F. "The Pardoner's 'Vernycle' and His 'Vera Icon'." *Modern Language Studies* 13 (1983): 34–40.

Rist, Rebecca. "Innocent III and the Roman Veronica: Papal PR or Eucharistic Icon?" In *The European Fortune of the Roman Veronica in the Middle Ages, Convivium Supplementum*, edited by Amanda Murphy, Herbert L. Kessler, Marco Petoletti, Eamon Duffy, and Guido Milanese, 114–125. Turnhout, Belgium: Brepols Publishers, 2017.

Rocacher, Jean. *Rocamadour et son pèlerinage: étude historique et archéologique*. 2 vols. Toulouse: Association les Amis de Rocamadour, 1979.

Rudy, Kathryn M. "Eating the Face of Christ. Philip the Good and his Physical Relationship with Veronicas." In *The European Fortune of the Roman Veronica in the Middle Ages, Convivium Supplementum*, edited by Amanda Murphy, Herbert L. Kessler, Marco Petoletti, Eamon Duffy, and Guido Milanese, 168–179. Turnhout, Belgium: Brepols Publishers, 2017.

—— "Virtual Pilgrimages in the Convent: Imagining Jerusalem in the Late Middle Ages." *Disciplina Monastica* 8 (Turnhout, Belgium: Brepols Publishers, 2011): 28–29.

—— "A Guide to Mental Pilgrimage: Paris, Bibliothèque De L'Arsenal Ms. 212." *Zeitschrift Für Kunstgeschichte* 63 (2000): 494–515.

Runciman, Steven. "Some Remarks on the Image of Edessa." *Cambridge Historical Journal* 3 (1931): 238–252.

Il Sacro Monte di Orta. Accessed April 21, 2019. www.orta.net/sacromonte/index.html.

Sand, Alexa. *Vision, Devotion, and Self-Representation in Late Medieval Art*. New York: Cambridge University Press, 2014.

Sanger, Alice E. "Sensuality, Sacred Remains and Devotion in Baroque Rome." In *Sense and the Senses in Early Modern Art and Cultural Practice*, edited by Alice E. Sanger and Siv Tove Kulbrandstad Walker. Burlington, VT: Ashgate Publishing Company, 2012.

Savigni, Raffaele. "The Roman Veronica and the Holy Face of Lucca: Parallelism and Tangents in the Formation of their Respective Traditions." In *The European Fortune of the Roman Veronica in the Middle Ages, Convivium Supplementum*, edited by Amanda Murphy, Herbert L. Kessler, Marco Petoletti, Eamon Duffy, and Guido Milanese, 274–285. Turnhout, Belgium: Brepols Publishers, 2017.

Schaus, Margaret, ed. *Women and Gender in Medieval Europe: An Encyclopedia*. New York: Routledge, 2006.

Schiaparelli, L. "Le carte antiche dell'Archivio Capitolare di S. Pietro in Vaticano'." *Archivio della Reale Società Romana di Storia Patria* 24 (1901): 393–496.

Schiller, Gertrud. *Iconography of Christian Art*. 2 vols. Translated by Janet Seligman. Greenwich, CT: New York Graphic Society, 1971–1972.

Scott, John Beldon. "Seeing the Shroud: Guarini's Reliquary Chapel in Turin and the Ostension of a Dynastic Relic." *The Art Bulletin* 77 (1995): 609–637.

Seubert, Xavier John. "Franciscans in Jerusalem: The Early History." In *Jerusalem 1000–1400: Every People Under Heaven*, edited by Barbara Drake Boehm and Melanie Holcomb, 240–241. New York: The Metropolitan Museum of Art, and New Haven: Yale University Press, 2016.

Sidgwick, Emma. "At once limit and threshold: How the early Christian touch of a hem (Luke 8: 44; Matthew 9: 20) constituted the medieval Veronica." *Viator* 45 (2014): 1–24.

Siew, Tsafra. "Translations of the Jerusalem Pilgrimage Route at the Holy Mountains of Varallo and San Vivaldo." In *Between Jerusalem and Europe: Essays in Honour of Bianca Kühnel*, edited by Renana Bartal and Hanna Vorholt, 113–132. Leiden: Brill Publishers, 2015.

Städel Museum, Frankfurt. Digital Collection. Accessed August 20, 2019. https://sammlung.staedelmuseum.de.

Stoenescu, Livia. "Ancient Prototypes Reinstantiated: Zuccari's *Encounter of Christ and Veronica* of 1594." *The Art Bulletin* 93 (2011): 423–448.

Storme, Albert. *The Way of the Cross: An Historical Sketch (The Holy Places of Palestine)*. 2nd ed. Jerusalem: Franciscan Printing Press, 1984.

Swan, Mary. "Remembering Veronica in Anglo-Saxon England." In *Writing Gender and Genre in Medieval Literature: Approaches to Old and Middle English Texts*, edited by Elaine Treharne, 19–39. Cambridge: D. S. Brewer, 2002.

Terra Sancta Museum. Accessed April 11, 2018. www.terrasanctamuseum.org.

Terry-Fritsch, Allie. "Performing the Renaissance Body and Mind: Somaesthetic Style and Devotional Practice at the Sacro Monte di Varallo." *Open Arts Journal* 4 (Winter 2014–2015): 111–132. doi:10.5456/issn.2050-3679/2015w07.

Thacker, Alan. "Rome of the Martyrs: Saints, Cults and Relics, Fourth to Seventh Centuries." In *Roma Felix—Formation and Reflection of Medieval Rome*, edited by Éamonn Ó Carragain and Carol L. Neuman de Vegvar, 13–50. Burlington, VT: Ashgate Publishing Company, 2007.

Thomas, Grégoire Marie. *Soulac et Notre-Dame de la Fin-des-Terres*. Bordeaux: Imprimerie de l'oeuvre de Saint-Paul, 1882.

Thompson, E. M. "Apocryphal Legends." *Journal of the British Archaeological Association* XXXVII, 239–253. London: British Archaeological Association, 1881.

Thompson, Nancy M. "The Franciscans and the True Cross: The Decoration of the Cappella Maggiore of Santa Croce in Florence". *Gesta* 43 (2004): 61–79.

Thurston, Herbert, S. J. *The Stations of the Cross: An Account of Their History and Devotional Purpose*. London: Burns & Oates, 1914.

Tobler, Titus. *Itinera hierosolymitana Crucesignatorum*. Geneva: J. G. Fick, 1877.

Tola, Fabrizio. "Parole e immagini nella devozione alla Passione di Cristo in Sardegna nel XVII e XVIII secolo: *Via Crucis* e processione dei misteri." *Theologica & Historica* 25 (2016): 535–561.

Van Asperen, Hanneke. "'*Où il y a une Veronique attachiée dedens*'. Images of the Veronica in Religious Manuscripts, with Special Attention for the Dukes of Burgundy and their Family." In *The European Fortune of the Roman Veronica in the Middle Ages, Convivium Supplementum*, edited by Amanda Murphy, Herbert L. Kessler, Marco Petoletti, Eamon Duffy, and Guido Milanese, 232–249. Turnhout, Belgium: Brepols Publishers, 2017.

—— "Praying, Threading, and Adorning: Sewn-in Prints in a Rosary Prayer Book (London, British Library, Add. MS 14042)." In *Weaving, Veiling, and Dressing: Textiles and their metaphors in the Late Middle Ages*, edited by Kathryn M. Rudy and Barbara Baert, 81–120. Turnhout, Belgium: Brepols Publishers, 2007.

Van Dijk, Ann. "The Veronica, the *Vultus Christi* and the veneration of icons in medieval Rome." In *Old Saint Peter's, Rome*, edited by Rosamond McKitterick, John Osborne, Carol M. Richardson, and Joanna Story, 229–256. Cambridge: Cambridge University Press, 2013.

Van Dijk, S. J. P., and J. Hazelden Walker. *The Origins of the Modern Roman Liturgy: The Liturgy of the Papal Court and the Franciscan Order in the Thirteenth Century*. Westminster, MD: The Newman Press, 1960.

Verstegen, Ian. "Between Presence and Perspective: The Portrait-in-a-Picture in Early Modern Painting." *Zeitschrift für Kunstgeschichte* 71 (2008): 513–526.

Il Volto Ritrovato (association). *Veronica Route*. Accessed July 18, 2018. www.veronicaroute.com.

Weddigen, Tristan. "Weaving the face of Christ: on the textile origins of the Christian Image." University of Zurich: Open Repository Archive, 2015. www.zora.uzh.ch/113276/1/Weddigen.pdf.

Weigert, Laura. *French Visual Culture and the Making of Medieval Theater*. New York: Cambridge University Press, 2015.

Weitbrecht, Julia. "The Vera Icon (Veronica) in the Verse Legend Veronica II: Medializing Salvation in the Late Middle Ages." *Seminar: A Journal of Germanic Studies* 52 (2016): 173–192.

Wharton, Annabel Jane. *Selling Jerusalem: Relics, Replicas, Theme Parks*. Chicago, IL: University of Chicago Press, 2006.

Wilpert, Josef. *Die römischen Mosaiken und Malereien der kirchlichen Bauten vom IV. bis XIII. Jahrhundert: unter den Auspizien und mit allerhöchster Förderung Seiner Majestät Kaiser Wilhelms II*. 4 vols. Freiburg: Herder, 1917.

Windeatt, Barry. "'Vera Icon'? The Variable Veronica of Medieval England." In *The European Fortune of the Roman Veronica in the Middle Ages, Convivium Supplementum*, edited by Amanda Murphy, Herbert L. Kessler, Marco Petoletti, Eamon Duffy, and Guido Milanese, 58–71. Turnhout, Belgium: Brepols Publishers, 2017.

Wittkower, Rudolf. "'Sacri Monti' in the Italian Alps." In *Idea and Image: Studies in the Italian Renaissance*, 175–183. London: Thames and Hudson, 1978.

Wolf, Gerhard. "'Or fu sì fatta la sembianza vostra?' Sguardi alla 'vera icona' e alle sue copie artistiche." In *Il Volto di Cristo*, edited by Giovanni Morello and Gerhard Wolf, 103–211. Milan: Electa, 2000.

—— "From Mandylion to Veronica: Picturing the 'Disembodied' Face and Disseminating the True Image of Christ in the Latin West." In *The Holy Face and the Paradox of Presentation*, edited by Herbert L. Kessler and Gerhard Wolf, 153–179. Bologna: Nuova Alfa, 1998.

Wood, Jeryldene. *Women, Art, and Spirituality: The Poor Clares of Early Modern Italy*. Cambridge: Cambridge University Press, 1996.

Zardoni, Raffaella, Emanuela Bossi, and Amanda Murphy. "The Iconography of the Roman Veronica. From the Repertoires of Karl Pearson to Veronica Route." In *The European Fortune of the Roman Veronica in the Middle Ages, Convivium Supplementum*, edited by Amanda Murphy, Herbert L. Kessler, Marco Petoletti, Eamon Duffy, and Guido Milanese, 286–301. Turnhout, Belgium: Brepols Publishers, 2017.

Zchomelidse, Nino. "Liminal Phenomena: Framing Medieval Cult Images with Relics and Words." *Viator* 47 (2016): 243–296.

Zissos, Andrew, ed. *A Companion to the Flavian Age of Imperial Rome*. West Sussex, UK: John Wiley & Sons, Inc., 2016.

Zwijnenburg, N. H. J. *Die Veronicagestalt in den deutschen Passionsspielen des 15. und 16. Jahrhunderts*. Amsterdam: Rodopi, 1988.

Index

Note: Pl. denotes a plate number; n gives the note number.